The Twain Shall Meet

To the students, teachers and administrators
at Teachers University, whose participation
made it possible to undertake this study
and
To my wife, Fang Meng,
whose inspiration and support
made it possible to complete it

The Twain Shall Meet

The Current Study of English in China

by
Donald J. Ford

McFarland & Company, Inc., Publishers
Jefferson, North Carolina, and London

British Library Cataloguing-in-Publication data available

Library of Congress Cataloguing-in-Publication Data

Ford, Donald J., 1951–
The twain shall meet.

Bibliography: p. 191.
Includes references.
Includes index.
1. English language–Study and teaching–China.
2. English language–Study and teaching–Chinese speakers.
I. Title.
 PE1068.C5F6 1988   428'.007'1051   88-42521

ISBN 0-89950-348-9 (lib. bdg.; 50# acid-free natural paper)

Manufactured in the United States of America.

McFarland Box 611 Jefferson NC 28640

Table of Contents

1. Introduction: English in China   1
2. The History of English Language Learning in China   12
3. How the Chinese Today View the Study of English   30
4. Laying a Good Foundation in Beginning English Courses   63
5. Learning from Abroad in Advanced English Courses   122
6. Learning to Teach English in Teaching
   Methodology Courses   143
7. Toward the Reform of English Language Programs
   in China: Future Prospects   166

References   187
Bibliography   191
Index   197

Top: Advanced (business) English composition class, University of International Trade and Economics (UITE), Beijing, fall 1984. Graduate students, 23 to 30 years old, met for three hours once a week for 20 weeks. Temperature indoors perhaps 58°. This class was cosponsored by the University of California, Los Angeles. Bottom: Graduation ceremony, UITE, February 1985 (this class had entered mid-year): B.A. degrees and graduate certificates. Woman at left is the teacher. Temperature indoors probably 50°.

Oh, East is East, and West is West,
and never the twain shall meet...

−Rudyard Kipling,
The Ballad of East and West, 1889

1
Introduction: English in China

> By nature men are pretty much alike;
> it is learning and practice that set them apart.
>
> —Confucius, *Analects*

> Reading is learning, but applying is also learning
> and the more important kind of learning at that.
> It is often not a matter of first learning
> and then doing, but of doing and then learning,
> for doing is itself learning.
>
> —Mao Tse-tung, *Quotations*

Why the Chinese Study English

From antiquity, education has occupied an important role in Chinese society. Confucius believed that through education, a person could learn to be virtuous, and his virtue could become a force for social harmony. Based on these principles, the Chinese developed a passion for learning and a corresponding admiration for education that is unmatched in the history of the world.

Much has changed in China since Confucius set down his principles for virtuous living. To Mao, virtue was measured by a man's actions in the midst of class conflict. For him, education was important mainly to instill revolutionary consciousness in youth, which they could best gain by engaging in productive work.

No matter how education has been defined in China, a strong commitment to it remains one of the bedrock principles of Chinese civilization. Today, the Chinese government operates the world's largest educational system, with over 200 million students enrolled at the primary and secondary levels alone.[1] Among the subjects that Chinese students study today, two would be familiar to both Confucius and Mao: Chinese history and Chinese language and literature. But the newest addition to the curriculum in Chinese schools is one that neither of these men ever studied: English. In the last ten years, the study of English has grown enormously from a few thousand specialists to millions of learners. In fact, some sources contend that there are more Chinese currently studying English than there are Americans. Estimates range as high as 250 million Chinese students of English.[2]

Americans have marveled at the rapid increase in English study in China, finding an irresistible lure in the knowledge that our language is being taught in a nation as distant and mysterious to us as China. Yet we know precious little about the purposes of English learning in China or the instructional practices employed to teach it. It is true that thousands of Americans have journeyed to China in the last ten years, including many who have taught English there, but they have only provided us with rough impressions of the study of English in China.

What has been missing up to now is systematic research into this question. In particular, there has been a paucity of curriculum research in China. Since curriculum is concerned with both the ends and means of education, research into the English language curriculum in China offers the prospect of discovering not only why the Chinese study English, but how they study it, and with what results.

For this reason, from September 1984 to June 1985, I conducted a case study of the English language curriculum in the foreign langauges department of a teachers college in the People's Republic of China. The rationale for my research was to investigate in detail the purposes and practices of the English curriculum in one institution in China so as to better understand what motivates Chinese to study English, what methods they use and how well they are learning it.

The university I chose is considered among the best teacher preparation centers in China. Mindful of the risks taken on my behalf by university officials and following standard research practice, I have chosen not to reveal the name of the university or of any participants in this study. Teachers University, as I have chosen to call it, is a comprehensive center for teacher preparation and educational research and development with schools of natural and physical sciences, social sciences and humanities. Large by Chinese standards, the university is under the direct control of the State Education Commisssion, formerly known as the Ministry of Education, a national government body with considerable power to decide educational policy. The English department is actually the largest section of the foreign languages department, which is under the school of humanities. In addition to English, the department has a sizable Japanese language section and a small Russian section. The English section consists of 200 students, including 170 undergraduates and 30 graduates, 42 faculty, including 5 foreigners, and 3 administrators—the Department Chairperson, Vice-Chair, and the English Section Head.

Since the scope of my research was limited to one institution, it is important to place this study in a larger context. Though I describe the historical development of the study of English in China in chapter two, a few words about the contemporary scene are in order. Among those who have visited China, a common anecdote is the one about eager young Chinese students, often armed with dictionaries, coming up to foreigners on the street or at tourist sites and asking if they might practice speaking English. Such conversations, though often brief and superficial, help to make a trip to China special because they provide virtually the only chance for foreigners who don't speak Chinese to interact with the local population.

I had many such conversations with Chinese young people during the course of two years of teaching and traveling in China. I found, as others have, that the Chinese give many reasons for studying English. Many do it out of curiosity about the rest of the world, especially the developed nations of North America and Western Europe. Others hope to find lucrative jobs in the growing tourist and foreign trade industries. Some harbor dreams of going abroad to study or even to live permanently. Despite numerous personal motives, nearly all Chinese give one reason why English has become so popular recently: it will help China modernize. Scientists and technical experts cite the huge knowledge base that is only available to those who understand English. Traders and industrialists stress the importance of English in world commerce. Those in the tourist industry mention the growing number of English-speaking tourists who visit China. Artists speak of the need for cultural exchanges to enliven the Chinese artistic scene. Whomever one talks with in China, the idea that English is an important tool which can help China modernize is virtually an article of faith.

Chinese extol the utility of English for both personal and political reasons. Without strong government support for English study, Chinese would not have the opportunity to learn it. Over the last decade, China has veered sharply away from Mao Tse-tung's radical socialism, which placed primary stress on self-reliance and a doctrinaire interpretation of Marxism. Mao's successor, Deng Xiaoping, favors a more pragmatic approach to politics. While still adhering to Marxist tenets, Deng is open to experimentation along the lines of Eastern European nations like Yugoslavia and Hungary. Never known as a theoretician, Deng built his career on pragmatism and concrete results. Unlike Mao, who loved philosophical debates, Deng is best known for his statement, "It doesn't matter whether the cat is black or white as long as it catches mice." Thus, China today has a leader who stresses results, regardless of the means employed to achieve them, rather than leadership which insisted on the purity of the means at the expense of the results.

One of the most important policy changes to occur in contemporary China has been Deng's so-called new "open door" policy, by which he intends to attract foreign capital and business to invest and trade with China. Under this policy, special economic zones like Shen Zhen, near the Hong Kong border, have evolved into modern, bustling centers of commerce and industry.

This policy has also attracted over $10.3 billion worth of foreign investment in industries, hotels and services, including $1 billion of direct United States investment.[3]

Since the number of non–Chinese who know Chinese is very small, the government realizes it must be prepared to do business in English, Japanese and other foreign languages. This has served an impetus to foreign language study in China. Apart from the economic incentives, though, Deng's open door policy has changed the entire Chinese perspective on foreigners and things foreign. Traditionally a self-enclosed nation, China, until quite recently, had little use for the rest of the world. Now, that philosophy of total self-reliance is under attack. Deng's followers believe that China will never modernize (without increased contacts with the rest of the world). By emphasizing China's need to become an active participant in the global family of nations, China's leaders have given the green light for its citizens to learn foreign languages and through them, to discover the rest of the world.

By all accounts, the Chinese people have responded to this new opportunity with unbridled enthusiasm. Though Chinese study a host of foreign languages, English is clearly the number one choice. Bookstores are mobbed with eager shoppers looking for anything written in English. In the public parks, English corners have appeared, where Chinese students of English gather to practice speaking. On radio and television, English conversation courses are popular fare.

The reasons for the popularity of English are both practical and symbolic. Always pragmatic, the Chinese look at the world today and see that English is spoken by more people (an estimated 750 million[4]) than any other language except Chinese. Moreover, English is the preferred language of world trade and commerce, science and technology and international relations. By embracing English as the second language of choice, the Chinese are largely recognizing the preeminent place of English as a world language. And because of China's enormous size, this decision has had an important impact on the growth of English usage in the world. If estimates are true, Chinese speakers of English may increase the English-speaking population of the world by one-third or more in the near future.

No less significant than the pragmatism of choosing to study English is the symbolic importance of the choice. The Chinese retain a surprising amount of goodwill toward Americans considering that our two nations were sworn enemies for three decades. Perhaps they see in us all that they are not—a young, vibrant, modern nation free of the shackles of tradition, rich in land and resources, peopled by dreamers and visionary thinkers who are free to pursue their ambitions wherever they may lead. I heard quite a few Chinese express the hope that they might become more like America in the future. Among the young in particular, interest in English is motivated at least in part by a loss of faith in the radical politics of socialist China. For example, student demonstrators demanding democracy in China have quoted Patrick Henry ("Give me liberty or give me death") and Abraham Lincoln ("Government of the people, by the people, for the people").[5] Through English, many hope to learn the secrets of the West's success, and to transplant and duplicate this success in China.

How the Chinese Study English

With so many reasons to study English, one would expect that the Chinese also have many methods and approaches to the subject. But this is only partially true. There are certainly differences between televised English courses such as "Follow Me," a production of the British Broadcasting Corporation which is seen by 100 million viewers on the Chinese Central Television Network, and the typical English lesson as taught by a Chinese instructor to a group of high school students. The former, employing trained foreign actors, takes a conversational approach which is heavily dependent on cultural norms and social settings, while the latter most likely relies on translation and the use of "Chinglish," a dialect of English that is characterized by direct, and often inappropriate, translations of Chinese into English, such as greeting someone by asking, "Have you eaten?"

These two examples serve to highlight the differences between the extremes, but in actuality, the teaching and learning of English does not differ so radically across China. In most classrooms, regardless of area or age level, the study of English is dominated by reliance on translation, memorization and grammatical analysis. In elementary schools, children memorize nursery rhymes and the words to English songs. In junior high, they study such topics as the difference between the present and present continuous verb tenses. By senior high, they translate Chinese sentences into English and portions of classics like Dickens' *Oliver Twist* into Chinese. Throughout the primary and secondary years, students are most likely to learn British English, because their textbooks teach British received pronunciation and their teachers are more likely to have learned this variant. The preference for British English is beginning to break down, though. As relations with the United States have developed, far more American teachers of English are now hired to work in China than are British instructors. This, coupled with a growing interest in America, has resulted in a tendency among young people to learn American accents and vernacular.

After high school, English study begins to diverge in many directions. A small percentage of students, about 4 percent of the total high school population, will pass the stiff college entrance examinations and go on to four year universities, most on full government scholarships. For this elite group, the future is bright. They will most likely study academic English, often with foreign teachers, and will graduate with at least a reading knowledge of English in their specialization. Students of business, for example, study the language of contracts, trade and marketing. Students of computer science learn technical English through such English-based computer languages as Fortran, Basic, and Pascal. Humanities majors learn to read classic works of literature by Shakespeare, Dickens, and Twain. Social science majors study American history, Western civilization, international law and related topics in English. For the college-educated elite, English is a tool of academic inquiry, a means to learn about the world, and a key to knowledge that is required for the modernization of China.

For the vast majority of Chinese adults, however, the study of English is a more practical matter. In trade schools and technical institutes, where far more students attend than at the elite universities, English courses are designed to provide a cursory, limited knowledge of the language of one's own field. Machinists may learn the names of tools and parts, for example, while tour guides learn the language of hotels and transportation. Among adults, however, the most common way to learn English is self-study, either with the aid of a textbook, radio or television. For self-learners, English is a private endeavor, motivated by a million private dreams and ambitions. For some, English study is the way out of a dead-end job or unemployment. For others, it is simply a way to relieve the boredom of every day life by exploring the exotic lure of life abroad. Whatever the reasons, the study of English is clearly growing in China and is a phenomenon that deserves the attention of the English-speaking world. By finding out why and how the Chinese study English, we can learn much about Chinese society as well as the future of our own society and the language that holds it together.

Research Purposes and Methods

The purpose of this study was to investigate the English language curriculum in China in order to answer two key questions: (1) For what purposes has English been taught in China? (2) What curricular and instructional practices have been employed to teach English in China?

To better understand the contemporary scene, I found it useful to examine past practices. In China, as elsewhere, the past continues to influence the present. Though revolutionary changes have swept China in the past four decades, they have not supplanted four thousand years of recorded history. While the history of English language study in China is comparatively short, spanning only about 180 years, it is a fascinating story that helps to explain a great deal about current Chinese attitudes toward English and English speakers. Accordingly, in the next chapter, I briefly recount this history from 1800 to the present.

The remainder of the book is devoted to the results of the year-long research study I conducted at Teachers University in northern China. For the sake of clarity, I would like to briefly introduce the theoretical underpinnings and research methodology that guided the research from conception to completion. Before beginning this research, I had to confront the question of exactly what the field of curriculum entails. Scholars have never fully agreed about this, and the field's scope has changed over the years, adding to the difficulty of clearly specifying its boundaries. After examining the large body of curriculum research, I chose to base my research on the work of two men whose conceptual model of curriculum is the most comprehensive and influential one available.

John I. Goodlad and his associates, building upon the work of Ralph W. Tyler, have developed, over a twenty year period, a conceptual framework for curriculum inquiry. Their paradigm encompasses five domains of curriculum inquiry which correspond to five different perspectives: the ideal (the work of scholars who create and define curriculum based on funded knowledge), the formal (expectations and values of those interested and concerned people outside the classroom), the instructional (the teachers' beliefs, attitudes and values), the operational (what actually happens in the class day to day as seen by a trained observer), and the experiential (what students experience in class and the outcomes achieved). It also includes four levels of curricular decision-making: societal (governing bodies at the national, state and local levels), institutional (a school's technical-professional staff), instructional (classroom decisions by teachers), and experiential (the students). A large body of data has already been collected in the United States using this framework.[6] Little attention has been paid, however, to the relevance, if any, of this heuristic model to curricula in other nations.

Ralph W. Tyler, in his seminal work *Basic Principles of Curriculum and Instruction*,[7] identified four fundamental areas of curriculum development: objectives, learning experiences, organization, and evaluation. According to Tyler, by raising questions about these four components, one can arrive at a clearly specified definition of what constitutes curriculum.

In the course of conceptualizing a major research project, "A Study of Schooling in the United States," Goodlad and his associates expanded on Tyler's original rationale. Besides the four components that Tyler postulated, Goodlad's associates added seven others: materials, content, teaching strategies, grouping patterns, time, space and class climate. Further, they identified nine other qualitative factors which exert an impact on the process of curriculum: description, decision making, rationale, priorities, attitudes, appropriateness, comprehensiveness, individualization, and barriers and facilitators.

Taken together, the Goodlad-Tyler conceptual framework is the most complete and authoritative model ever to be developed in the field of curriculum. Still, this conceptual model falls short of a true theory of curriculum. It has not yet reached the stage where it is accepted among experts in the field as a verity, and it lacks the rigor needed for a theory, including the ability to explain and predict curricular practice. Still, it is an excellent place to begin an investigation of curriculum.

While the theoretical framework of this study is based on the work of Tyler and Goodlad, it should not be viewed as an attempt to replicate their work in China. Rather, in conceptualizing this research, I chose those elements of the Goodlad-Tyler model which appeared to have the greatest potential for a case study of English curriculum in China. In particular, of the nine qualitative factors identified by Goodlad, I chose to focus on three: description, decision making and attitudes.

I also decided to limit my research to four domains of curriculum inquiry: the formal (administrators), instructional (teachers), operational (observation), and experiential (students). I endeavored to describe in detail the curriculum from each of these perspectives and explore relationships among them. Additionally, I determined which curricular decisions are made at the societal, institutional, instructional and experiential levels. Finally, I investigated an important attitude—satisfaction—among administrators, teachers and students.

Besides these changes, I also added two elements to my study which set it apart from Tyler and Goodlad's work. First, I chose to take a sociolinguistic approach to observation based on the work of anthropologist Dell Hymes.[8] This entailed spending one month observing classes and writing down everything I saw and heard, and then recording one class session on either audio or videotape for subsequent detailed analysis. My observations focused on the language used, including the social and cultural elements of speech, to discover the types of language and the behavioral regularities of the Chinese classroom. This allowed me to better understand the implicit or hidden curriculum, two terms used by scholars to refer to the implicit values that schools teach and the unwritten rules by which the curriculum is learned.[9] For example, schools teach literature, but they also implicitly teach attitudes and values about literature that affect student perceptions and beliefs.

Second, I decided to investigate student achievement. My own interest in this topic was reinforced by the fact that Chinese educators also place great importance on student achievement, considering it the best single gauge of a curriculum's worth. As a result, I developed and administered a criterion-referenced test[10] of students' achievement in reading English to accurately assess the extent to which they were mastering two of their college's objectives in this area of basic English skills. This test was given to all freshmen, sophomores and juniors when I first arrived, and again six months later. Scores were then compared to determine if students were making measurable progress in learning to read English.

Research Significance

Like any research, this study raised a number of theoretical and methodological issues. Of greater importance, however, is the practical significance this study had for two groups. First, the research proceeded in the context of increasing concern in China with the quality of education. Recently, government and educational leaders have announced a commitment to reforming Chinese education at all levels to make it more effective and cost-efficient. Among the steps already taken has been an increased emphasis on scientific research in education to better understand the current status of education and pinpoint existing problems. In this context, the results of my study, which I reported back to administrators, teachers and students at Teachers University, proved useful to them in that the results stimulated discussion of the department's curriculum, provided scientific information about curricular practices and their effectiveness, and indicated areas of satisfaction and dissatisfaction with the curriculum as various groups perceived it. Moreover, I also shared my research methodology with officials, teachers and graduate students in the department, who found aspects of it useful in evaluating English curriculum in China. In particular, department administrators decided to adopt the criterion-referenced test that I developed and now use it as a yearly evaluative tool to judge the effectiveness of the reading curriculum.

The second way that this study has practical significance is the insight it provides to educators in the United States regarding the teaching of English in China. Americans will undoubtedly find the purposes and practices of English curricula in China a fascinating topic. Why would a nation as different from us as China suddenly become enamored with the study of our language? The answer to that question reveals a story of rapid change in China that can shed light on this important nation. In addition, Americans can learn about themselves by understanding the perceptions that Chinese have of us and our language. Finally, since the number of Chinese students studying in the United States has grown rapidly in the last few years, there is a need for a better understanding of the educational experiences of these students before they came to the United States.

Since I will be using certain terms throughout this book which have several definitions, I will define, for the purpose of this study, the following terms:

Curriculum: A set of intended and unintended learnings, including both the field of knowledge embraced by the term . . . and the human processes and products of curriculum making.[11]

Curricular organization: The systematic building up of learning experiences over time and across different courses and subject areas.[12]

Educational objective: A change in the behavior of learners that an educational institution seeks to bring about.[13]

Evaluation: The process for determining the degree to which changes in the learners' behavior are actually taking place.[14]

Learning experience: The interaction between learners and the external conditions in the environment to which they can react. Learning takes place through the active behavior of the student.[15]

Sociolinguistics: The study of the social and cultural aspects of language use, including both the rules of a language (linguistic competence) and the rules of a given culture that dictate how the language is used in specific contexts (communicative competence).[16]

Chapter Outlines

To make it easier to access particular topics covered, I conclude this chapter by describing the layout of this book. Broadly speaking, the book is divided into three parts. First, in Chapter 2, I present the history of the English language in China. Second, the results of my investigations at Teachers University are presented in chapters 3 through 6. Finally, in Chapter 7, the conclusions of the study are presented.

Chapter 2 is devoted to a brief overview of the history of English curriculum and instruction in China from 1800 to the present. This chapter is designed to provide a clearly focused backdrop to current curricular efforts, thus enabling readers to better understand the historical context in which this study was conducted. Starting with the earliest educational efforts by Western missionaries in China, English language programs in China are traced from their modest beginnings in the mid-nineteenth century to their rapid growth in the early twentieth century, sudden decline after the Chinese revolution in 1949 and their recent comeback after 1976.

Chapter 3 presents the Chinese perspective on the study of English. It is based on research results from questionnaires and interviews I conducted with Chinese administrators, teachers and students, and a detailed analysis of one textbook compiled in China for use in beginning English. The views of administrators were explored in a survey and interviews with department officials. The perspectives of teachers are based upon results of a questionnaire and interviews with teachers in the department. Students' experiences with English were investigateed two ways: a survey, and interviews. Finally, to conclude Chapter 3, a comparative analysis of the views of all three groups is presented to identify similarities and differences in the perspectives of administrators, teachers and students.

Chapters 4, 5 and 6 describe in detail what I learned from observations conducted in seven English department courses. The results for beginning English courses, including those taken in the first two years of undergraduate study, are presented in Chapter 4. Advanced English literature courses are examined in Chapter 5. In Chapter 6, the preparation of English teachers is considered.

Finally, Chapter 7 presents the conclusions of this study, based on the results reported in chapters two through six. Answers to both of the research questions posed in the introduction are presented and discussed, and the results of my research are considered in light of the recent educational reform movement, with an eye toward the future of English in China.

2
The History of English Language
Learning in China

Introduction

Though much has been written about the impact of foreigners on China in the past two centuries, surprisingly little attention has been given to the role of the English language as a growing medium of communication between foreigners and Chinese, given the fact that English played an important role in the development of China's relations with the West and in the emerging modern educational system of China. Three important themes emerge from the historical literature. These will be presented first and then discussed in detail to show how they affected the teaching and learning of English in China over time.

The most important theme in the record of the past two centuries is that of the role of the English language in China as inseparable from the broader social and political relations between China and English-speaking countries, especially Great Britain and the United States. As these broader relations developed and changed over time, so too did the purposes and practices of English instruction.

A second theme is that of the missionary nature of the teaching of English in China. Before 1949 such work was primarily carried out by American and British missionaries whose main purpose was not English teaching per se, but rather the conversion of Chinese to Christianity. Besides this primary purpose, English was also promoted by missionaries as a way to introduce Western ideas to China and as a way to undermine Chinese traditions that they opposed. This theme is particularly important in understanding the origins of English in China and the reactions of Chinese to the language and culture of Great Britain and America.

The third theme is that of the tremendous variances in China's response to English teaching—from outright rejection, resistance, and reluctant acquiescence to active promotion as a means of modernizing China. The variety of Chinese responses has been dependent, as previously noted, on relations with English-speaking countries, and also on internal political and social developments in China.

The Context of English in China

A sizable literature on Sino-American and Sino-British relations in the nineteenth and twentieth centuries has accumulated over time. This includes modern works on Western imperialism in China[17] and a number of earlier works, among the best of which are a three volume history of international relations in the Qing dynasty by Morse[18] and a two volume history of the Qing dynasty's notable personages by Hummel.[19] These works, among many others, provide a chronicle of the rapid changes in China as a result of Western imperialism's penetration into and increasing control over China's economic and political life.

Initial contacts in the eighteenth century revolved around the growing trade between foreign nations and Chinese coastal cities of the southeast, especially Guangzhou. Though the Portuguese initiated this trade, they were gradually supplanted by the British. In 1840, the British began a war with China after the latter demanded that Britain stop selling opium in China. The war resulted in a stinging defeat for China, which was forced to give up Hong Kong and open other ports to foreign traders. From this point on, Western powers demanded that China open more of its territory to trade and allow foreigners virtually unlimited access to China. Whenever China refused to acquiesce to new demands, Western forces invaded China, heaping one defeat upon another. By the end of the nineteenth century, China had also been defeated by its neighbor and former disciple, Japan, and a scramble was underway to carve China up into foreign spheres of influence.

These growing foreign pressures, combined with increasing domestic rebellion, led to the downfall of the Qing dynasty in 1911 and the founding of China's first republic. But the new government had no more success in controlling China's destiny than its predecessor. Foreigners continued to usurp Chinese territory, leading eventually to the Japanese invasion of Manchuria in 1931 and all-out war with Japan in 1937. Domestically, China became hopelessly fragmented, with provincial warlords vying for control. In the late 1920s, a bloody civil war broke out between the Nationalists and the Chinese communists, a conflict which raged on and off for twenty years until the communist triumph of 1949 put an end to Western domination over China. In the words of Mao Tse-tung, China had stood up after more than a century of humiliation.

It was in this context of growing foreign domination that the English language was introduced to China. Along with foreign gunboats and troops came merchants, diplomats and missionaries, each with their own agendas.

But all brought to China their native languages, among the most influential of which was English. Beginning with coastal colonies and treaty ports, the English language began to penetrate and spread throughout China, both as the result of conscious policy and incidental expediency.

The best source for the earliest period of English in China is Poon Kan Mok's 1935 doctoral dissertation, *The History and Development of the Teaching of English in China*.[20] Mok traces the origins of English in China to the early 1700's, when pidgin English developed in Guangzhou to facilitate the growing trade between England and China. Mok notes that a pidgin dialect developed primarily because foreigners refused to learn Chinese and made no formal effort to teach English to the Cantonese. Though severely limited, pidgin English gradually supplanted Portuguese as the language of commerce in south China.

The first formal effort to teach English in China was begun by the protestant missionary Robert Morrison, possibly as early as 1807.[21] Originally sent from England to learn Chinese so he could translate the Bible, Morrison arrived in Guangzhou in 1807 and struck up friendships with local Cantonese traders, with whom he exchanged language lessons.

But it was not until 1835 that a school was founded to teach English in China. This first effort, the Gutslaff School, was begun by Morrison in Macao, already a Portuguese colony. In 1839, the first American school was founded in Macao by Samuel Brown, a Yale graduate who came to China to conduct missionary work. Three years later, after the Opium War, Robert Morrison founded the Anglo-American College in the new British crown colony of Hong Kong.[22]

These schools taught a handful of Chinese boys (and, in the case of the Gutslaff School, girls as well). The subjects included English grammar, reading, pronunciation, composition, English and American history, Western music, mathematics and the Bible. The students ranged in age from 8 to 18. The primary purpose in teaching English, like other missionary schools which followed, was to use the language as a tool to preach the gospel and win converts in China. Robert Morrison believed that the study of English could pave the way for Christianity by allowing Chinese to more easily grasp the key concepts of the Christian outlook on life and by enabling them to read the English Bible and other religious materials in their original form. Samuel Brown carried this argument even further, promoting English instruction as a means to break down what he called the superstitious and heathen Chinese way of life.[23]

The Growth of English: 1842–1900

Mission schools could not have been established in China without the protection they received from the first unequal treaties forced onto China in the

1840s by the British. These treaties usurped territory from China, opened port cities to trade and guaranteed that the activities of foreigners would not be regulated by China. But it was the second round of unequal treaties in 1858 and 1860 which directly spurred the growth of English schools in China. Besides opening five more ports to foreigners and extending extraterritoriality (the principle that foreigners were not subject to Chinese laws), these treaties contained a toleration clause which guaranteed protection to Christian missionaries and their converts and a translation clause which mandated that all future agreements with China must be rendered in a foreign language, either English, French, German or Russian, depending on the nation involved. Later a United States–China treaty signed in 1868 allowed Americans to build schools in China and set up the first formal educational exchange program between China and a foreign country.[24] As a result, a small number of Chinese went to Yale University and an increase occurred in the number of American-run schools in China. By the end of the decade, missionaries had set up a total of 32 schools enrolling about 800 Chinese students.[25]

Before 1858, China's official policy toward English teaching was one of complete rejection. Foreign-run schools were forbidden by law. Although foreign languages were not in themselves deemed illegal, the Chinese saw no use for them, regarding them as inferior to their own language and viewing those who spoke them as barbarians.

This attitude underwent a change as the result of the translation clause. China quickly recognized that it needed a corps of reliable English interpreters and translators, and believed that the few Chinese who knew English at that time could not be trusted with this important work. Thus, in 1862, Prince Gong, acting on the advice of Li Hong Zhang, a prominent Qing reformer, set up the first Chinese-run English language school in Beijing.[26]

Called the Tong Wen Guan (Government Translators School), it took over the site of an old Russian school founded in the eighteenth century, and began to teach English, Russian, and French. In its first five years, the school's sole purpose was to train interpreters and translators. About 30 students attended the school during this period, ten of whom studied English.[27] All of them were sons of the Manchu nobility (known as the Eight Bannermen). The teachers were foreigners, since qualified Chinese could not be found. During these early years, the school trained very few competent interpreters, due to frequent staff changes, the low quality of instruction and a lack of motivation among students. In fact, many of the students attended the school against their will. For most, the study of foreign languages seemed a useless and even treasonous pursuit. They attended the school only because they had failed the civil service examination and had no other way to enter the ranks of officialdom. Additionally, they were given generous stipends and comparatively luxurious housing as an enticement to attend. Despite these incentives, 20 of the students failed the first examination in 1868 (a translation from

English to Chinese) and were dismissed from the school. The following year, five of the remaining ten students were also dismissed.[28]

These problems notwithstanding, China opened two more Tong Wen Guan by 1864, one in Shanghai and one in Guangzhou. In 1867, the Zongli Yamen (Foreign Affairs Office), which directed the Tong Wen Guan, decided to reorganize the schools as colleges, expanding them to include courses in Western science and technology.[29] The reasoning behind this move was that China's continued strength was dependent upon the adoption of Western technology, particularly in the military, a view which became known as the self-strengthening theory.[30] Mok sums up Chinese motives as follows:

> The one and only value of teaching English was the national value ... the value of knowing one's opponent ... and of learning his strength in war in order to meet him on equal ground.[31]

In 1869, W.A.P. Martin, an American missionary from Indiana University who had taught at the Beijing campus for four years, took over the presidency of the college. Because it was forbidden to teach religion at the school, Martin resigned his missionary post and became a full-time educator, directing the Tong Wen Guan until his retirement in 1894.[32] Under his direction, the newly-formed college matured into a more effective center of Western learning. At the same time, Martin found ways to circumvent the regulations banning religion, ensuring that students got a more sympathetic view of Christianity than they otherwise would have.

Among Martin's first acts was a thorough reorganization of the curriculum. An eight year program was developed. In the first three years, students studied one foreign language and Chinese. The foreign language courses were subdivided as follows:

1st year — elementary reading, writing and speaking
2nd year — reading, grammar, translation and speaking
3rd year — translation, speaking, world geography and world history

In the fourth year, students had courses in translation, arithmetic and algebra; in the fifth year, courses in physics, geometry and trigonometry; the sixth year, mechanics, calculus and navigation; the seventh year, chemistry, astronomy and international law; and in the eighth year, courses in astronomy, geology, mineralogy and political economy. Throughout the last four years, students also had a course in translation.[33] A shorter five year curriculum was also offered. This curriculum was the same as the last five years of the regular curriculum, with the exception that Chinese mathematics was added. Nearly all of the courses in mathematics and science were taught in English, since few of the foreign teachers were sufficiently proficient in Chinese. Students were evaluated by means of a monthly written test and annual exams in each subject area. Monetary prizes were given to students who did well on exams, and those who did poorly for a year were dismissed.

By 1879, enrollment had risen to 103 students,[34] and stayed at about that level until the school's demise during the Boxer Rebellion of 1900. Though the Tong Wen Guan began in a modest one-story building, it soon expanded its facilities. In 1873, a printing office was established which published numerous translated works over the next two decades.[35] In 1876, a chemistry laboratory was built and in 1888 an observatory and physics lab were added.[36] A small library begun in the 1870s gradually grew to a collection of 3000 books and a fairly complete periodical room with Chinese and foreign language magazines and newspapers.[37]

Despite progress, the school faced many serious problems throughout its existence. It was the object of vitriolic criticism by some Confucian scholars, especially Wo Ren, the Grand Secretary of Hanlin Academy, the Confucian center of learning. He was opposed to the employment of foreigners, missionaries in particular, and rejected the rationale behind the school, namely the self-strengthening theory.[38] Besides fending off constant attacks from conservative officials, the Tong Wen Guan also experienced difficulty in attracting good students and providing a uniformly high quality instructional program. The problem of student recruitment was complicated by several factors. First, very few students wished to attend the school; they did not want to forego a traditional Confucian education which would prepare them for the civil service examinations.

This problem was alleviated somewhat in 1887, when Martin convinced the Zongli Yamen to include Western mathematics and science in the government's triennial exam. Those who chose to take this test were eligible for government service.[39] In practice, however, few Tong Wen Guan graduates obtained permanent government jobs until after 1900, having to settle instead for part-time employment or, in some cases, spending years at the Tong Wen Guan as resident graduates waiting for job assignments which never materialized.[40] Indeed, the Qing government made very poor use of its modern-trained personnel. Many graduates never got an opportunity to use their knowledge.

Regarding the poor quality of instruction, Biggerstaff cites three contributing factors.[41] First, course content was often superficial and little attempt was made to ensure that students received the kind of broad training which would prepare them for government service. Proficiency in English was usually too low to enable students to follow technical lectures in the advanced subjects, contributing to low student morale. Second, the lack of student motivation made teaching even more difficult. One American professor complained that 30 percent of his students were regularly absent from his English classes.[42] Third, some of the teachers were untrained missionaries or diplomats who had no interest in teaching and did so in their spare time only to earn extra money. Of course most of the permanent faculty, including Dr.

Martin, were dedicated pedagogues who did the best job they could under the circumstances but they could not totally offset the damage done by their less dedicated colleagues.

Criticisms of the Tong Wen Guan became a howling chorus after Japan's victory over China in 1895. Though China's humiliating defeat left little doubt about the need for Western learning, many officials believed that the Tong Wen Guan was not providing the kind of education required. Liang Chi Chao, a prominent reformer of the time, argued that the prevailing form of Western education had failed China because of the superficiality of the curriculum and the neglect of Chinese culture.[43] He put forward a new principle for future efforts: let Chinese education serve as the foundation and Western education as a useful tool.

This position was adopted by the Zongli Yamen, which decided to draw up new regulations for the college in 1895. Their main thrust was to move the focus of the curriculum from foreign language study to Chinese. Henceforth Western subjects, wherever possible, were to be taught in Chinese and English was to be taught only in the first three years. To strengthen Chinese study, the rules declared that Chinese should be the foundation of translation and that Sundays were to be devoted exclusively to Chinese study. Furthermore, professors were instructed to report all absences from class and keep monthly grades on all students. Those who did not show an aptitude for Western learning were dismissed. Finally, the five year curriculum was dropped. All students would have to complete the Chinese and foreign language courses before taking courses in the sciences.[44]

It is difficult to judge whether these reforms made a difference. Certainly the quality of students began to improve, primarily due to the fact that enrollment was opened to Chinese (as well as Manchus) and the desire for Western learning was on the upswing. At the same time, eleven students from the Tong Wen Guan were sent abroad for further study in 1896, a sign that the government still did not believe students were receiving the kind of education required.[45]

In any event the Tong Wen Guan was shortly to experience its demise. In 1900 the Boxers (an ultranationalist group) went on a rampage in Beijing, attacking the Tong Wen Guan and the new Imperial University, severely damaging both. The school was closed down. In 1902, after the Boxer Rebellion had been put down by foreign forces, the Tong Wen Guan was transferred to the new Imperial University and became the foreign languages department.

While the Tong Wen Guan never achieved the influence its founders had hoped for, due to the unfavorable atmosphere toward Western learning which prevailed in the nineteenth century, it certainly was not a total failure. As the first modern school created by China, it helped to spread Western learning among the upper classes and served as a model for subsequent efforts, especially at Beijing Imperial University. Second, it helped to train China's modern foreign service. Already by 1898, 47 of its graduates had acquired provincial posts as translators and interpreters. After 1900, several graduates reached the rank of Minister of overseas legations and a few obtained leading posts in the national government.[46] Third, it formed the basis for foreign language curriculum and instructional practice in China. Many textbooks written or translated by its professors and resident graduates became standard works at other modern colleges. The emphasis on teaching languages through translation and grammatical drills became the basis of instruction and continues to persist in China to the present day.

Finally, the Tong Wen Guan clearly illustrates the dilemmas that China confronted as it took its first steps toward modernization. Born out of a sense of frustration and promulgated as a way for China to regain superiority over the West, it was simultaneously an object of scorn and unrealistic expectations. Its supporters hoped it would enable China to selectively borrow what it needed from the West while discarding ideas which were unpalatable to China. But its detractors pointed out the incompatibility of Western and Chinese education and insisted the latter be stressed, even when this impeded modernization. Caught on the horns of this dilemma, the Tong Wen Guan was unable to reach a satisfactory synthesis of the old and the new. Instead, the two forces were constantly at odds, and as a result, students often graduated without a firm foundation in either type of education. Despite these problems, China never abandoned the hope that a happy medium could be found. In fact, nearly one hundred years later, the current government of China is still searching for ways "to make foreign things serve China."

The Growth of Missionary and Modern Education

The activities of missionaries in China have been the focus of much research and writing in this century.[47] From very small beginnings in the mid-nineteenth century, mission schools grew rapidly toward the end of the century and experienced their heyday after the fall of the Qing dynasty. By 1918, there were 13,000 foreign-run schools in China enrolling 350,000 students, including 12 institutions of higher education with over 1,000 students.[48] In the 1920s, however, the growth of Chinese nationalism spurred increasing demands for control of foreign-run schools. After 1927, missionary schools were required to have a Chinese director and a majority of Chinese on their governing boards. Further, strict limitations were placed on the schools' proselytizing activities. Many mission schools became Christian in name only, secularizing their curriculum in the face of growing antiforeign and antireligious sentiments.

The origins of Christian colleges are discussed in detail by Jessie Lutz.[49] Like Mok, she notes that the primary reason Christian colleges were established in China was the hope of converting Chinese to Christianity.[50] The specific educational objectives of these colleges were summarized by Calvin Mateer, founder of Tengzhou College (also known as Jilu College) in Shangdong province, the first missionary college in China, begun in 1864. At a conference of Protestant missionaries in 1877, he outlined five objectives of Christian education in China[51]:

1. To train native ministers
2. To train teachers for Christian schools
3. To introduce Western science, arts and civilization to China
4. To gain access to the higher classes in China
5. To make the native church self-reliant

The curriculum of these schools was usually patterned on the small denominational colleges in the United States and England from which most missionaries had graduated. Typically, it included courses in Chinese, Latin, Greek, English, mathematics, philosophy and religion. By the 1890s, English literature, Western history and natural sciences had been added, often by substituting these for Latin and Greek. At first, textbooks were scarce and materials were generally teacher-made. The Bible was the only textbook widely used before 1900. Libraries were virtually nonexistent until the twentieth century. One effort to improve this situation was begun in 1877. The General Conference of Missionaries set up a Schools and Textbook Series Committee in Shanghai to compile and translate textbooks for use in all Protestant colleges. By 1890, they had published about 30,000 copies of books and charts, mostly translations of Western books into Chinese.[52]

The teaching of English in Christian colleges was often an afterthought, since the primary purpose was religious training for Chinese converts in their native language. In fact, the introduction of English was originally spurred by expediency as much as any purposive intent. Most of the missionaries did not know enough Chinese to teach the advanced courses in religion, philosophy and science, so they taught them in English, relying on a bilingual student or aide to translate for them. A second motive which emerged in the 1870s was the demand for English among the Chinese urban middle class who could get relatively well-paid jobs in foreign firms if they knew English. These people were willing to pay to learn it.

Always strapped for funds, Christian colleges, beginning with St. John's University in Shanghai, opened their doors to non–Christian Chinese who wanted to learn English. Besides generating badly needed revenue through tuition, the colleges hoped to elevate their lowly status among the Chinese middle and upper classes and to use English classes as a lure to attract potential converts. But the issue of using English as the medium of instruciton was hotly debated among missionaries. Calvin Mateer, for example, argued that English classes secularized the Christian colleges and detracted from their main religious work. He believed that English classes would attract students who were more interested in finding lucrative jobs than in learning to live Christian lives and that the colleges which offered English were serving the mercenary interests of foreign merchants. Further, he argued that students who studied English rather than Chinese would not be able to exercise much influence with their countrymen.[53]

On the other side of this debate, a number of rationales were offered to defend the teaching of English. In the view of St. John's University officials, the Chinese would study English one way or another, and offering it at Christian colleges increased the chances that more converts would be won.[54] Further, English study would enhance Chinese understanding of Western science and civilization, thus creating a more receptive attitude toward Christianity.

Some missionaries steadfastly defended English teaching as a means to undermine Chinese traditions which they opposed. One of the most vocal proponents of this view was Samuel Brown of the Morrison Society, head of an English school in Macao. Rabidly anti–Chinese, he declared that English teaching could liberate the Chinese mind from

> the bondage of superstition . . . broaden it and save it from petrification . . . instill into it imagination, affection, manliness and a Christian conscience.[55]

Brown frequently criticized the Chinese language, calling it "imprecise and heathen".[56] In his view, Chinese could never be a language of science and technology. If the Chinese ever hoped to modernize, they would have to adopt English or at least romanize Chinese.

This debate was never fully resolved, because it was rooted in the deep philosophical differences among the diverse missionary groups active in China. In 1910, the World Missionary Conference declared, "missionary educators are sharply divided about the question of which language should be used as the medium of instruction."[57] There seem to have been four fairly distinct positions on the use of English. At one extreme were those like Mateer who refused to teach English at all. At the other extreme were those like Brown who refused to teach Chinese. Between these two extremes, two other positions seem to have represented the majority views. One was that English could prove a useful lure to attract non–Christians to mission schools. The other was that a foundation in English and other Western subjects was required before successful proselytizing efforts could be undertaken. This was the view of W.A.P. Martin and other Westerners who taught at the Tong Wen Guan. In the end, most Christian colleges strove for some type of bilingual education, with the goal of educating students in both languages. The extent to which this was achieved varied considerably.

To illustrate this, two colleges which epitomized the two extreme positions will be considered. At St. John's University, all instruction, except in Chinese language courses, was given in English. As a result, its graduates were among the country's best in English and were in great demand in the foreign-dominated economy of Shanghai. But these graduates were often criticized for their lack of literacy in Chinese. Some critics charged they had no more than a primary school knowledge of their own language.[58]

At the opposite extreme, instruction at Tengzhou College was conducted exclusively in Chinese until 1906. Moreover, its students learned *bai hua* (Chinese vernacular) three decades before it was popularized by Chinese literary figures of the May 4th (1919) movement,[59] The only reason the college began to teach English was that students went on strike to demand it in 1906. Even after they had won this concession, only 6 percent of the students were studying English by 1908.[60]

Though these early efforts in missionary education were significant for the pattern they set, the total number of students enrolled remained small until the Imperial Edict of 1905 abolished China's Civil Service Examination, and with it, the rationale for more than 1,000 years of Confucian education. Without a national examination to prepare for, Chinese no longer saw any use in studying the classics and they began to flock to Christian colleges in unprecedented numbers. The fall of the Qing dynasty in 1911 accelerated the rush to these schools. Between 1900 and 1918, there was a four-fold increase in the number of students enrolled in foreign schools.[61] By 1924, more than half a million Chinese were enrolled in foreign schools, 8 percent of all students in China.[62] At least half of them studied English.

The vast majority of these students were enrolled in primary schools, most of which were run by Catholic missionaries. From the beginning, Catholics concentrated their educational efforts at the primary level, setting up prayer schools to teach the catechism.[63] Conversely, Protestant missionaries concentrated on secondary and collegiate education. In 1899, of the 40,000 students enrolled in mission schools, 4,000 were secondary students and only 200 were in colleges.[64]

This ratio began to change after the Chinese government set up its first modern school system in 1903. An ambitious national school system was envisioned, based on the model of Japan, encompassing primary, secondary, and tertiary institutions. All students at the secondary and tertiary levels were required to study a foreign language, with English the most popular choice, followed by Japanese and French.[65] The curriculum of the new school system was highly ambitious. Students were to spend five years in lower primary, four years in upper primary, four years in middle school and at least four years of college, a total of 17 years of schooling.[66] In reality, few students got beyond the lower primary level. Of those who went on to complete upper primary, only 5 percent entered middle school.[67] In fact, secondary education remained a weak link in the Chinese school system throughout the Republican period. The government put most of its efforts into primary and tertiary education. Several new colleges were founded after 1900, the most influential of which was Beijing University, founded in 1902.

To strengthen the emerging national school system, a Ministry of Education was established for the first time in 1905, as part of an administrative reorganization of the government.[68] In theory, the ministry had the power to establish and regulate schools, set the curriculum, select textbooks, determine graduation standards and appoint and dismiss educational officials.[69] In practice, however, the Ministry of Education had limited control over provincial authorities, especially after the fall of the Qing dynasty. The authority of the central government became weak, with virtually autonomous warlords emerging as powerful provincial rivals to the central authorities. In particular, after the death of Yuan Shi Kai (second president of the republic) in 1916, China lapsed into a period of civil war for the next decade. During this time, the Ministry of Education continued to issue policy edicts, but they had little impact outside the environs of Beijing.

Reflecting the chaotic political situation of the time, the school curriculum underwent four major revisions between 1903 and 1922. In general, the thrust of these revisions was to cut down on the number of course offerings and to reorganize education more along American lines. This was partly due to the growing American influence in China, as well as bitter Chinese resentment toward Japan's efforts to assume control of Germany's spheres of influence in China after World War I. In 1919, John Dewey visited China, introducing his progressive ideas to Chinese educators. Later, Dr. Paul Monroe spent time in China and had a significant influence on Chinese education. In 1922, China adopted the American system of education, with six years of primary education, six years of secondary (three junior and three senior), and four at the college level.[70]

China's new modern school system quickly came into conflict with missionary schools, especially those at the primary and secondary levels. Before 1907, the Chinese government's attitude toward foreign schools was one of uneasy toleration. But once China had established its own system, pressure began to mount against the existence of a parallel school system operated by foreigners. Since Catholics ran most primary schools, they were the first target of criticism. Chinese considered these schools to be in direct competition with their own primary schools, and increasingly demanded that foreign schools be taken over and incorporated into the Chinese system. It was particularly irksome to China that missionaries were teaching religion to Chinese children too young to make informed judgments.[71]

Despite growing dissatisfaction with foreign schools, early efforts to regulate them met little success. Missionaries simply ignored government edicts and relied on the protection provided them in foreign spheres of influence. For example, in 1907, the National Board of Education decided not to recognize the goals or curriculum of foreign schools. In 1917, the Ministry of Education ruled that non–Christian Chinese should receive equal treatment at Christian colleges, and that no compulsory religious training be offered.[72] Neither of these decisions was enforced.

It was not until the 1920s that China became powerful enough to control foreign schools. The May 4th (1919) movement was a tremendous boost to Chinese nationalism. The founding of the Kuomintang and Communist parties in the early twenties added further impetus to the anti-imperialist movement in China. In 1925, the Ministry of Education began to insist that foreign-run schools register with the government. Additionally, it set four conditions for the future operation of foreign schools: (1) the director or vice-director of the school must be Chinese, (2) a majority of the board of directors must be Chinese, (3) the school should not have as its purpose the propagation of religion, and (4) religious courses must not be compulsory and the curriculum must conform to Ministry of Education standards.[73]

In 1927, after the Kuomintang captured Nanjing and took control of the government, even stricter regulations were put in place. Most foreign primary schools were taken over by the government. Foreign high schools and colleges could operate only if the president and at least two-thirds of the board of directors were Chinese. Also, all schools were required to teach courses in Sun Yat Sen's three principles and the history of the Kuomintang, and offer military training to all students.[74] By 1933, all but one of the Christian colleges had complied with these new regulations. The one dissenter was St. John's, which steadfastly refused to register until 1948, despite numerous student strikes and demonstrations against its continued operation.[75]

By the 1930s, then, the religious goals of the Christian schools had been rejected by all but a handful of Chinese. Most foreign primary and secondary schools were taken over by the government and incorporated into the growing modern educational system of China. Foreign colleges were allowed to continue, since they were seen as providing a necessary function which China could not yet duplicate, but they came under the control of Chinese Christians and were forced to secularize their curricula. As a result, missionary education took on a new look. Colleges began to concentrate on quality instead of quantity and consciously tried to divest themselves of their foreign character.[76] Nevertheless, the goal of these schools continued to be, as before, to make China a Christian nation.[77]

When full-scale war broke out between Japan and China in 1937, educational institutions in China suffered greatly. By 1939, all but one of the Christian colleges had been occupied or threatened by Japanese forces.[78] Many colleges along the central coast were badly damaged, and staff and students were forced to flee into the interior. A number of Christian colleges set up wartime colleges in Sichuan or Yunnan province, often by banding together. Others sought refuge in Shanghai's international settlement, which was safe from Japanese attack until the Allies entered the war in 1941. Under such adverse conditions, educational quality suffered greatly, with few books or facilities available.

After the war, vast areas of eastern China lay in ruins. Many schools had been gutted by bombings and looted. The Christian colleges were better off then their Chinese counterparts, however, in that they received substantial sums of money from abroad to rebuild. In fact, despite the heavy damage, most of the Christian colleges reopened by 1947, and several new ones appeared. But their future was short-lived. By then, the Chinese communists were engaged in an all-out civil war with the Kuomintag, and the tide was turning in favor of the communists. In September, 1948 communist forces occupied Shangdong Christian University, the first foreign college to fall to them.[79]

By the end of 1949, all foreign colleges were in communist hands. Religious teaching was forbidden in 1950, Marxism became a required course, and professors had to submit detailed teaching plans to Party officials for approval.[80] Despite these measures, some Christian colleges were allowed to stay open until the summer of 1952, when China expelled all missionaries and formally took over the Christian schools.[81] Some of the colleges were reorganized and opened under new names, while others were incorporated into new Chinese colleges.

Though the Christian colleges clearly failed in their primary goal of converting masses of Chinese to Christianity, their educational activities left an important legacy in China. First, they led the way in introducing Western science, medicine, engineering and civilization to China. Second, they were the first educational institutions in China to admit women. Third, they authored and introduced a number of textbooks and teaching methodologies which became part of the curriculum of many Chinese schools and universities until the communist triumph in 1949.

English in the People's Republic Period: 1949–1976

Writings on education in the People's Republic of China have tended to focus on the issues of development, nationalism, equity, Marxism and Soviet relations rather than the English curriculum and instruction.[82] The reasons for this are twofold. First, the Chinese communists drastically reduced the importance of English, especially during the 1950s, when the Cold War chilled Sino-American relations and the Soviet influence was at its height. During this time, Russian became the primary foreign language taught in China, with English a distant second. After the Sino-Soviet split in 1960, English reemerged as the primary foreign language in China, but the English curriculum consisted almost exclusively of texts drawn from Marx, Lenin and Mao. In 1964, the Ministry of Education established a seven year program for the teaching of foreign languages, giving English top priority in recognition of its increasing popularity around the world.[83] Starting at that time, secondary and college students were required to study a foreign language. But when the Cultural Revolution broke out in 1966, the study of anything foreign reached its nadir in modern Chinese history.[84]

A second reason for the paucity of writings about English in the People's Republic is that information about it became extremely hard to come by after 1949. Few foreigners were allowed to visit China; even fewer had an opportunity to live there. In place of firsthand information, the methodological tools of China watchers were limited primarily to tenuous inferences based on policy documents and the mass media in China and interviews with Chinese refugees in Hong Kong.

One of the few firsthand accounts of English teaching was written by R.F. Price, an Australian educator who taught English in China from 1962 to 1964.[85] He was among the first foreigners to be hired to teach in China after 1949, aside from the few foreigners who had remained in China after the communist triumph. He reports that by 1965, about 12,000 college students were studying foreign languages at specialized language institutes in China, about 2 percent of the total college enrollment.[86] In addition, most comprehensive universities in China also began to offer English classes after 1962. At the college where he worked, Beijing Second Foreign Language Institute, about half of the students studied English. He states that the goal of the English curriculum was to acquire a working knowledge of the language, without acquiring foreign ideas. In 1962, Chen Yi, speaking to a group of foreign language students, stressed the need for them to learn to think in the foreign language, but hastened to add that this did "not mean learning the way of thinking of the foreigner."[87]

Accordingly, the English curriculum was based almost entirely on Chinese materials translated into English. The only materials from abroad were drawn from left-wing publications in Great Britain and the United States and consisted of such topics as racial discrimination and the labor movement. Most curriculum planning was done locally with mixed results.[88] There appeared to be very little effort at standardization of the English curriculum. Even within one school, English classes did not all use the same materials.[89]

Teaching methods were based on the direct method (using the foreign language as the medium of instruction), but continued to emphasize the grammar-translation approach that had dominated Chinese foreign language instruction since the nineteenth century. Typically, students would be given a text, asked to memorize it, and their understanding would be checked by translating sections from English to Chinese. Key grammatical structures were presented in the form of drills and translation exercises. Texts were sometimes recorded for later listening in language laboratories and students could be heard reciting texts aloud in their spare time.[90] In general, the focus was on learning about English, not learning to use it.

By 1965, some experiments with the audio-lingual method were underway at Beijing First Foreign Language Institute, which tried out a new curriculum based on a sequenced presentation of grammatical points, oral pattern drills and a controlled vocabulary. Though evaluation of students' oral proficiency demonstrated the superiority of this approach to the older method, its adoption was cut short by the Cultural Revolution.[91] An additional hindrance to curriculum reform was the resistance of Chinese teachers. Price attributes this to fear of the unknown, and wariness toward straying from the text, due to the potential for political criticism.[92] In general, Chinese teachers fiercely clung to their traditional role of lecturing from behind a lectern to a passive group of learners. Though Price does not mention it, the key to meaningful English curriculum reform in China would appear to be the necessity of redefining traditional teacher and student roles.

Contemporary English Curriculum: 1976–1986

The year 1976 was a watershed in recent Chinese history. After the death of Mao Tse-tung that year and the downfall of his allies, the Gang of Four, China made an abrupt shift away from the policies of the Cultural Revolution and thereby dramatically altered the status of English in China. Although China had already begun to seek contacts with foreign countries by the early 1970s, with Nixon's 1972 visit most prominent, it was not until after 1976 that large numbers of foreigners began to visit and live in China as part of a new open door policy initiated by Deng Xiaoping, whose goal is to speed up modernization. In particular, since the reestablishment of diplomatic relations with the United States in 1979, a host of American teachers, students and scholars have visited or worked in China. From their accounts, a better understanding of English language curriculum in the People's Republic Period can now be reconstructed.

Along with the growing number of foreigners, writings on English language instruction have proliferated in recent years as the importance of English has dramatically risen in China. These writings generally fall into two categories. The first, and by far the most numerous, are anecdotal accounts written by visiting foreigners[93] or by foreigners who have taught English in China.[94] While these accounts are useful in getting an impression of the learning of English in China, they are not based on systematic research and their conclusions are tentative at best.

A second category of writings, far fewer in number, have attempted to employ some defensible research methodology in studying aspects of English language teaching and learning in China.[95] For example, Barendsen has written about the college entrance examinations which were reintroduced in 1978, including in his account a copy of the English examination and the study outline which was distributed in China prior to the exam. From this, it is possible to infer the major purposes and goals upon which the English examination was based. These were primarily knowledge of English grammar, reading comprehension and translation between Chinese and English.[96]

Price, in a similar vein, reviewed several English language textbooks used in China to determine their goals and objectives and the methodology upon which they are based.[97] Like Barendsen, he concludes that grammar, translation and reading comprehension appear to constitute the major content of the formal English curriculum in China. He found that the grammar translation method of teaching predominates, with some evidence of audio-lingual approach in a few texts. These findings are substantiated by the more anecdotal accounts of numerous foreign visitors and English teachers in China.

The only piece of research to deal with other aspects of the English language curriculum in China is a doctoral dissertation published by Janene Scovel in 1982.[98] She studied changes in the English language curriculum from 1949 to 1982 with the purpose of identifying the extent and nature of change and the forces for stability in these programs over time. Her data sources included her own experiences as an English teacher in China during the 1979–80 school year, interviews with American China specialists and visiting Chinese scholars in the United States, Chinese documents on English language curriculum translated into English, and a questionnaire sent to 50 Chinese teachers of English at five universities in the PRC. Of these sources, the interviews appear to have yielded the most useful data.

Her questionnaire, which attempted to trace changes in teachers' beliefs about language structure, skills and purposes, and teachers' practices regarding Western literature, methodology and instruction, was badly flawed in two ways. First, based on expediency, she did not administer the questionnaire herself. Rather, she sent them in batches of ten to five universities where she had foreign or Chinese contacts and asked her contact person to administer the questionnaire to volunteers and mail them back to her. Thus, her subjects were all self-selected and undoubtedly answered the questions knowing full well that the contact person would read the answers and that they would be sent by mail out of China. Such a data collection method would exert strong pressure on respondents to give politically acceptable answers.

Second, and more seriously, she asked respondents to rate these variables over a 30 year period of time divided into three eras: 1949–66, 1966–76, 1976–81. Getting respondents to accurately answer questions about their current beliefs and practices is hard enough; asking them to rate the preceding 30 years of Chinese history is an impossibility. Anyone who knows anything about China is aware that a major axiom of political faith there is that the current policies, whatever they happen to be, must perforce be the best policies available. To indicate otherwise is to invite serious political repercussions. In particular, Scovel should have known that it is impossible to get anyone in China today to publicly say anything favorable about the Cultural Revolution. Yet, she blithely invited teachers to do just that and subsequently ran the results of her questionnaire through a series of statistical tests, the required assumptions of which she clearly had not met.

It is little wonder then that she reports statistically significant changes for five of six variables when comparing her first and third eras, and significant changes in four of six categories between second and third eras. Incredulously, she found no statistical difference between the Cultural Revolution and the present regarding the teaching of Western literature, although it is widely known that this was banned during the Cultural Revolution.[99]

The only useful results emerging from her study that I can see are that pedagogical practices have not changed very much in China since 1949 and that Chinese scholars visiting the United States report they would be reluctant to introduce more modern practices upon returning home, due to social pressures to maintain the traditional practices and a feeling that practices suitable to the United States may not work in China. The first of these results has also been cited by a number of authors of anecdotal accounts.[100]

The contemporary era, then, has witnessed the explosive growth of English language teaching in China. Today, about 150 million students in primary, secondary, adult schools and colleges are enrolled in formal English courses, either full or part-time.[101] One result has been a rather large number of anecdotal accounts of English language curriculum by foreign visitors and teachers and a much smaller number of systematic research reports. Further, the research that has been done either focuses solely on the formal curriculum or is based on such shoddy research methodology that the reported results are, at best, on a par with impressionistic accounts. No foreigner has yet investigated the instructional, operational or experiential curriculum of a single institution to find out how the formal curriculum is interpreted and taught by teachers and how it is experienced by students.

John Hawkins, a prominent expert on Chinese education, described, in a recent article, important research on Chinese education which needs to be done[102]:

> Scholars interested in the relationship between pedagogical theory and practice will want to study the apparent contradiction between official Chinese interpretations of socialist pedagogy and actual educational practices and outcomes.

This is indeed an important topic, because it appears that curricular practice in China, at least as it relates to foreign languages, has changed little over the past century, despite numerous attempts by the Chinese communists to radically alter traditional teaching methods, including the replacement of virtually all college teachers for a period of time during the Cultural Revolution. The old adage, "the more things change, the more they stay the same" aptly applies to the teaching of English in China over the past century.

3
How the Chinese Today View
the Study of English

In the preceding chapter, I showed how the Chinese government's attitude toward the English language has varied over time, and discussed the effects of this on the teaching and learning of English. In this chapter, the focus shifts to the contemporary scene and to the views of those who administer, teach and study English at the university level. This chapter reports, for the first time, the results of scientific research into the opinions of Chinese administrators, teachers and students regarding the study of English. Data were gathered over a period of one academic year, 1984–1985. The results reported here were based on 152 completed questionnaires and 23 one-on-one interviews with administrators, teachers and students in the English department.

To set the stage, the first section of this chapter briefly outlines the government's view of the study of English, represented by the State Education Commission, formerly the Ministry of Education. This agency of the national government exercises broad administrative and legal powers in the conduct of education. It is responsible, among other things, for establishing university graduation requirements and course offerings and for compiling and issuing required textbooks in some key courses. Since Teachers University is under the direct control of the State Education Commission, unlike colleges under local or provincial control, Teachers University feels the influence of national government educational officials more than most institutions of higher learning.

The second section of this chapter presents the views of three English department administrators, which were gained from a six page questionnaire and hour-long interviews. Their perceptions and preferences on a variety of curricular and instructional issues are discussed.

The third section is devoted to the views of English instructors at Teachers University. They reflect on their philosophy of education, psychology of learning, the curriculum, administration and decision making, among other issues. A total of 16 teachers completed eight-page questionnaires and 7 teachers agreed to be interviewed in 45 to 60 minute individual sessions.

The fourth section presents the views of undergraduate students who were majoring in English. Their opinions about courses, textbooks, teachers, administration, facilities, motives for learning English and quality of their education are presented. A total of 133 students, freshman through senior, completed seven page questionnaires and 14 randomly selected students were interviewed.

Finally, the fifth section is a comparison of the views of administrators, teachers and students to identify major areas of agreement and disagreement.

The Government's View

The English department's overall mission, assigned by the State Education Commission, is to prepare Chinese students to become English teachers at the secondary or collegiate level. To accomplish this mission, the department has devised three major subject matter objectives:

(1) to become fluent in the basic skills of speaking, listening, reading and writing
(2) to recognize important elements in the literature and culture of English-speaking countries
(3) to apply principles of English language teaching

Additionally, the department, like all other educational institutions in China, regards one other objective to be important: to prepare for the social, moral and political responsibilities of adulthood. These four objectives form the guiding principles of the English curriculum.

Students take a common core curriculum throughout their undergraduate program, with few electives available. In the third and fourth years, students may choose two elective courses, Stylistics and Lexicology, and in the fourth year, students' experiences diverge somewhat in two other areas: practice teaching and the senior thesis. The course load is quite heavy throughout the four year program. Students take 12 to 18 hours of English courses per week, plus 4 to 8 hours of Chinese language and politics, for a total of 18 to 24 hours of classroom instruction per week. In the third and fourth years, students also take a second foreign language (French, German, Japanese or Russian) for 4 hours per week, raising the total course load to between 24 and 28 hours per week. Furthermore, school is in session six days a week for 40 weeks per year, divided into two 20 week semesters. As a result, students spend between 600 and 640 hours per year in English instruction in the first three years, and about 480 hours in the fourth year, accumulating nearly 2400 hours of English instruction in their undergraduate program. This certainly represents an intensive approach to language study, and is probably the main factor in explaining student gains in English proficiency.

The Teachers University English department curriculum is presented below (does not include other language courses):

Year One:	*Hours*
Intensive Reading I	6
Intensive Reading II	4
Extensive Reading	2
Spoken English	2
Listening Comprehension	2
	16

Year Two (1st semester):		*(2nd semester—add):*	
Intensive Reading I	6	Grammar	2
Intensive Reading II	4		16
Extensive Reading	2		
Listening Comprehension	2		
	14		

Year Three (1st semester):		*Year Three (2nd semester):*	
Intensive Reading I	6	Reading & Composition	2
Extensive Reading	2	History of Amer. and Brit. Lit.	4
Grammar	2	Selected Readings of Amer.	
Reading & Composition	2	and Brit. Literature	2
History of Amer. and Brit. Lit.	4	Reading & Vocabulary	2
Introduction to Literature		Elementary Stylistics (elect)	2
in English	2	Teaching Methodology	2
	18		14

Year Four (1st semester):		*Year Four (2nd semester):*	
Reading & Composition	2	Selected Readings of Amer.	
Selected Readings of Amer.		and Brit. Literature	2
and Brit. Literature	2	European Literary Masterpieces	2
European Literary Masterpieces	2	Translation	2
Translation	2	Lexicology (elective)	2
Teaching Methodology	2	Senior Thesis (5 weeks)	4
Practice Teaching (6 weeks)	5		12
	15		

To get some sense of the relative time spent on each of the major objectives, the courses can be divided into three groups: basic skills, literature, and pedagogy. Basic skills include all courses in the first two years, plus the composition, reading, vocabulary and translation courses of the last two years. These account for 71 percent of a student's total instructional time in English. Literature courses include those offered in the last two years on American, British and European writers, accounting for 17 percent of the total instructional time. In addition, Western literature is an element of Intensive and

Extensive Reading in the second and third years. Pedagogy courses, comprising teaching methods and practice teaching, account for about 8 percent of the total time, with the remaining 4 percent of the time devoted to the senior thesis.

This breakdown is only a rough estimate, of course, since individual teachers may stress a number of objectives in one course. But it does give a sense of the department's view of the relative importance of its three major objectives. Clearly, basic skills development receives the greatest emphasis in the formal curriculum, accounting for more than twice the amount of instructional time devoted to the other two objectives. This is attributable most of all to the students' low English level upon entering the program. Before they can attempt to master objectives in literature and pedagogy, students must first have a solid foundation in basic English skills. Literature is given the next largest amount of time, and overshadows basic skills development in the fourth year. The least emphasis is given to pedagogy. This appears to be an anomaly for a department whose overall mission is to train English teachers. Apparently, university officials believe that two courses in teaching methodology and six weeks of practice teaching are sufficient training.

The exact content of most English courses is left to the discretion of the teachers. They choose textbooks to be used, supplementary materials, the nature of learning opportunities and methods of evaluation. They are required to exercise discretion within the limits suggested by the course titles, but are not overly restricted in other ways. One course, however, is an exception to this pattern—Intensive Reading I. This course is taught from a common textbook which the administration has designated as the only one to be used. This course stands out in another way, also. It is given more time than any other course: 6 hours per week for a total of 5 semesters. Judging strictly by the amount of time devoted to it, Intensive Reading I can be considered the most important single course in the English curriculum.

As one important piece of the English curriculum, the Intensive Reading I textbook was examined in detail, using Ralph W. Tyler's four components of curriculum as a yardstick by which to judge the material. It will be recalled that these consist of: objectives, learning experiences, organization and evaluation.

Unfortunately, the course title is a misnomer. It is not, strictly speaking, a reading course, but an introductory course in all four basic language skills. The name Intensive Reading comes closer to describing the teaching method employed, but even in this respect, it does not accurately represent the course. One Chinese teacher of this course describes its scope as "covering everything," certainly not much of a hyperbole. Many Chinese educators have also arrived at the conclusion that the course is misnamed. At a recent conference in Shanghai, English language experts from around China proposed that the course name be changed to Comprehensive English, a term that more accurately describes its content.[103] To complicate matters further, the department uses the designations 'I' and 'II' after Intensive Reading to indicate whether the teacher is Chinese or foreign, respectively. In fact, the two courses are quite distinct. Intensive Reading II is truly a reading course, and foreigners are given wide latitude in teaching it.

The textbook designated by the department for Intensive Reading I is simply called *English,* and comes in four volumes. Published by the Shanghai Foreign Languages Institute in 1979 and 1980, it represents contemporary Chinese approaches to English language learning. The text is one of several that are on an officially-approved list published by the State Education Commission. All university English programs are required to use one of these texts in beginning Intensive Reading I. Teachers are required to cover two volumes in the first semester, and one volume per semester thereafter to complete the book by the middle of year two.

The *English* series takes an audio-lingual approach to language learning, supplemented by grammar-translation activities and some communicative gambits like role playing. In the introduction, the authors present the major purposes of the book, though they do not mention any specific objectives. The first purpose is to present a sequential introduction to English syntax based on its perceived difficulty for the Chinese student of English. The second purpose is to develop oral skills through the memorization of sentence patterns and repetition of substitution drills, an approach to language study which is classically audio-lingual. The third major purpose is to "cultivate reading and writing ability" through intensive reading of Chinese and Western sources and a controlled writing program organized loosely around the précis. This last purpose does not receive much attention until volumes 3 and 4, when it begins to dominate the first two. The authors also state their opposition to oral translation as a teaching device unless it is clear that students are having difficulty understanding the content in English. In sum, the textbook stresses oral skills first, then written skills, taught mostly through the medium of English, and presents learning experiences in the form of pattern and substitution drills, and detailed analysis of texts. Thus, while broadly falling within the audio-lingual paradigm, the textbook also incorporates aspects of the grammar-translation approach which has traditionally exercised such great influence on foreign language teaching in China.

It is convenient to discuss the series in two parts: volumes 1 and 2, and volumes 3 and 4, since the focus of the last two volumes differs from the first pair. The first two volumes have, as their major objective, to memorize aspects of English syntax. A second major objective is to become fluent in everyday spoken English. The third objective, and least emphasized, is to read various texts with comprehension.

The learning experiences presented to students in the textbook are divided into eight parts. Opportunities for memorizing syntax are presented through a section called Language in Context, which offers a series of short dialogues or sentence patterns designed to illustrate one discrete point of English syntax. This section is the nucleus of each lesson, according to the authors. As an example, Lesson 5 of Volume 1 presents short sentences containing illustrations of the use of "too," "both," "all," "this," "there," "who," and "where." In some cases, students read and repeat sentences like: "I'm a student. You're a student, too. We're both students." In other cases, they answer questions using "there" ("Is there a book on the desk?").

Further learning experiences for objective one are offered in three other sections of each lesson: Notes, Written Work, and Language Points. The first of these offers explanations of syntactic points like use of "both" versus "all" and the subject, object and possessive pronouns. Some notes provide Chinese translations of words and phrases in the Text or grammatical explanations in Chinese.

This latter practice seems to contradict the authors' proclaimed opposition to translation as a teaching device, but they resort to it sparingly. Written Work provides further opportunities to practice grammatical points. In Lesson 5, the written work consists of a fill-in-the-blank exercise concentrating on the proper use of the articles "a," "an" and "the." The Language Points section presents substitution drills to supplement the grammar illustrated in Language in Context.

Of the four learning experiences devoted to objective one, only two appear to give effective and appropriate practice in the objective. Those are Language in Context and Written Work. The former provides contextual illustrations of the grammatical points to be learned, while the latter provides an opportunity for students to practice using new grammatical structures. The other two sections, Notes and Language Points, do not seem to provide meaningful practice on the objective. The inclusion of Notes simply focuses student attention on translation and Chinese, while the Language Points section is more appropriate as a way to practice speaking English, although in a highly artificial context.

Opportunities to learn the second objective—becoming fluent in oral English—are presented primarily in the Oral Work section of each lesson. In Lesson 5, Volume 1, the oral work consists of activities like: reading and memorizing short dialogues about classroom life, and asking questions about students and objects in the classroom. Another opportunity to develop oral English is the Intonation, Rhythm and Pronunciation section of each lesson. Lesson 5 provides practice in phrase stress by asking students to repeat short sentences which are marked with "Basic tone patterns."

Of these four activities, only one provides any practice approximating real-life conversation—asking questions. The other activities are highly contrived and would not ensure, in and of themselves, that students could speak English any better after completing them. In particular, memorizing set dialogues, a common feature of the audio-lingual approach, does not provide any practice in real communication, since people rarely recite from memory when they talk to others.

The third objective—to read texts with comprehension—is promoted through two sections of each lesson: the Text, and the Words, Phrases and Expressions sections. The Text in volumes 1 and 2 generally consists of a short dialogue or prose selection followed by questions. In Volume 1, the texts are mostly drawn from Chinese sources or based on Chinese life. Out of a total of 24 lessons, 19 have texts about China. In Volume 2 the texts shift to Western topics or sources. Of the 18 lessons in Volume 2, 14 are about Western life. The number of prose selections gradually increases until they predominate over dialogues by the end of Volume 2.

An example of a text in Volume 1 is a dialogue entitled "Talking About the Vacation" from Lesson 15. In the 250 word dialogue, two Chinese students discuss their current vacation, telling what they have and have not done as a somewhat forced and obvious illustration of the present perfect tense, that lesson's major grammatical objective.

An example of a text from Volume 2 is a 620 word excerpt from a South African short story entitled "Saturday Afternoon," which is presented in Lesson 15. The story describes the fate of an interracial couple on a street corner in Johannesburg, who are accosted by two white youths and beaten up. Following the text are nine comprehension questions, consisting of six questions about factual details and three inference questions (e.g. "What have you learned from this story about life in South Africa?").

The latter example is a more appropriate learning experience than the first because students are asked to apply two important reading skills—identifying factual details and drawing logical conclusions—which are indispensable to fully comprehending reading materials. The first example, which only offers practice in vocabulary, is incomplete, because students may be able to define all the individual terms in a passage without seeing how they fit together to create overall meaning.

The other vehicle for reading comprehension is the Words, Phrases and Expressions section, which is basically a vocabulary list of new items in the lesson. In Volume 1, word lists range from about 40 to over 80 words, while in Volume 2, word lists range from about 60 to 100 items. This is an enormous amount of new vocabulary to present in one lesson, especially considering that teachers cover at least one lesson per week. Moreover, the vocabulary lists contain no definitions, translations or examples of the items, so they seem to provide little opportunity for vocabulary growth. In the back of each volume, a selected vocabulary list gives Chinese translations for some difficult English items in the texts.

Organization of the first two volumes is based primarily on continuity, that is, reiterating content in several types of activities, and on grammatical difficulty, though the authors never present their rationale for the sequence which emerges. Volume 1 begins with the verb "to be," and moves to pronouns, question words, the verb "to have," simple present tense, telling time, use of "there" and "here," possessives, present continuous tense, conditional tense ("would"), and the modals "can" and "shall." The authors contend that students should already have a foundation in English before beginning this volume, but they seem to take little for granted except a knowledge of the English alphabet. Like many other audio-lingual textbooks, *English* treats each grammatical point as discrete and independent from other rules of grammar. Once a rule has been presented and presumably learned, the authors do not come back to it at all in Volume 1 and only briefly in two review lessons in Volume 2.

In the area of evaluation of student learning, *English* leaves much to the individual teacher. The Written Work section of each lesson is the major evaluation device presented. It usually requires students to show mastery of the lesson's grammatical points and would probably be assigned as homework by most teachers. In Volume 2, the Revision lessons could be used as an evaluation tool, but the authors do not mention this. To evaluate student progress in speaking and reading skills, teachers would have to develop their own methods.

Volumes 3 and 4 of *English* are used in the second and third semesters of Intensive Reading I. While maintaining the same basic purposes and objectives of the first two volumes, the second year textbook places greater emphasis on purpose three: developing reading and writing skills. The objectives of volumes 3 and 4 can be stated in their order of importance as follows: (1) to read Western and Chinese fiction and nonfiction with comprehension; (2) to memorize aspects of English syntax; (3) to write précis and paragraphs; (4) to become fluent in oral English; (5) to translate between Chinese and English.

The major difference between the first and second year volumes is the emergence of the Text as a major organizing criterion of each lesson. Most reading and writing exercises are based on the Text in the later volumes rather than grammatical content. The latter, while still important, is presented through a section called Language Structure which is loosely tied to the lesson's Text.

The learning experiences of each lesson in Volume 3 are divided into nine sections. Opportunities to master reading comprehension skills are presented in four of the nine: Text, Notes, Comprehension, and Discussion. The texts consist of 400- to 1200-word passages drawn from a variety of sources, both Western and Chinese. Western sources outnumber Chinese by 13 to 3. Fiction predominates, including excerpts of works by Dickens, Lamb (his Shakespeare), O. Henry, the British writer Jerome K. Jerome and South African author William Plomer. Other texts feature biography, science, history and travel. Max Adeler and Agnes Smedley are examples of nonfiction writers represented in Volume 3.

The Notes section, as before, is a compendium of vocabulary items, especially idioms, which are either defined in English or translated into Chinese, often accompanied by examples. The comprehension section presents questions about the text which are mostly of a factual nature (who, what, when, where, how?), but also feature inference, opinion, and vocabulary questions. The Discussion section raises more open-ended questions about the Text to stimulate class discussions.

An example of some of the reading comprehension activities is Volume 3, Lesson 12, which presents a 1000 word adaptation of "King Lear," based on Lamb's *Tales from Shakespeare*. The prose text summarizes the classic tale in modern language. The Notes section following the text includes brief biographies of Charles Lamb and William Shakespeare, and definitions of five idioms. The Comprehension section presents 12 questions about the text, including 10 based on factual details and 2 based on inference. The Discussion section raises three topics which require knowledge of vocabulary, inference, opinion and classification.

The comprehension skills emphasized in Lesson 12 are more advanced than those of the first two volumes, although the format of learning experiences differs only by the addition of the Discussion section. Volume 4 continues the gradual introduction of more complex reading comprehenison skills using the same four learning experiences as Volume 3, plus a new opportunity contained in a Vocabulary section. Once again, fiction predominates the texts in Volume 4, including excerpts from Guy de Maupassant, W. Somerset Maugham, Nikolas Monssarat, E. Braithwaite and Charles Dickens' *Oliver Twist*. Additionally, one drama excerpt by J.B. Priestly is included, along with nonfiction by Edgar Snow, a biography of Madame Curie, and other articles on science, writing and travel. Of the 16 lessons in Volume 4, 14 are drawn from Western sources, with a heavy emphasis on British writers. Most of the texts are from nineteenth or early twentieth century works, but a few are drawn from contemporary sources.

Of the four opportunities to practice reading comprehension in volumes 3 and 4, all but the Notes section are appropriate. The texts present a wide variety of writing styles and content, reflecting the diverse purposes for which students are being trained to read with comprehension. The comprehension questions and discussions provide good opportunities to identify factual details, draw logical conclusions, state opinions, recognize main ideas and define vocabulary in context, all important reading skills. The Notes section, however, provides no practice in these skills and only gives some background information which may help students indirectly in comprehending the texts.

The second objective of volumes 3 and 4 is memorizing aspects of English syntax. This receives somewhat less focus than in volumes 1 and 2, but remains a major aspect of each lesson. It is presented through the Language Structure section of each lesson, which is second only to the Text in the amount of space devoted to it. Volume 3 covers such syntactic points as gerunds, past participles, perfect participles, nominative clauses (infinitives, attributive classes), adverbial clauses, subjunctive mood, comparative adjectives and passive voice. In Volume 4, the Language Structure section includes sentence combining exercises, and drills on the use of verb forms, prepositions, adverbs, and articles. Most learning experiences are in the form of fill-in-the-blank or sentence completion exercises, except the sentence combining practice which, as the name implies, requires students to combine two or three short sentences into one longer one. All of these activities are appropriate, given the objective sought.

The third objective – writing skills – is supported by learning experiences in the form of précis writing and paragraph exercises. Volume 3 introduces the précis in Lesson 9, and incorporates this as a new learning experience in most lessons thereafter. Students are instructed to jot down a list of the main points of the text and write these up, using their own words as far as possible, into a 160 word summary. The first few précis exercises list the main points for the students, but later exercises do not.

In Volume 4, two new learning experiences are offered in some lessons to practice writing skills. These are: Sentence Combining (one part of the Language Structure section), and Paragraph Writing Exercises. In Lesson 12, for example, the Paragraph Writing Exercise presents two faulty paragraphs which students must revise, correcting both organizational and grammatical errors.

Of the activities devoted to writing skills, the précis writing comes closest to approximating real-life situations in which students may be asked to write. Sentence combining and revision of faulty paragraphs present micro skills which may help students to improve their writing ability, but do not lead to direct application of writing skills in contexts in which students may use them in the future.

The fourth objective – oral English – is presented through a section called Communication Activity. This usually offers learning experiences in the form of short dialogues, role playing and question-making. Lesson 3, Volume 3, for example, presents three short dialogues with several blanks. Students are instructed to work in pairs and read the dialogues, supplying the appropriate word in the blanks. Lesson 8, Volume 4, requires students to role play elements of the lesson's text on the Apollo 11 moon flight. The role-playing and question-making activities are far more appropriate speaking practice than memorization of dialogues and substitution drills, because they come closer to using the language in meaningful, real-life situations. Unfortunately, only some of the lessons include such communicative activities, and they receive less emphasis than audio-lingual drill and practice.

The fifth objective involves translation, and becomes increasingly important in Volume 4. Students are given opportunities to translate between English and Chinese, with Chinese to English exercises predominating. Lesson 8, Volume 4, for example, has a translation section which asks students to translate five sentences from Chinese to English, and to translate a short essay on the solar system from English into Chinese. While these activities provide appropriate practice of the objective sought, I question the inclusion of translation at this stage of the English curriculum. It tends to focus student attention on their native language, not English, and serves as one more barrier between the student and the target language. Further, this seems to contradict the authors' declaration that translation should not be used as a method of instruction.

As previously mentioned, the organization of volumes 3 and 4 differs from the first two in that the Text becomes the major organizing vehicle for each lesson. Most reading, writing, speaking, grammar and translation activities are based on the content of the Text. But little sequential organization occurs. Texts are not organized thematically, nor are they based on any apparent sequence of difficulty. Topics range randomly over a large content area. In Volume 3, some attempt is made to coordinate the text with the lesson's major syntactic focus, but in Volume 4, the texts are not closely related to grammatical activities.

Although evaluation is again given short shrift in volumes 3 and 4, it at least receives more attention than in the first two volumes. Most written work still focuses on syntax and grammar exercises which would probably be assigned as homework. The addition of the précis provides teachers with one method of evaluating students' writing and reading development that was lacking in the first two volumes. Additionally, Volume 4 includes paragraph and translation exercises which could be used to evaluate writing and translating skills. But teachers would still have to rely on their own methods of evaluation to assess student progress in spoken English and in reading comprehension. The authors have little to say about evaluation, leaving this aspect of the curriculum to teacher discretion.

To sum up, in many ways the *English* series attempts to be all things to all people. It takes an audio-lingual approach with eventual focus on all four language skills. At the same time, it incorporates many elements of the grammar-translation approach which appeal to those teachers who still prefer the traditional, while adding some activities like role playing associated with contemporary communicative approaches to language learning. This might best be termed an eclectic textbook, and could easily be used by different teachers in a variety of ways. But an underlying preoccupation with grammar, specifically syntax, pervades all four volumes. Emphasis is placed on knowledge about the language rather than communicative use of the language. At best, students practice pseudo-communication in a controlled environment. One might argue that this is enough for a foundation course in basic skills, but it is hard to justify devoting so much time to linguistic acquisition without sufficient opportunities to apply the language in real-life situations in which English is likely to be used.

Overall, the last two volumes of *English* are better than the first two, because they present learning activities which are more likely to result in students' mastering the objectives sought. But this still leaves one question unanswered: Is this the right course for beginning students of English? I do not think so. The course has too many objectives, even for six hours per week, and focuses too much on linguistic competence at the expense of communicative competence. With so much to accomplish, teachers would probably be forced to emphasize a few objectives while downplaying others. This could easily result in students getting limited practice in some basic skills, especially speaking and listening.

The Views of Administrators

The perspectives of administrators were investigated two ways, in a survey and via interviews. The administrator survey was designed to explore a large number of variables affecting the formal and institutional curriculum, to provide background information for further investigation. A total of 25 variables were included in the survey, divided into four sections: demographics, educational background, institutional curriculum and administrator's educational beliefs. The interviews were designed to explore some important issues in detail, especially the decision-making process in the department and the extent of administrator satisfaction.

It was determined that three department administrators have charge of the curriculum and other academic affairs. These are: the Chairman of the Foreign Languages Department, the Vice-Chairman, and the Head of the English Section. All three persons received surveys and returned them. Of these three, two also taught courses in the English section, so their perceptions and beliefs, as reported here, actually overlap those of instructors in the department. These two individuals were also subsequently interviewed. The Department Chair declined my request for an interview.

Administrator Survey Results

A number of the important findings in each of the four categories of questions will be presented. Starting with demographics, it was found that the average age of administrators was 52, and that they came from families in the professions or government. Regarding educational background, it is interesting to find that none of the respondents report majoring in, or taking in-service courses in, the field of educational administration or related educational disciplines. This suggests that administrators perform their jobs without benefit of formal preparation in the areas of administration and management. In fact, all three department administrators are also part-time teachers in the department and must assume both administrative and instructional duties. The respondents are veteran teachers with an average of 28 years experience, but they have far less administrative experience, averaging only seven years. They teach courses in either Russian, Western literature or Lexicology. Two of the three administrators had studied abroad and both reported that their career expectations had been fulfilled.

Responses to questions about the institutional curriculum reveal considerable variation among rspondents on some variables, but their views were quite close on others. Regarding department goals, administrators indicated that they felt five of six listed goals were important, with basic skills development accorded the greatest importance, followed by social, cultural, pedagogical and personal development. Vocational development was the only goal that a majority of administrators did not regard as important. Perhaps this is because vocational development has traditionally been the prerogative of the government, which assigns students to jobs upon graduation without the students' or the university's consent.

Administrators also rated the importance of individual courses. They unanimously agreed that Intensive Reading I and II were the most important courses, followed by Composition and Translation. Regarding evaluation, two administrators reported visiting classrooms at least 10 times a year, but the other administrator never observed classes. Of the many sources of information on student progress, administrators unanimously believed two were most valuable: student work habits and study skills, and student aptitudes and interests. Test results and student behavior were also cited as very valuable sources of information.

In assigning an overall grade to the department, administrators gave an average grade of B−. When asked to rate their satisfaction with various elements of the curriculum, however, administrators were mildly satisfied with only three elements: objectives, use of classroom space and time and class schedules. They were least satisfied with teaching techniques and learning activities, two areas where they report teachers exercise considerable decision making power.

Regarding an important aspect of the institutional curriculum—their power to decide academic matters—administrators indicated they exercised some control, but not complete control over the department. Among other important influences, administrators cited two at the social level and one at the institutional level which had a lot or some influence. The social influences were lists and descriptions of mandated courses, and government-sponsored examinations. At the institutional level, department officials were rated to have more influence than university officials, but two respondents rated both as having a lot of influence on the department curriculum. Teachers' background, interests and experiences – the most important instructional level variable – was also rated influential. There was a split of opinion on the role of students. Perhaps most interesting of all is the rating of Communist Party organizations' influence. They were deemed to have no influence on the curriculum by two respondents, and only some influence by the other respondent. If true, this result shows a significant change in the management of university education, which has been dominated in the past by Party organizations and members.

Administrators expressed mild dissatisfaction with extracurricular activities in the department. They report that the most common activity is the showing of films (which the department does nearly once a week), while sports programs and meetings of the whole department are rare. Administrators listed a variety of activities they would like to provide, including guest lectures and discussions of various academic subjects, discussions among faculty of teaching experiences, and school activities related to the reform of education.

In part three of the survey, adminstrators were asked to rate their agreement with a series of statements that were grouped into two variables: belief in student participation, and belief in teacher concern for students. On the first variable, administrators mildly agree, while on the second, they strongly agree. In particular, administrators strongly agreed with the following: "Student initiation and participation in planning classroom activities are essential to the maintenance of an effective class atmosphere." They also strongly agreed that "The best learning atmosphere is created when the teacher takes an active interest in the problems and affairs of students."

This appears to support an active role for students, but two-thirds of the respondents indicated that "Good teacher-student relations are enhanced when it is clear that the teacher, not the students, is in charge of classroom activities." So, while strongly supporting some student initiation and participation in the classroom, administrators still see the teacher as the central decision making figure in instructional matters. At the same time, they strongly believe that teachers should take an active interest in the problems of students.

Administrator Interview Results

During interviews, which were conducted at the end of my stay at Teachers University, the two administrators I talked with confirmed many of the findings reported above and also expanded on two areas of interest: satisfaction and decision making. Regarding their satisfaction with the curriculum, both administrators reported that they were most satisfied with the basic skills courses taught in the first two years. They believed students definitely needed such courses and that they were generally being taught by competent teachers. They felt less satisfied with the course offerings in the last two years, especially the literature courses.

One administrator cited the quality of teachers in upper division courses as the key problem facing the department. This administrator believed that some teachers were not knowledgeable about Western literature or were poorly trained to teach it. The other administrator was also concerned about the literature course offerings, but for different reasons. This person indicated that too much emphasis was placed on literature, to the exclusion of other areas of importance, such as linguistics and teacher preparation. As for the biggest problem confronting the department, this administrator named lack of resources, both human and financial, which was impeding the department's efforts to improve teaching standards and provide students with a better learning environment.

Regarding institutional-level decision making, both administrators mentioned two areas where they were active: course offerings and materials. They indicated that their administrative responsibilities include drawing up a curricular plan for the department which specifies which courses will be offered, how many semesters and hours per week will be devoted to these, who will teach them, and which students will be assigned to them. They also indicated that all texts and teaching materials used in the department are supposed to be cleared by administrators, though one of the two I interviewed admitted that materials in some of the advanced courses are not scrutinized. Additionally, one administrator said that department officials were responsible for any reforms of the curriculum that might be undertaken. Indeed, this administrator believed that without the initiative of department officials, no significant reform was possible in the department.

Views of English Instructors

Of all the groups who influence education, none has a more direct impact on students than their teachers. The perceptions and beliefs of classroom teachers are critical to understanding what students are taught and how they are taught. To investigate these questions, data were collected from instructors in the English department via survey and interview. In this section, I will first discuss the results of the teacher survey, and then mention the additional information I learned during interviews about the department curriculum. Interview data were also gathered about the specific courses taught by each teacher; these data will be discussed in chapters 4 through 6.

Because less than half the faculty completed surveys, and those who did not included many older teachers with little experience in dealing with foreigners, these results cannot be interpreted as representing the views of the whole faculty. Rather, they mostly represent the views of younger faculty members, those who have been abroad, those who are Americans, and those whom I observed teach. Analogously, interview results only reflect the views of the seven teachers I observed, who were generally young, world travelers, or American.

Teacher Survey Results

The survey explored 27 variables which were divided into six sections. These were: demographics, teacher preparation, decision making process, department curriculum, course curriculum and teacher beliefs. As noted, respondents tended to be young, with an average age of 40 and a range from 27 to 55. The department had a number of veteran teachers over 55, perhaps as many as one-fourth of the faculty, but they all refused to participate in this study. Of those surveyed, 73 percent were from professional or government families, 7 percent were from working class families, and 20 percent were foreigners, all Americans.

Those who completed surveys tended to have less academic training for their positions than American college instructors. Only 15 percent of the Chinese (2 of 13) held graduate degrees, while all of the Americans had M.A. or Ph.D. degrees. The other Chinese instructors only had a B.A. or equivalent. Thus, Chinese teachers of third and fourth year courses are often teaching students with virtually the same educational level as themselves, certainly not an ideal situation. Still, 94 percent of the teachers reported that they had taken some classes since they began teaching, usually in the field of grammar or language structure, which was also the most commonly cited college major of teachers. As for why they entered the profession, the largest number cited interest in English or in teaching. A second reason was simply job assignment, cited by about one-third of respondents. About the same percentage said their career expectations had not been fulfilled, and a check of the data reveals that teachers who cited job assignment as the reason to enter teaching were most likely to report career dissatisfaction.

Teachers basically agreed about four important department goals: social, basic skills, cultural and pedagogical development. There was less agreement about personal development as a department goal and a majority disagreed that vocational development was a goal. When asked to rate their personal view of the same goals, teachers indicated that all six goals were important, but pedagogical, personal and vocational development were less important than the other three. By a large margin, teachers cited basic skills development as the single most important curricular goal.

Half the teachers appear to be basically satisfied with the department,

giving it an average grade of B. But the other half gave the department a C
or D, indicating that some teachers are not very satisfied, among them the
Americans. Regarding the instructional curriculum, teachers report the
greatest satisfaction with setting objectives, selecting content, and scheduling
classroom time use. They were least satisfied about selecting materials, grouping students, and selecting learning activities. Teachers tended to rate the content of their courses as very useful, and they rated the materials and strategies
they rely on most as the most useful.

As for instructional decision making, teachers report a lot of influence in
two areas: instructional strategies and daily schedule and activities in their
courses. They also report having considerable control over evaluation of
students and content of their courses. Areas where teachers exercise little or no
control include the department schedule and course offerings, preparing the
budget, managing funds for instruction, and use of classroom space.

When asked to rate the quality of institutional decision making, teachers
mildly agreed with statements like "In faculty meetings, there is a feeling of 'let's
get things done'" and "Decisions are made by people who have the most adequate and accurate information." Teachers most strongly agreed with the statement, "When decisions are made, it is usually clear what needs to be done to
carry them out." Despite mildly positive ratings like these, a majority of
teachers disagreed that "problems are recognized and worked on; they are not
allowed to slide."

These responses seem to signal a decision making process characterized by
fairly clear lines of authority and implementation of decisions, but some
tendency to avoid confronting and tackling all the problems the department
faces. Furthermore, a significant minority of 30 to 40 percent consistently rated
the quality of decision making as low, suggesting a group of instructors who
are not very satisfied. Once again, the American teachers tended to rate the
department more negatively on decision making, and also gave the department
the lowest overall grade. It is not surprising, then, that none of the Americans
chose to remain at the university for another year.

Teachers were also asked to rate the influence of the government, university, faculty and students on what they teach. Unsurprisingly, teachers rated
their own background and interests as most influential, followed by students'
interests and abilities. At the social level, government-recommended
textbooks were cited as most influential. This is particularly true of two
courses—Intensive Reading and Teaching Methodology—where teachers use
textbooks approved by the State Education Commission. At the institutional
level, teachers cited department curriculum guides (actually, descriptions of
course content) as most influential, followed by department officials.

Regarding the curriculum of their own courses, teachers report using a
variety of materials, activities and strategies to teach students. Textbooks are
the most common materials employed, followed by worksheets, periodicals

and tape recordings. As for activities, teachers are most likely to have students listen to them talk, take tests and quizzes, have discussions and practice speaking and reading English. The most common strategies employed are the direct method (in which students listen and speak directly in English), memorization and translation.

To evaluate student progress, most teachers rely on homework and written tests. Few ask students to write reports or perform in class. Teachers also report working with the whole class most of the time, though some also have students work alone at times. Hardly any small group work occurs.

Finally, teachers, on average, express mild agreement with two curricular beliefs: that students should participate in classroom decisions, and that teachers should show concern for their students. For example, teachers strongly agreed with the statement, "Student initiation and participation in planning classroom activities are essential to the maintenance of an effective classroom atmosphere" and most agreed with the statement, "The best learning atmosphere is created when the teacher takes an active interest in the problems and affairs of students."

Regarding student participation, however, teachers disagreed that students are better motivated when they feel free to move around the room. Once one sees a Chinese classroom, this sentiment is easy to understand. Most are so overcrowded that there is not enough room for people to get up and move around. A second exception to the general pattern of responses is that teachers agree that they should be in charge of the classroom, not students. This suggests that while teachers are willing to consider student opinions and suggestions, they are not generally willing to give substantial decision making power to students alone.

Instructor Interviews

During interviews, I explored the issue of curricular decision making further. Teachers' responses, when considered in light of survey results, tended to support the view that each of the four major educational domains—government, administrators, teachers and students—has some influence on the curriculum. Moreover, each domain appears to have fairly clear areas of responsibility. At the governmental level, teachers report that decisions are made regarding some textbooks and educational funding. At the university level, decisions are made regarding management of the budget, student enrollment and assignment to classes, and course descriptions and offerings.

As for instructors' own influence, teachers rate themselves high. They report relying on their own interests and backgrounds, more than any other single variable, to help them choose objectives, materials, content, learning experiences, teaching strategies and methods of evaluation. But they also appear to consider the interests and abilities of students, thus indicating some concern for the needs of students. Furthermore, most of the teachers indicated that students should have some say in what they learn and how they are taught, but few could give specific examples to illustrate student decision making in their courses.

As for teacher satisfaction, most interviewees basically felt good about the job they were doing in their classes. The one curricular area where teachers were least satisfied was materials. Several complained about the scarcity of good materials or the problems involved in getting materials duplicated and distributed to students on time. A few instructors also expressed concern over the methods they were using, and asked me for suggestions on how to teach some topics.

Teachers were far less satisfied about the department curriculum as a whole, especially course offerings and facilities. Several teachers believed the department should be offering a wider variety of courses, including some in linguistics and Western history and culture, to give students a broader perspective. Another complaint about courses was that students were spending too much time in class, and did not have enough time for independent study or extracurricular activities. Regarding facilities, teachers frequently complained about the lack of office and classroom space. They also felt the department's small library was inadequate and that some facilities, like the language lab, were not being efficiently used.

The Views of Students

No curriculum study would be complete without the perceptions and preferences of students, for they are the major clientele of education. The views of students were explored in a seven page questionnaire which was completed by 133 undergraduates in the English department, and in interviews with 14 randomly selected students. In this section, the results obtained from these sources will be presented and discussed. Additionally, since the interviews included questions about specific courses in the department, those portions of the student interviews are presented in chapters 4 through 6.

Student Survey Results

An important source of data on the perceptions of students was the student survey, which was completed by 78 percent of the students in the English section. It was personally administered to 11 classes of students in the department, which were chosen as a purposive sample of all those taught in the undergraduate program. The survey was designed to assess a large number of variables affecting the curriculum so as to provide baseline data from which to explore issues in detail. The survey covered 22 variables in total, divided into four sections: demographics, class specific curriculum, class climate and department curriculum.

Of the three surveys, the student version was completed by the largest number of respondents and yielded the best data. Accordingly, the more interesting findings are worth describing in detail. The students of this department are nearly two-thirds female and range in age from 17 to 26, with a mean age of 20. The first two years have a higher enrollment than the last two, suggesting a recent increase in the department's size.

Regarding the instructional curriculum of the 11 classes surveyed, students expressed many similar views, but on some issues, they held significantly different opinions. Among similar views, regardless of subject, were student preferences in materials, learning activities, teaching strategies, and grouping, and opinions about the usefulness of content. In the class climate section, students, on average, reported similar ratings of class organization, and extent of student decision making. Moreover, males and females held substantially the same view on these issues.

Overall, students preferred the following types of materials (in rank order): newspapers/magazines, television/radio/video, and films/pictures. They least liked worksheets and textbooks. This indicates a bias towards visual aids and other materials that engage oral/aural language skills. At the same time, students enjoy reading contemporary materials.

In their preferences for learning activities, students also indicate an interest in visual, oral and aural activities. Their three most preferred activities in rank order were:

1. field trips/visits out of school
2. listening to guest speakers
3. watching films or videos

Like students everywhere, they least enjoy taking tests and quizzes, but more surprisingly, they also do not generally care to listen to student reports.

The teaching strategies students prefer most reveal a strong oral bias. In rank order, they like:

1. speaking in English
2. telling how things are similar or different around the world
3. reading in English

They least like memorizing as a strategy and listening in English, although the latter was reported to be the most common strategy employed in their courses. In the area of strategies, students show an interest in active class participation, with the exception of reading.

Regarding grouping, students overwhelmingly expressed a preference for individual class work, with 76 percent stating they liked working alone very much. They least liked working with the whole class, but teachers reported in their survey that students are grouped this way 61 percent of the time. For a country with such a strong collectivist ethic, this finding is surprising. One would expect students to enjoy group activities most, but they report just the opposite. One student told me that she spends her whole school life with the same group of students. They not only take every class together, but also share the same dorm, eat together, and socialize together. For this reason, students enjoy opportunities to work alone in class.

A third area where students generally agree is the usefulness of their subjects, with the majority rating them as useful (76 percent). Still, more students rated courses "useless" than rated them "very useful" (17 to 8 percent).

On the class climate variables, no statistically significant differences between classes emerged from two of the variables: class organization and student decision making. Regarding the quality of class organization, students were evenly divided in their assessment. A majority of students agreed with statements like "We know exactly what we have to get done in this class"; "We know why the things we are learning in this class are important"; and "Our teacher gives us good reasons for learning in the class." Students also overwhelmingly disagreed with the following negative statement: "We don't know what the teacher is trying to get us to learn in this class."

Conversely, a majority of students agreed with critical statements like "Many students don't know what they're supposed to be doing during class"; "The grades I get in this class have nothing to do with what I know"; and "This class is disorganized." Moreover, students also disagreed that "things are well planned in this class." These findings suggest that students are generally aware of the objectives of their courses, but do not think they are well-planned or organized.

Despite this split in opinion, students did not rate particular subjects significantly better or worse on this variable when an Analysis of Variance was run blocking students by subject. One reason no significant differences emerged is that student answers tended to form a favorable response set (the tendency for people to give yes answers on questionnaires), and this variable was represented by more negative statements than the other three. In fact, of the five negative statements included on class organization, students disagreed with only one. By the same token, students disagreed with only one of the six positive items related to class organization.

Divided opinions also emerged from the questions about student choice and student decision making. Roughly half the students said they sometimes could choose their own books, materials and equipment in their courses, but one-third reported they never could. However, the percentages reporting these findings did not differ significantly among course subjects surveyed. Regarding the extent of student decision making in class, students were equally split into two groups. A majority agreed with statements like "We are free to talk in this class about anything we want"; "Students help make the rules for this class"; and "Sometimes I can study or do things I am interested in even if they are different from what other students are studying or doing." On the other hand, a majority of students disagreed with the following: "We can decide what we want to learn in this class" and "Different students can do different things in this class."

This suggests that the issue of student decision making is a controversial one among students. Their responses varied widely on these items, including sizable numbers of students who strongly agreed and strongly disagreed with statements like those listed above. Undoubtedly, perceptions about one's decison making power are affected by one's view of the appropriateness of assuming a decision making role. If one believes that decision making is the teacher's prerogative, then one might well be satisfied with a limited role, and even perceive that role to be larger than it really is. Traditionally, Chinese students have played a passive role in the classroom, deferring to their teachers in most matters. The survey results on this variable, when viewed in light of Chinese tradition, are a bit surprising. Though students do not report a strong decision making role, neither do they report having no influence in curricular decisions at the instructional level.

Despite consensus on many issues involving their courses, students in diverse subjects also report some important differences. Among these, three variables reveal statistically significant differences: interest in subject, teacher concern for students and knowledge of results. Additionally, reports of which materials, activities and teaching strategies are actually used in courses reveal a number of important differences.

In responding to the question: "How interesting or boring for *you* is what you are learning in this class?", students overall reported that their courses were "sort of interesting" (42 percent). But 32 percent said courses were "sort of boring," while only 20 percent chose "very interesting." To determine if these differences were statistically significant, a one-way Analysis of Variance was run, using interest as a dependent variable and blocking students by year in college as an independent variable. The results showed a significant difference between years. ($F = 3.93$, $p < .01$). An examination of mean ratings for each year shows that students in the first two years rate their courses "sort of interesting," while those in the last two years rate them "sort of boring."

To explore this issue further, a second ANOVA was run, this time blocking students by subject. Again, the results showed significant differences among students of various subjects ($F = 2.3$, $p < .03$). A post-hoc analysis using Tukey's HSD procedure did not, however, reveal any significant differences in the group means among the eight subjects tested. Still, a number of interesting trends emerged. The two subjects which students rated as most interesting were Extensive Reading and Spoken English. For both of these subjects, student ratings were clearly in the "interesting" category. Conversely, the two subjects with the lowest ratings were Grammar and Teaching Methodology. Both of these subjects were rated by students in the "sort of boring" category. One other subject, Composition, was also rated sort of boring. All other subjects were rated in between these two extremes. These results suggest that students find three of their subjects, Grammar, Teaching Methodology and Composition, sort of boring, while they rate all other subjects, on average, as sort of interesting. It should also be noted that all three of the least interesting classes were taught to juniors and seniors, which may suggest that they rate their experiences in the department significantly lower than freshmen and sophomores do.

Two of the class climate variables—teacher concern for students and knowledge of results—also revealed statistically significant differences between students of different years. Overall, students mildly agreed with statements about their teacher's concern for them such as "The teacher makes this class enjoyable for me"; "The teacher listens to me"; and "The teacher is fair to me." But a one-way Analysis of Variance blocking students by year in college revealed significant differences ($F=6.63$, $p < .001$). While students in the first, second and fourth years all mildly agreed their teachers showed concern for them, those in the third year tended to agree with the negative statement, "I wish I had a different teacher for this class." To further pinpoint differences, a second ANOVA was run, blocking students by class. Once again, significant differences emerged among the 11 classes surveyed ($F=3.1$, $p < .002$).

When a Tukey HSD test was performed on class means to detect any significant differences, one class, Composition, was determined to have a significantly lower rating on teacher concern than all others. The fact that the composition teacher was a foreigner may be happenstance, or an isolated example peculiar to the dynamics of that particular class. The other foreign teacher whose class was surveyed received a higher than average rating on this variable. But it certainly contradicts a commonly-held assumption among both foreign and Chinese teachers of English that students always prefer to have native speakers as teachers. As for the other classes, the two with the highest ratings on teacher concern were Spoken English and first year Extensive Reading. It will be recalled that these two courses also rated highest on interest level, suggesting a correlation between student perceptions of the teacher's concern for them and their interest in the course.

The last class climate variable—knowledge of results—follows a different pattern. The Analysis of Variance of this dependent variable, when blocked on year in college, also showed statistically significant differences ($F=4.72$, $p < .004$), but in this case, an examination of means for each year reveals a decline in ratings from the first through the fourth year, with a particularly sharp drop between the second and third year. Once again, overall opinions tended to mildly agree with statements like "The teacher tells us how to correct the mistakes in our work"; "This teacher lets us know when we have not learned something well"; and "We know when we have learned things correctly." But students in the third and fourth year are less likely to agree with such statements. By the fourth year, students are evenly divided on this variable between those who agree and those who disagree.

Once again, a second ANOVA was run, using subject as a blocking factor, to determine precisely which subjects were rated significantly higher and lower on knowledge of results. The second ANOVA was also significant ($F = 2.7$, p $< .01$). A post-hoc Tukey HSD test of subject means revealed that one subject, Spoken English, was rated significantly higher than all others when alpha was set at .05. In two other subjects, Listening and Intensive Reading, students also generally agreed that they knew how well they were learning. The subject rated lowest on knowledge of results was Literature. Students in two literature classes, on average, disagreed that they knew how well they were doing in this course.

The subject with the second lowest rating was Teaching Methodology, where students also tended to disagree. The overall trend in the data suggests that students of the first two years felt they had greater knowledge of results than those in the last two years. Still, students only rated three courses as providing adequate knowledge of results: Spoken English, Listening, and Intensive Reading. In the other five subjects, students tended to disagree that they had sufficient knowledge of results. This suggests weaknesses in the evaluation procedures of most of the courses taught in the department.

Given the range of courses surveyed, one would expect to find that students report using different materials, engaging in different activities and experiencing different teaching strategies in their various courses. This, in fact, was the case for each of these class specific curricular variables. At the same time, there are some striking similarities in the materials, activities and strategies used in several subjects.

The most commonly used materials were worksheets, which students reported using in all 11 classes. Two other commonly used materials were textbooks and mimeographed materials. In 9 of the 11 courses, students report using either a textbook or other texts. In Spoken English and Listening, however, no texts are used. Instead, students listen to tapes, watch videos, and use worksheets.

Besides Speaking and Listening classes, students also report watching videos in their Teaching Methodology course, and listening to tape recordings in their Intensive Reading I class. Other subjects do not use these audio-visual materials, relying on texts instead. One other difference is the use of newspapers and magazines in Extensive Reading. Additionally, Extensive

Reading and Western Literature students report having no textbooks for these courses. Instead, they use mimeographed materials, mostly duplicated from single copies of textbooks owned by the teachers of these courses.

Regarding learning activities, students in all 11 classes report that they "listen to the teacher when he/she talks or shows how to do something." Another common activity is "practice speaking English," which students do in all classes except Listening and Grammar. A third common activity is taking tests or quizzes and writing answers to questions. Tests and quizzes appear to be particularly used in Intensive Reading, Spoken English and Grammar courses, while writing essay answers is more commonly reported in Extensive Reading and Composition.

Three important differences also emerge in the learning activities that students report engaging in. First, listening to recordings is only reported in Intensive Reading, Spoken English, and Listening, all courses in the first two years. Second, watching videos is an activity in only three courses, Spoken English, Listening and Teaching Methodology. Finally, class discussions are reported occurring in two courses, one in the fourth and one in the third year: Selected Readings in American and British Literature, and Teaching Methodology. The literature course is taught by a foreign teacher, while the methods course is taught by a Chinese teacher who conducts class discussions, and the entire course, in Chinese.

Regarding teaching strategies, students were asked to tell how often they engaged in seven commonly used foreign language teaching strategies. Of the seven, the most frequently reported was listening in English, which was always or often used in Extensive Reading, Spoken English, Listening and the first year Intensive Reading course. Reading in English was the most frequent strategy in the History of American and British Literature and in Composition. Translating between Chinese and English was the most common strategy in Grammar and also often used in the second year Intensive Reading course. Writing in English was most often done in the Selected Readings of American and British Literature and Teaching Methodology courses. Finally, memorizing was often used as a strategy in Intensive Reading and in Teaching Methods.

The most interesting thing about the findings on teaching strategies is that in no course did students report that they spent most of the time speaking in English or telling how places, people and ideas are the same or different around the world. Regarding speaking, one-third of the students said they seldom or never did this in class. Regarding cross-cultural comparisons, more than two-thirds of the students reported they seldom or never did this. Considering the importance of culture in second language learning, the latter finding is particularly disturbing. If students of English do not report discussing cross-cultural experiences in their courses, then one is left wondering whether they do so elsewhere. It seems doubtful, given the relative isolation of China, even in an era of so-called "openness" to the outside world. Perhaps this is a clue to the widely-reported phenomenon of "Chinglish," a dialect of English spoken in China which is characterized by such culturally inappropriate (for English) expressions as greeting someone by asking, "Have you eaten yet?" (This is appropriate in Chinese.)

The findings on materials, learning activities and teaching strategies also raise one additional issue of great importance. In each case, there is a large mismatch between what students report doing, and what they say they would prefer to do. Based on survey data alone, this mismatch between what is and what students wish would be represents the major source of their disenchantment with the department's curriculum. For example, in the area of materials, students report using worksheets and texts most often, but they would prefer to use newspapers or magazines, and watch films, television or videos. Regarding learning activities, students report listening to the teacher, taking tests and quizzes, and practicing speaking English. But they would rather go on field trips, listen to speakers who come to class and watch films or videos. As for teaching strategies, most students report that they currently listen in English, read in English, memorize words, names, places, etc. and translate, but they would rather speak in English, and talk about cultures around the world. In sum, students prefer audio-visual and participatory approaches to English learning, but they are more likely to get approaches based on listening, reading, and writing instead. This is a major mismatch between preferred learning styles and the teaching styles actually in use. It goes a long ways towards explaining the low overall assessment (C−) that students gave when asked to assign a grade to the department.

In part three of the survey, students were asked questions about the department-wide curriculum, including course offerings, extracurricular activities, objectives, and overall assessment of the department's quality. Students were asked to judge the department's course offerings in two ways: how much they liked each subject, and how important each subject was to them. In both categories, students of different years held roughly similar views, with only minor variations. Overall, the best liked courses in rank order are:

1. Extensive Reading
2. Listening
3. Intensive Reading II

Among fourth year students, Spoken English followed Intensive Reading II as the two favorite courses. The courses which were disliked most in rank order are:

1. Grammar
2. Intensive Reading I
3. Teaching Methodology

In the first and second year, Intensive Reading I was cited as most disliked. Since those students have not yet had Grammar and Teaching Methodology, they tended not to comment on these courses.

The question regarding the importance of course offerings drew different responses, depending on the students' year in college. Overall, ratings of importance in rank order are as follows:

1. Intensive Reading I
2. Extensive Reading
3. Listening

The two least important courses, according to students, are: Teaching Methodology and Grammar. But an examination year by year shows some different rankings. First year students ranked Spoken English and Listening as most important, second year students chose Listening and Intensive Reading I, third year students, Extensive Reading and Intensive Reading I, and fourth year students, Extensive Reading and Spoken English.

To gauge the extent to which course offerings are mandatory, students were asked to indicate how many semesters of each course they had taken through fall semester, 1984. Allowing for some incorrect calculations by students, results show that courses in the first two years are all required, and that students take the same number of semesters of each. In the third and fourth year, this pattern continues, but a few electives are allowed in Composition and Western Literature, and the Lexicology course is an elective taken by only a small handful of students. The variation in Composition results from an elective course in Stylistics offered to third and fourth year students. The variation in Western Literature reflects the fact that some students choose to take extra courses in this area, beyond the four required to graduate.

Turning to the goals of the curriculum, students were asked to rate the importance of six goals both from the department's and their own points of view. In choosing the most important one, both for the department and for themselves, all 11 classes agreed on basic skills development. Regarding other goals, students rated all of them as important, but not necessarily in the same order. To students, the second most important goal is personal development, but in their view, the department stresses social development second.

The greatest dispute is over vocational development. Nearly half the students thought that the department viewed this as unimportant, but only 23 percent rated it unimportant themselves. The importance of getting a useful job rises sharply in the third and fourth years, as students begin to look beyond graduation. The differing responses on this objective reflect the current social debate on the best way to train students for specific jobs. At this writing, students are still being assigned by the state to jobs upon graduation with little or no say in the process. Even department administrators fret that they have little say in the matter. But, several experiments are under way to allow universities more flexibility in placing students and to give the best students more say in decisions regarding their future employment.[104]

Two questions in part three were of a general evaluative nature. Students were asked to indicate the one best thing about the university from a choice of eleven. Nearly half the students chose "nothing." The only two that drew more than token responses were "my friends" and "extracurricular activities other than sports." Areas more directly related to the curriculum like courses, teachers, administrators and facilities only managed to draw 18 percent of the total responses to this question. These responses illustrate more vividly than any other single item the extent to which students are dissatisfied with their educational experiences.

This discontent is also apparent in the overall grade they gave the department: C –. This barely passing grade is even more significant because fully half the students gave the department a 'D,' or failing grade. Clearly, many students are not at all pleased with the education they are receiving.

The last question on the survey asked students to rank ten motives for learning English in China. These were divided into three a priori groups: instrumental motives (using the language as a tool to accomplish something else), integrative motives (learning the language to become part of its culture) and passive motives (learning the language because one has to). Results differed slightly for some classes, but overall, students rated an instrumental motive – to help China modernize – as the most important. This is hardly surprising. A commitment to this broad goal is the raison d'être of all activity in the People's Republic. But surprisingly, the next two most important motives were both integrative: interest in English language, literature and culture, and a desire to understand foreigners better.

The extent to which students cite integrative motives for studying English is unexpected. For years, the Chinese government has been criticizing Chinese who "worship foreigners and foreign things." A strongly-stated desire to integrate oneself into another cultural tradition is considered politically unacceptable, even in the more open environment of the mid-1980s. Of course, neither of the reasons listed goes so far as to express preference for a foreign culture, but the fact that students are highly motivated by interest in Anglo-American culture and peoples is in sharp contrast to what one hears on this topic from the officially-controlled Chinese mass media, which often depicts America as "the evil society," a nation full of dope, derelicts, bums and bag ladies.[105] Students' interest in life abroad does, however, certainly reflect support for the new "open door" policy currently in vogue in China.

The least important reasons for studying English are also enlightening. Students rated two instrumental motives least important: to fulfill family wishes, and to become an English teacher. In particular, this last finding demonstrates the dilemma facing many students at Teachers University. Most do not want to become English teachers, and yet that is precisely what most of them will end up being. But this dilemma does not only confront students. Teachers and administrators must also try to reconcile their own efforts and views with the fact that students are being prepared to work at something that most of them would rather not do. I am led to conclude that the dilemma caused by forced employment in the teaching profession is another important source of student dissatisfaction with the English curriculum.

Conclusions: Comparisons of Three Views of the English Curriculum

The results of the surveys and interviews discussed above reveal a number of important similarities and differences among administrators, teachers and students. These include both the perspectives they have about the curriculum and the beliefs they hold about learning English. In general, teachers and administrators reported similar perspectives and beliefs about the curriculum, but these differed sharply from what students reported.

When teacher and student survey results were compared, significant differences emerged in six areas: grouping patterns, materials, learning activities, teaching strategies, course usefulness and overall department grade. Regarding grouping patterns, students reported overwhelmingly that they prefer to work alone. A total of 76 percent of the students said they liked to work this way very much, while only 8 percent said they liked very much to work as a whole class. On the other hand, teachers report grouping students as a whole class 61 percent of the time, while only 54 percent of the teachers said they ever had students work alone. Furthermore, teachers thought small group work was the most useful, but reported that they rarely grouped students this way.

Turning to materials, both teachers and students generally agreed about the materials actually in use in their courses, but differed sharply when asked to state their preferences. When students were asked to rate a list of materials according to how much they liked to use them, they chose newspapers and magazines, videos, and films as their favorites. Teachers, however, rated textbooks, other books, and newspapers and magazines as the most useful materials. Here, students and teachers agree only on newspapers and magazines. When the least preferred materials are considered, sharp differences also emerge. Students reported they least liked worksheets and textbooks, the two most widely used materials in the department, while teachers thought that games and simulations, and videos were least useful. These results indicate a major conflict between student preferences and the materials actually in use, and also differences in the preferences of teachers and students. Considering that teachers reported making most decisions about materials, it appears they chose materials which least appealed to students.

When learning activities were examined, a similar pattern of disagreement emerged. While both teachers and students basically agreed about the activities actually in use, their preferences were markedly divergent. These are presented below in two tables:

Student Choices	*Teacher Choices*
1. Field trips	1. Speaking English
2. Guest speakers	2. Reading English
3. Films or videos	3. Listening
Least Liked	*Least Useful*
1. Tests	1. Making recordings
2. Student reports	2. Field trips

In this case, students and teachers do not agree on any of the activities, neither most nor least preferred. Another interesting finding is that few of the preferred activities of students and teachers were actually used very often. Of the three favorite student activities, only the third, watching films and videos, was something a majority of students actually reported doing. Of the three most useful activities cited by teachers, only the third, listening to the teacher, was a common activity in all of the classes. Though teachers thought students should practice speaking and reading in class, these two activities, especially speaking, did not actually take place very often.

Learning activities were one area of the curriculum where students and teachers both reported that students had some say. Yet, it does not appear from the data that students were participating in many activities that they enjoyed doing. Even more surprising, teachers were not always using activities that they themselves rated to be the most useful, though they clearly believed they could, along with students, choose whatever activities they liked. This raises an intriguing question. Why were students engaging in activities that neither they nor their teachers rated as appropriate?

One answer appears to be the kinds of teaching strategies employed. It should be obvious that a direct relationship exists between learning activities and teaching strategies. Certain strategies suggest one set of activities, while other strategies suggest different kinds of activities. For example, teachers who used translation as a teaching strategy were not likely to have students practice speaking English in class. Conversely, teachers who believed students should talk about culture would be required to include activities involving speaking.

When teacher and student preferences in teaching strategies were compared, major differences emerged. These are summarized on page 60 in table form:

Student Choices	*Teacher Choices*
1. Speaking	1. Reading
2. Talk about culture	2. Writing
3. Reading	3. Listening
Least Liked	*Least Useful*
1. Memorization	1. Translation
2. Listening	2. Memorization

Of the top three choices, only reading in English appears on both student and teacher lists. Of the least popular strategies, memorization appears on both lists. But students rated listening in English as one of the least liked strategies, while teachers rated it among the most useful. Clearly, students prefer strategies that involve speaking and reading, while teachers did not list speaking as one of the most useful strategies. Furthermore, if one compares the strategies actually in use to those listed above, it is clear that teachers generally use those strategies that they rate highly. Both teachers and students reported that students often read, wrote and listened in English. Regarding translation and memorization, however, teachers and students reported different things. About two-thirds of the students said that they often memorized words, sentences, names and places, but less than half the teachers reported requiring this often. For translation, a similar pattern emerged. This could well be the result of the self-selected teacher sample, which probably included more teachers opposed to traditional grammar-translation approaches to teaching than was true of the department as a whole. Still, these results show that teachers generally favored approaches to teaching that tend to make students passive learners, while students preferred more active strategies. Consequently, teachers were not very likely to chose student-centered learning activities when they preferred to use teacher-centered strategies.

On two other survey questions, statistically significant differences between teachers and students emerged. These were usefulness of courses and overall department grade. Aggregate student and teacher responses were compared, using a one-way Analysis of Variance. Regarding usefulness, teachers rated their courses significantly higher than students did ($p < .004$). While teachers rated their courses "very useful," students gave them only a "useful" rating. This indicates that both believe courses are useful, but teachers feel much stronger about this than students do.

Finally, regarding overall assessment of the department as measured by a letter grade, students and teachers were far apart. Teachers rated the department significantly higher overall than students did ($p < .002$). While teachers gave the department a grade of B– (2.4), students only gave it a C– (1.5). This indicates that teachers are far more satisfied with the department than students are. When administrator responses to this same question are compared, they agree with teachers. Administrators also gave the department a B– (2.5).

Though teachers and administrators agreed on most curricular issues, they differed considerably on two questions, the extent to which they were satisfied with elements of the curriculum and the amount of control teachers exercised over curricular elements. In general, administrators were less satisfied with some elements of the curriculum than teachers were. For example, only one-third of the administrators were satisfied with the way students are evaluated, but over half the teachers reported satisfaction with this component. Regarding content, a similar pattern emerged. Administrators tended to be mildly dissatisfied with this component, while teachers were generally quite satisfied with the content of their courses.

But the biggest disagreement between teachers and administrators came over learning activities and teaching strategies. None of the administrators were satisfied with these two components of the curriculum, but half the teachers were, including 25 percent of the teachers who reported being "very satisfied" with the teaching strategies they used. These responses indicate that administrators see more problems with the curriculum than teachers do, especially in the areas of content, learning activities and teaching strategies.

When teachers and administrators were asked to rate the amount of control that teachers have over curricular decisions, they both reported that teachers have considerable control over materials, content, evaluation, and teaching strategies. Regarding objectives, however, teachers reported less control than administrators thought they exercised. For learning activities, the opposite occurred. Teachers generally felt that they exercised complete or considerable control over this component, while administrators thought that teachers only exercised some control in this area.

In conclusion, the survey results demonstrate that students have perspectives on the curriculum that are significantly different from the teachers' and administrators'. They are far less satisfied with major elements of the curriculum such as objectives, learning experiences, teaching strategies and organization. Analysis of the results revealed that student dissatisfaction is due to several factors, including the mismatch between students' preferred learning styles and the actual teaching styles employed by instructors, the lack of student interest in becoming teachers and the forced employment of Teachers University graduates in the teaching profession, and the lack of student decision making power which led some students to feel they had no control over the most basic aspects of their education. Of all the problems facing the department, the most serious is the dissatisfaction of students.

As for teachers and administrators, comparisons of the survey and interview results demonstrated that administrators were less satisfied with the department curriculum than teachers were, but that both groups were mildly satisfied. Further, analysis of teacher survey results showed that three distinct groups of teachers worked in the department. One group included older Chinese teachers of English who had never been abroad and had little experience with foreigners. This group generally chose not to participate in this research study, but to the extent that they were represented at all, they were the most satisfied group of all those included in this investigation. A second group of instructors included younger Chinese faculty and those who had been abroad. This group was more critical of the curriculum, and expressed less satisfaction with the way the department was run. The third group was the American teachers, who were by far the least satisfied adults in the department.

In the area of curricular decision making, both administrators and teachers have fairly clear realms of authority. Administrators, for example, make decisions regarding the department budget, course offerings, enrollment and class schedules of students, and the recruitment and assignment of instructors. Teachers make decisions regarding content, evaluation, teaching strategies and learning activities of their own courses. Decisions regarding objectives and materials appear to be shared among three levels: the government, the university and the faculty. State Education officials decide the overall purposes of the university, and these in turn guide administrators in formulating goals for the department, while teachers are generally free to determine the specific objectives of the course they teach. Regarding materials, government officials and department administrators largely determine the textbooks for two courses—Intensive Reading I and Teaching Methodology—while decisions about materials in other classes are mostly left to teachers.

Students get to make very few decisions about the curriculum or other aspects of their school life. Occasionally, their teachers may solicit their opinions about particular materials, learning activities or content, and students may sometimes choose their own materials, but that is the extent of student decision making power.

4
Laying a Good Foundation in Beginning English Courses

Introduction

Whenever they begin to learn a new subject, the Chinese have a cliché to describe this process: *da hao ji chu*, meaning "lay a good foundation." As noted in Chapter 3, the English courses taken by undergraduates in the first two years at Teachers University are beginning courses which are designed to provide a solid foundation for more advanced courses in the junior and senior years, and beyond. The results reported in this chapter describe what I learned about the purposes and practices of beginning English courses in China through observation of what occurs in these courses day to day.

Over a period of four months, observations were conducted in seven courses offered by the English language section of the foreign languages department at Teachers University. A total of 70 hours of observation took place; 60 of those hours were naturalistic observations in which I sat in the back and took detailed notes of what I saw and heard, and 10 hours were recorded on audio or video tape for subsequent discourse analysis. It was my original intention to arrive at an interpretation of what I saw that teachers and students would both agree with. In fact, I found this was impossible, due to substantive differences between the perspectives of teachers, students and myself. So, to compensate for a lack of consensual interpretation in most courses, I also report the opinions regarding these courses which were expressed by teachers and students in interviews.

Observations were conducted with the 11 components of curriculum identified by Goodlad and Tyler as a guide. My specific purpose was to discover how these components are defined in English courses in China. Accordingly, the results described in this chapter and the following two chapters include evidence regarding the 11 curricular components listed on page 64 in the order they are considered:

1. objectives
2. materials
3. content
4. learning activities
5. teaching strategies
6. evaluation

7. grouping patterns
8. organization
9. time
10. space
11. class climate

The courses chosen for observation included the following:

First Year
Extensive Reading
Intensive Reading I

Second Year
Intensive Reading I
Listening Comprehension

Third Year
Teaching Methodology

Fourth Year
Stylistics
Selected Readings of American
and British Literature

In this chapter, the four beginning courses in the first two years of the undergraduate curriculum are described in detail: Extensive Reading, Intensive Reading I (first year), Intensive Reading I (second year), and Listening Comprehension.

In Chapter 5, the two literature courses of the fourth year—Stylistics and Selected Readings of American and British Literature—will be described in detail. Finally, in Chapter 6, the Teaching Methodology course of the third year will be described.

FIRST YEAR: EXTENSIVE READING

I entered a crowded classroom with 19 desks arranged to form four rows facing the front. The room was spartan in appearance, with a bare concrete floor, concrete walls, two windows that didn't quite close, and four fluorescent lights, only two of which worked, dangling by chains from the ceiling. Students had tried to brighten the room up a bit by hanging maps, calendars, Chinese calligraphy and a bulletin board on the walls, but nothing could disguise the fact that this had been a cheaply constructed room with little attention to aesthetics. A few students looked up and greeted me; others continued to read their books. One student, the class monitor (a kind of student representative), steered me down a narrow aisle to a vacant seat in the back. We all waited for the teacher to arrive.

A woman in her thirties entered and mounted a podium at the front of the room. She assembled her notes and books on the lectern, turned around and wrote the words, "America on Wheels" on the blackboard behind her. Then she faced the students. The class monitor announced in Chinese that class was ready to begin and whispering voices became silent. The teacher pointed to the phrase on the board and asked, "What do you think this title means: America on Wheels?"

A girl answered, "America is on wheels."

"But what does that mean?" the teacher persisted.

Another girl offered, "Americans do everything in cars."

"Oh, I see what you mean," the teacher responded. "America on wheels; China on bicycles." The class laughed appreciatively. "Let's look at the first paragraph," she said, and then began to read aloud:

> Early automobiles were sometimes only "horseless carriages" powered by gasoline or steam engines. Some of them were so noisy that cities often made laws forbidding their use because they frightened horses.

The teacher then proceeded to define the term "horseless carriage" as an early name for automobile, and translated the word "forbid" in Chinese. She talked at length about the early days of automobiles in America, quoting from a book she had in front of her.

So began one session of Extensive Reading, a required course for students in the first two years of the undergraduate curriculum. Unlike Intensive Reading, which is largely an introductory course in grammar, Extensive Reading is truly a reading course designed to improve students' reading comprehension skills and acquaint them with important people, places and events in Western history.

I observed five quite different class sessions over a period of ten weeks. The course did not meet for five weeks, including one month-long stretch, due to an illness in the teacher's family. A substitute teacher was finally located after one month, and taught two sessions of the course I observed. This teacher was a recent graduate of the department in her very first teaching assignment. Later, the regular teacher returned and was observed twice more. Normally, this course was taught to three separate classes of about 15 students each who comprised the freshmen year. But during the substitute's tenure, all three groups met together. The differences in teachers and class sizes radically altered the climate of the sessions I observed. I was unable to interview the substitute, so the comments reported here are those of the regular teacher.

When I asked this instructor what she hoped students would learn in her class, she cited two goals: "enlarge their vocabulary" and "reinforce their reading comprehension ability." Two students I interviewed in one first year class also mentioned learning about vocabulary and reading comprehension, but they both added one other important thing they had learned—knowledge about America—its authors, history and culture.

After observing this class five times and talking to the teachers and students, I arrived at the following five objectives, listed in rank order of importance:

Objective 1: To define vocabulary items in context

Objective 2: To recognize important people, places and events in American and European history

Objective 3: To identify factual details in reading materials
Objective 4: To draw inferences based on reading materials
Objective 5: To summarize main ideas presented in reading materials

Though I identified more objectives than the teacher or students did, we all basically agree about the course's important purposes. The major difference is that I identified three separate reading comprehension skills taught during sessions I observed, while the others did not differentiate among reading skills. Additionally, the teacher did not mention the second objective, although she always devoted some time to explaining the people, places and events introduced in the materials. Perhaps she simply forgot to mention this as an objective, or considered it a minor one in comparison to the two she stated. Students, however, listed knowledge about America as the most important thing they had learned in the course.

The materials employed while I observed represented a variety of content and styles, one of the specified curricular requirements of the course. In this way, students were intended to gain wide exposure to fictional and nonfictional writing in English. All but one of the pieces were written by twentieth century American writers. Each week, students were given a different piece to read. These were mimeographed, often from one original copy, and served as the "textbook" of the course. Some of the materials included study questions; others contained only the text. From what I learned, students in Extensive Reading were asked to read short stories, poems, essays, newspaper and magazine articles and a few original pieces written by teachers in the department.

The content of the five lessons I observed reveals the breadth of reading materials offered in this course. They included three short stories, one biography, and two essays on American technology. The exact content is listed below:

> *Session One:* "In Another Country," by Ernest Hemingway, a 1500 word short story which describes the experiences of wounded soldiers in World War I.
>
> *Session Two:* "In the Cart," by Anton Chekhov, a 2600 word short story which describes a teacher's life in a small Russian village around the turn of the century.
>
> *Session Three:* "Lincoln's Birthday," an anonymous 2300 word biography of the life of Lincoln, drawn from a contemporary American magazine.
>
> *Session Four:* "America on Wheels," an anonymous 700 word history of the automobile in the United States with accompanying discussion questions, and "Airplanes: Yesterday, Today and Tomorrow," an anonymous 600 word history of the airplane, also with discussion questions.

Session Five: "The Lottery," by Shirley Jackson, a 2500 word short story about a bizarre ritual in a small American town, with comprehension questions covering both factual details and inferences.

Students were presented with several learning activities each week, some of which differed considerably, depending on who taught the course. Though all five objectives were supported by learning activities, some received more attention than others. The learning activities I observed are presented below, according to the objective they were perceived to support:

Objective 1: To define vocabulary items
1. students define vocabulary by orally paraphrasing the meaning
2. students ask the teacher to define vocabulary they don't know
3. students listen to the teacher define vocabulary or give translations

Objective 2: To recognize people, places and events in Western history
1. students listen to the teacher explain author's life and background of reading materials
2. students compare life in China and abroad (one week only)

Objective 3: To identify factual details
1. students listen to the teacher explain details
2. students answer questions orally about details

Objective 4: To draw inferences
1. students listen to teacher draw inferences
2. students answer inference questions orally

Objective 5: To summarize main ideas
1. students present oral summaries of reading materials (four weeks)
2. students prepare written summary of materials (two weeks)

It should be noted that some of these learning activities were more effective than others. Those that appeared to work best engaged students actively, requiring them to talk or write. When students simply listened to the teacher, they had little opportunity to master the behavior implied by the objective. Unfortunately, students spent far more time listening to their teachers than they did talking or writing themselves. This was especially true for objectives one and two.

The main reason students were so inactive was the teaching strategies employed in the course. Though I saw a total of five strategies in use, one of them — explication of text — occupied more time than any other. This involved the teacher reading from the text and stopping to explain vocabulary and meaning line by line. With this strategy, students became passive listeners. The only activity they could engage in was to take notes of what the teacher said, and less than half the students were observed to do so. Others followed along in their texts, looked up at the teacher, or idly stared around the room. Besides this strategy, teachers were observed to use four others sparingly. These were:

> (1). drill and practice: the teacher posed oral questions about vocabulary, details, inferences, etc. and students gave short answers
>
> (2). translation: the teacher translated English vocabulary items into Chinese
>
> (3). discussion: the teacher posed open-ended questions and invited students to talk about them
>
> (4). retelling: the teacher asked students to retell or summarize portions of the materials orally

Of the strategies employed, the last two—discussion and retelling—most actively engaged students in the learning process, but were the least often used. Drill and practice, while suitable for some objectives like defining vocabulary, did not appear to work very well in helping students understand the historical and cultural background of materials and the deeper meanings implied in them. It also seemed to bore students when used in excess. Translation as a teaching strategy has been criticized for years because it focuses student attention on the native language rather than the target language and offers little opportunity to practice using the target language. Though the regular teacher had studied abroad in the United States and was aware of contemporary criticism of translation, she used it quite frequently to explain the meaning of new vocabulary items. This practice did not help students to master any of the course objectives, but perhaps did serve to make difficult materials more accessible to students and to build up an amiable class climate, since both teacher and students were more comfortable conversing in their native language.

To evaluate the extent to which students were mastering objectives, the teacher relied primarily on a final examination which required students to read texts and answer essay questions about them. Aside from this, I observed no written evaluation in the sessions I attended. Student homework was not collected by the teacher, and only one quiz was given. In lieu of this, the teacher relied on oral evaluation of student responses in class to judge progress. The regular teacher appeared to use oral evaluation effectively, commenting on almost every student response, either by praising correct answers or asking other students to correct wrong answers. The substitute teacher did this less frequently, so that during her sessions, students received virtually no evaluation of any kind.

Evaluation was one of the biggest weaknesses of this course. The final exam may have told the teacher what students knew at the end of the course, but it provided little productive feedback to students. They had few clear indications from the teacher, week by week, how they were doing in the course. The teacher also made no attempt to determine how much students knew at the outset, and how much they had learned throughout the semester. In the last session, which was videotaped, the teacher made a point of evaluating student understanding of the materials via a short true-false test at the beginning of the period, but this was the only week that such a procedure was observed, and was probably added that day because I was videotaping.

Though the size of classes varied from week to week, the grouping patterns employed by teachers did not. Students were always grouped for instruction as a whole class. They did no small group or paired work at all, and only worked alone when taking the true-false quiz. Still, variations in class size were an important influence on the class climate. The two sessions when the whole first year met together were characterized by far less student participation in the lesson, more student side talk and whispering, demonstrably fewer interested students and consequently, a much more frustrated teacher. The small class sessions of 14 to 16 students each were vastly more effective. Though students did not get many opportunities to talk, they appeared to follow the lesson more intently and were not observed to talk much among themselves or otherwise fail to pay attention to what was going on. Part of this difference must also be ascribed to the substitute teacher's lack of experience. She was extremely nervous and proved unable to get and hold student attention for very long. But she was asked to teach in very crowded, difficult conditions which would have tested the abilities of a far more experienced instructor.

Because of cancellations and changes in teachers, I had trouble assessing the organization of this course. During the ten weeks I was attempting to observe classes, Extensive Reading was characterized by a complete lack of organization. From one week to the next, I never knew if the course would meet, where it would meet or who would teach it. Students told me they were just as confused. In fact, one week when I was told the course would meet, I showed up to find the whole class waiting for the teacher. She never arrived, and students pressed me to teach them instead that day. Though I was not prepared to teach, I answered their questions about life in America for an hour or so.

Under more normal circumstances, the course was designed so that each lesson was self-contained and could be completed in two hours. Most of the lessons I observed were divided into three parts: an introduction, in which the teacher introduced the material to be read and the author or other background information, a vocabulary activity, in which the teacher presented new vocabulary items from the lesson, and an explication of the text, in which the teacher went through the materials line by line, stopping to explain meanings and structures. Occasionally, other elements were added, such as discussion or retelling.

Judging by the three organizational principles identified by Tyler—continuity, sequence and integration—the course was poorly organized. The only apparent continuity (the reiteration of curricular elements over time) was the fact that similar activities and strategies were employed from week to week to teach the course. But even this limited continuity was broken by the fact that the course did not meet for five weeks and had two different teachers. As for sequence (the vertical organization of curricular elements from the simple to the complex), the materials and content of the course exhibited no apparent sequential organization.

Materials were certainly not organized thematically, chronologically or by reading difficulty, three of the most common ways to sequentially arrange a reading course such as this. Other curricular elements also did not appear to be organized in any demonstrable sequence. Rather, it was as if each lesson existed independently of all others. Within each lesson, though, some sequencing occurred. Typically, the teacher began the lesson with an overview of the content, introduced new vocabulary, and then proceeded to determine meaning.

Regarding the broader vertical organization of this course—the way it relates to other reading courses in the department—I also did not discover any evidence of sequence. Though students take four consecutive semesters of Extensive Reading, the department has no plan for these courses. Instead, it appeared that the teachers of Extensive Reading drew materials from whatever sources were at hand, and taught these in whatever order they liked. One unfortunate result, according to some students, was that they sometimes reread the same materials in two or more courses.

The third organizational principle, integration, was even less in evidence than the other two. Integration implies that curricular elements are organized horizontally across lessons, units and subjects so that students get a more unified and complete understanding of all the elements under study and learn how these apply to what they have learned from other sources. There was none of this in the sessions I observed. Teachers did not even review previous lessons, let alone attempt to synthesize student learning or help them to apply what they had learned. So little variety in learning activities occurred that students had few chances to broaden their knowledge or approach the objectives from different perspectives. Of course, it should be noted that integration is usually the hardest organizational principle to document, because evidence of it only emerges over long periods of time. Despite this fact, of all the curricular elements at work in this course, organization was clearly the weakest link, resulting in an inefficient learning environment.

The allocation and use of time in this course varied from week to week, but it was possible to make some overall estimates of time use. I determined that teachers talked about 90 percent of the time, with the remaining 10 percent divided between student talk and occasional individual written work.

The percentage of time devoted to each of the five objectives was estimated as follows:

Objective	Percent Time
Vocabulary	35
History and culture	20
Factual details	20
Inference	15
Main ideas	10

The last curricular element to be considered is space. As indicated, it was always at a premium. Classrooms were overcrowded even in the best of circumstances, but when 40 students tried to squeeze into a room with 20 desks, the results were chaotic. Teachers were always separated from students by a podium and lectern, and were never seen to step down and approach students while class was in session. This barrier between teacher and students was both physical and psychological. The teacher stood above students and assumed the role of authority. Students rarely questioned their teachers, and when they did, teachers invariably insisted they were right.

Though students made attempts to decorate at least one of the classrooms I visited, the results still left much to be desired. Rooms were often dirty, poorly insulated from noise, poorly lit and without heat. In one classroom, none of the lights worked, so everyone relied on whatever natural light happened to enter through three windows along one wall. In another class, two of four lights were out of order, making for a very dim classroom. Cold was endemic in winter and nothing insulated the classrooms from heat in summer. During the two months I observed this course, from March to May, classroom temperatures varied from a low of 51 degrees F. to a high of 79. Of course, the poor conditions bothered me as an American far more than they appeared to bother the Chinese, who are used to living in places with insufficient space, heat and light. But the uncomfortable, poorly-lit classrooms used in this course did nothing to make learning a pleasant experience for students.

Discourse Analysis

To examine the "hidden" curriculum and the class climate in greater detail, the last session I observed was recorded on video tape for subsequent discourse analysis. By carefully examining and analyzing the tape, I was able to pinpoint behavioral regularities which affected the implicit curriculum and class climate, and to assemble a series of statistics that shed light on the ways in which the teacher and students interacted. For each utterance, I identified the following sociolinguistic characteristics, based on the work of sociolinguist Dell Hymes[106]:

(1). setting
(2). sender (speaker)
(3). receiver (audience)
(4). message form (question, response, assertion, etc.)
(5). amount of time
(6). topic
(7). tone (mock, serious, laudatory, critical)
(8). style (archaic, formal, informal, intimate)
(9). channel (oral, written, kinesic, English, Chinese)

It was not easy to convince the teacher to allow me to videotape, since she had never been taped before and viewed the prospect with some dread. Though she reluctantly agreed, she used the opportunity to prepare and teach one of the best lessons I observed in the department. Students appeared to cooperate in this effort by participating more actively than I had seen them do before in this course. The result was a much better than usual class session, with more student talk and more attention to comprehension skills. The teacher also had students take a true-false pretest, something she had not done before. In sum, the videotaped lesson was atypical. Nevertheless, it provides interesting insights into the interactions between the teacher and students.

The setting of this lesson was a small classroom which was "home" to one first-year class. A total of 15 students and two observers, in addition to myself, were present. The teacher taught "The Lottery," a short story by Shirley Jackson. The overall climate prevailing during this lesson was quite positive, though serious. The teacher encouraged students to participate and they responded eagerly in most cases. This was quite a contrast to some of the sessions I had observed earlier, particularly those taught by the substitute. During those two sessions, students kept up a constant murmur of conversation which annoyed the substitute to no end. The climate of those sessions was marred by student disinterest and disrespect and teacher frustration. A number of testy exchanges between teacher and students occurred. Students complained that the teacher did not explain the lesson well, that the materials were too difficult and that they were bored. When the regular teacher taught them, however, students generally responded favorably. They appeared to respect her, and thus paid more attention to what she had to say.

The hour and a half lesson was divided into four parts. First, the teacher introduced the story and the author and asked students to briefly summarize the plot. Second, students took a short quiz on factual details in the story, which the teacher corrected in class. Third, the teacher asked students to answer a series of inference-based questions which followed the story. Finally, the teacher explained the text line by line, stopping to define vocabulary and interpret the meaning of each paragraph. Thus, the teacher appeared to be seeking four objectives in this lesson:

Objective 1: To summarize main ideas
Objective 2: To identify factual details
Objective 3: To draw inferences
Objective 4: To define vocabulary in context

The results of the discourse analysis reveal, despite greater student participation than usual, that the teacher dominated the lesson, doing 87 percent of the talking, initiating most questions, making most of the explanations and assertions and all of the directives. Students primarily participated by responding to teacher questions. If someone were led blindfolded into this classroom, he could quickly tell who the teacher was simply by hearing who did most of the talking. Furthermore, student talk was not equally distributed. Though 12 or 15 students spoke at least once, six of the students did most of the talking and received most of the teacher messages that were directed at individual students. One student in particular, a boy, did more talking than anyone else. He also made the only two assertions not stated by the teacher. At least half the students were primarily passive listeners throughout the lesson, speaking only when they were called upon to give an answer on the true-false quiz. Also, most student talk occurred in the first hour of the lesson during the quiz and inference sections. Once the teacher began her explication of the text in the last half hour, students said virtually nothing thereafter.

Further insights are gained by looking at the tone, style and channel used in the lesson. The tone was serious throughout. Students laughed only once, and that was when one of them made a mistake. The teacher switched to a laudatory tone eight times when she praised the answers of several students. She did not make a critical remark, even when students made errors. The style was generally formal. The teacher did not use colloquial or informal language except when she read dialogue from the story. Students answered in complete sentences. The channel was mostly oral throughout the lesson. The teacher wrote two things on the board: the title of the story and the author's name, and the word "sinister," a new vocabulary item for students. The teacher also resorted to using Chinese 12 times during the lesson, accounting for about two of her 74 minutes of talking. Each time she used Chinese, it was to give a translation for a new vocabulary item.

The teacher and two students were asked during interviews to rate the class climate of Extensive Reading. The teacher, who instructed all three classes of the first year, rated each differently. On a scale of one to ten, with ten being best, the teacher gave class one, which I videotaped, the highest mark, a seven. She gave class two a four and class three a five. In explaining her ratings, the teacher commented:

> In class one, the atmosphere is more relaxed and more active than the other classes. They ask more questions. But they are not as good as the older students I have taught. Class two is rigid and shy, especially the girls tend

to be shy. Class three is in the middle of the other two, better than two but worse than one. Students seem to like literature best, but they also like some popular science, biographies and some poems. Non-fiction on science and technology is not too popular.

The two students were asked to identify the one best and one worst thing about Extensive Reading. For best thing, one student said, "I like the materials best, because they include many kinds of things, some new things we haven't had before." The other student cited the teacher, saying, "she taught us how to understand the writer's ideas and style."

For worst thing, both students agreed that some materials were too difficult. One said, "I don't like so many new words in the materials. It prevents me to understand them well, especially science articles." The other student agreed, saying, "Some [materials] have so many new words, I can't understand it. For example, poems, especially old ones, are very difficult in meaning."

These assessments of class climate are in basic accord. Both teacher and students recognize the importance of the right materials, and give credit to each other for the basically positive climate in class one.

Furthermore, it would seem there is a connection between the difficulty level of materials and the extent to which students are active. When fairly simple short stories and popular science were presented, students tended to be active, responding to questions and even initiating some of their own. When materials were difficult, however, like the Lincoln biography and the Chekhov short story, students were less active and considerably more frustrated. This suggests that the teacher and department administrators should pay greater attention to choosing materials which are within the range of students' ability. Based on the sessions I observed and the results of the reading test, first year students seemed to be reading comfortably at about a fifth to sixth grade reading level. When materials exceeded this level, students became frustrated and so preoccupied with unknown vocabulary that they were not able to appreciate the information contained within the materials.

Decisions about materials were complicated by the fact that the regular teacher and the English Section Head had different ideas about appropriate reading materials for this class, and neither seemed to take the opinions of students into account. The regular teacher preferred to choose short stories, like the Hemingway and Jackson pieces she taught. The Section Head thought students should be reading nonfiction, and chose the Lincoln biography and pieces on American technology while the substitute was in charge of the class. Meanwhile, two students I interviewed said they did not feel they had any say in how or what they learned, and they were bothered by this. Attention to student opinions and closer cooperation between teachers and administrators would result in a better selection of materials.

Summary

Because of the many changes and disruptions affecting this course, it is difficult to rate its overall effectiveness. When the regular teacher taught materials within the range of students, the course appears to have been fairly successful on at least two objectives: defining vocabulary in context, and identifying factual details. Both of these objectives received considerable curricular attention and were supported by a number of learning activities. When the substitute taught, however, students did not seem to be making much progress on these two objectives. Instead, they did better on objective five, summarizing main ideas. This is because the substitute emphasized main ideas more than the regular teacher did, and the materials she taught contained so many new vocabulary items for students to define that they could not easily identify factual details.

As for the other two objectives, neither teacher appeared to be having substantial success, primarily because of inappropriate learning activities and teaching strategies. Objective two, recognizing important people, places and events in Western history, arguably one of the most important objectives of this course, was marred by the fact that students had few chances to practice the behavior—recognizing—implied by the objective. Instead, teachers did all the talking about Western history, and students were simply passive listeners. Only once, in the lesson about automobiles and airplanes, did the teacher encourage students to actively participate in a comparative discussion of the role of these two technologies in China and the United States. By using comparisons, students were able to see the different roles these technologies play in the two societies.

The final objective, drawing inferences, suffered from the lack of time devoted to it, and the lack of good inference questions to accompany most materials. Only the last lesson on "The Lottery" contained any inference questions, and these proved to be useful stimuli for discussion. But too many of the inferences were drawn or identified by the teacher, leaving students, once again, in a passive listening mode. The results of the reading test indicate that students were poor at drawing inferences and were making no substantial progress on this very important objective.

Overall, then, this course was most effective at teaching lower level reading skills like defining vocabulary and identifying factual details. When higher level skills like drawing inferences and summarizing main ideas were presented at all, they were done so in ways that did not encourage student learning. Finally, the extent to which students learned about Western culture and history from this course was limited to recognizing a few key names, places and events. Teachers generally did not delve into the cultural context of the materials to any great extent, either because they themselves were unfamiliar with this context (which seemed to be true of the substitute) or because they failed to see the importance of doing so. Thus, the focus of the course dictated that students would have greater opportunities to learn lower level reading skills than to go beyond these to a full appreciation of the materials they read.

FIRST YEAR: INTENSIVE READING I

A male teacher in his late twenties entered the room and mounted the podium. The students, who had been chatting quietly in Chinese, fell silent. "Good morning," the teacher said.

"Good morning," the 16 students replied in unison.

"It's chilly this morning, isn't it?" the teacher observed. "Let's begin reading our new lesson, 'Night Marching'. Any volunteers?" The teacher waited. "No one?" Again he paused. "Come on, Xiao Li, read the first paragraph." Xiao Li began to read in a soft voice, just barely audible above the noise coming from the hallway. As she read, the teacher and most students followed along in their books.

This was a first year course in Intensive Reading, a subject considered by administrators, teachers and students to be the most important of all those offered in the undergraduate program, and one which students attend six hours a week, more than double the time allotted to any other course. The classroom where the course met was "home" to the group of 16 students. They took all their courses in this room, and had decorated it themselves. On one wall was a map of China and a small calendar. On the opposite wall hung a world map and examples of student essays under the heading "Love Life, Love Youth." At the front, beside the blackboard on either side hung two paper scrolls of Chinese calligraphy. The classroom was medium-sized, containing 22 desks, and a table at the front with three reel-to-reel tape recorders sitting on it. Two windows facing south admitted most of the room's light. Four fluorescent bulbs hung from the ceiling overhead, but only two of them were on.

As the two hour lesson proceeded, the teacher asked students to read a 500 word text aloud, one paragraph at a time, and then went line by line through the text, explaining vocabulary and grammatical structures, and often using Chinese, either to give translations of new words or to test the students' ability to translate orally from Chinese to English. Occasionally, the teacher asked students to raise questions about the text, or directly quizzed them in a drill and practice format, but most of the time he went through the text himself, referring to copious notes he had prepared in order to explain the finer points.

I observed five two-hour sessions of this course in the spring semester, attending the same day for five consecutive weeks. The first four sessions, I observed and wrote down what I heard and saw. The fifth session I recorded on videotape for subsequent discourse analysis. Each week, the teacher and students did similar things, as has been described above. During the remaining four hours the course met each week, students engaged in other activities, including practicing spoken English through reading and recitation of dialogues and substitution drills, doing grammatical exercises, writing down material dictated by the teacher, and writing translations of sentences from Chinese to English and vice versa. Due to schedule conflicts, I was unable to attend on any of the days when these activities occurred.

As I have previously indicated, the name "Intensive Reading" is a misnomer. This six hour course is really a comprehensive introduction to English grammar, with attention also given to reading, writing, speaking and translation. When asked to name the most important things he wanted students to learn in the course, the teacher cited the following in rank order of importance:

(1). good pronunciation and intonation
(2). ability to talk in English
(3). correct usage of words and expressions
(4). ability to write dictations well
(5). translating between Chinese and English

When two students in the course were asked to state what they had learned so far, both named "usage of new words and phrases" as the most important thing. One student also cited learning pronunciation, writing and knowledge of science, but the other student was unable to name anything else he had learned in the class.

Based on my observations and conversations with the teacher and students, I arrived at the following five objectives, listed in rank order:

Objective 1: To identify grammatical functions and meanings of new words and expressions.
Objective 2: To become fluent in spoken English
Objective 3: To translate between Chinese and English, both orally and in writing.
Objective 4: To memorize portions of texts and the meaning and spelling of new words.
Objective 5: To read aloud from texts with correct pronunciation and intonation.

In comparing the objectives as perceived by the teacher, students and myself, a number of differences emerge. First, students listed fewer objectives, which indicates that they do not believe they are learning some of the things that their teacher wants them to. Secondly, while the teacher and I agree about four of the five most important objectives, we disagree about their relative importance. The teacher places speaking skills first, but I saw little evidence that the teacher devoted a great deal of time to them. In fairness to the teacher, speaking received more stress on days when I was not present.

I concluded from the time actually spent on each objective and the activities and strategies used in class, however, that identifying grammatical functions and meanings of new words was by far the most important objective of the course. Further, I chose the behavior "identify" instead of "use," because I saw no evidence that students were required to actually use grammar or new words to create messages of their own. One other difference between my list and the teacher's involves dictation. While the teacher considered this one of the important objectives, I did not see any dictation going on during the time I observed and students said they only did this once a week for about 30 minutes. Thus, I do not count it among the five most important objectives of the course.

The materials for this course included a Chinese-compiled textbook, entitled *English*, Volume 3 (see description in Chapter 3, under "Government's View"), and teacher-made worksheets which focused on grammar and translation. The textbook was the only material used during the sessions I observed, and the teacher stuck closely to it most of the time.

The content of the five lessons which were observed is as follows:

Chapter Two: "Napoleon's Questions," a humorous text about a Swedish soldier in Napoleon's army who makes a fool of himself because he does not know any French. This 400 word text was one that the students had studied before in middle school.

Chapter Three: "Helicopter," a 500 word description of the functions and advantages of helicopters as a means of transportation, written in the style of general science for the layman.

Chapter Four: "Night Marching," a 600 word excerpt from a book by Agnes Smedley about the Chinese Communists' Long March in the 1930s. This was a topic that students had studied repeatedly throughout their school years.

Chapter Five: "From Los Alamos to China," a 500 word excerpt from a 1979 speech by Joan Hinton, sister of China scholar William Hinton, who describes how she worked on the Manhattan Project, became disillusioned with the United States, and left to become a citizen of China. Though the exact details of her life were new to students, the events she described and her political tone were both eminently familiar.

Chapter Six: "Albert Einstein," a 700 word biographical sketch of the life of Einstein, including details of his personal life and a brief summary of his scientific accomplishments, written for the layman.

In addition to the texts, each lesson contained vocabulary and translation drills based upon the content of the text, oral drills and dialogues tangentially related to the texts, and grammatical exercises which were mostly unrelated to the content of the text. During the sessions I observed, the teacher focused exclusively on the text of each lesson and the accompanying notes, which explained grammar and definitions in greater detail. Though most of the lessons also contained reading comprehension questions on the text, the teacher only went over these in class once.

Altogether, this course included seven kinds of learning activities, although I only observed five of them in use. The activities students engaged in were:

(1). listening to the teacher explain the text (and sometimes taking notes)

(2). reading the text and pattern drills aloud

(3). translating from Chinese into English and occasionally vice versa

(4). asking the teacher questions about the lesson

(5). answering the teacher's questions about meanings and functions of words

(6). writing down material from the text dictated by the teacher

(7). listening to tape recordings of the text by native English speakers

The last two activities were not observed, but according to the teacher and students, dictation was a weekly exercise in the last half hour of each week's class, and students listened to tape recordings after class in their spare time.

The teaching strategies employed in this class were of five types. The most common strategy was to use a grammar-translation approach to language teaching. In this approach, the teacher explained grammatical structures line by line, stopping to illustrate certain points by writing examples on the board. The teacher also spent a good deal of time on oral and written translation. The teacher would make up a sentence in Chinese, recite it aloud, and ask students to translate it into English. Additionally, students were given worksheets each week which contained translation exercises or were asked to translate portions of the text from English into Chinese. An example of the grammar-translation aproach in action is given below:

> T: [Reads text] "Because helicopters do not require any special place to land, they can be used in looking for people lost in the heart of the jungle or trying to find likely places to sink wells which will yield petroleum." Now, let's look at this sentence. What is "jungle"? [Pause.] It means "tropical forest." What about "looking for"? What part of speech?
>
> S1: Attributive.
>
> T: Yes, attributive. What about "heart of jungle"? [Pause.] That means the center part. Now look at "sink." It's an intransitive verb usually, but here it is used transitively, "sink wells." How about "trying to find likely places"? What function?
>
> S2: Present participle.

T: Yes, that's right. Present participle used as adverbial of manner. [Pause.] Here's a sentence: *Ta bu zhi dao ta de shu ben zai nar, suo yi ta qu zhao ta.* Xiao Wang [student's name]?

S3: He doesn't know where his schoolbook is, so he goes looking for it.

T: "Went looking for it" is better [repeats her translation].

Another teaching strategy, less commonly used than the first, was to have students read aloud from their textbooks, either prose passages, dialogues or substitution and pattern drills. This strategy is closely associated with the audio lingual approach to language teaching and was the one that the textbook's authors recommended. The teacher made only limited use of it during the sessions I observed, but claimed to use it more often during oral English practice which occurred on days I did not attend.

The final two teaching strategies were used in combination with the others mentioned above. These were to invite student questions about the text, and to ask students questions about the function or meaning of words. The latter has already been illustrated above in conjunction with the grammar-translation approach. The former occurred more sporadically. Some weeks the teacher began his explication of the text by asking for student questions. Other weeks, he did not. The time devoted to this depended very much upon the students' initiative. One week, student questions occupied only five minutes of class time, but the last class session, which was videotaped, featured 40 minutes of student questions and teacher answers. During the interview, the teacher indicated that he was experimenting with having students ask more questions as an alternative to going line by line through the text. But, whether he initiated the questions or students did, the topics covered were quite similar. Students typically asked for the meaning of words, phrases or whole sentences that they were having trouble understanding. The teacher's answers usually involved specifying the parts of speech of various words and phrases, and sometimes paraphrasing the meaning or translating it into Chinese.

To evaluate the extent to which students were learning the major objectives, the teacher relied most heavily on written evaluations of student homework and results of tests and quizzes. These types of evaluation, however, only indicated student progress in three of the five objectives, those involving translation, memorization and identification of grammar and definitions. To evaluate student ability to translate between Chinese and English, the teacher gave written translation exercises to students every week. These were graded by the teacher and returned to students. The scores formed one part of a student's overall grade in the class.

To evaluate memorization of new words and portions of texts, the teacher gave students weekly dictation exercises. These usually were taken directly from the lesson's text, and since students knew this, they were encouraged to memorize the text so as to reproduce it without error on the dictation. Again, the teacher collected dictation exercises and counted the scores toward students' overall class grade. Another memorization test frequently used was the spelling test, which required students to correctly spell new vocabulary from the lesson.

Finally, to test students' ability to identify grammatical functions and meanings of new words, the teacher often distributed worksheets with grammar or vocabulary exercises, mostly with a fill in the blank format. A sentence would be given with a word missing, and students would have to supply the correct form of the word that could be used in that context. These were also sometimes collected and graded.

The two objectives which the teacher did not evaluate through written means were those relating to pronunciation and spoken English. These were only evaluated orally by the teacher. Sometimes, he asked other students to comment as well, encouraging them to listen for mistakes made by their classmates.

The teacher employed oral evaluation in two other ways also. First, the teacher frequently checked students' understanding of words or grammatical forms by asking them to orally translate sentences from Chinese to English. Thus, if the teacher wanted to know whether students understood a new word like "arise," he would give several Chinese sentences using the equivalent term and ask students to translate them. Of course, such a method does not ensure that students could use the words correctly in forming new English sentences. In fact, students and teachers often disagreed about the best way to translate Chinese into English. The students' attention in these oral exercises was clearly focused on the technique of translation rather than on the correct usage of the word in English. A second kind of oral evaluation occurred when the teacher asked students questions and then evaluated their responses. This was the least frequent method of evaluation, however. When used, its purpose was to check student ability to recognize and identify grammatical forms.

The various kinds of oral evaluation gave immediate feedback to students, and were useful in that way, but the teacher did not count these toward the course grade. Knowing this, students might well have paid less attention to the evaluation they received in this form. In fact, as the class proceeded, I observed about half the students taking notes of the teacher's oral comments at any one time. The rest listened, but did not write them down. Further, since oral evaluations covered a large number of new words and grammatical forms, it is doubtful that students remembered more than a few of them.

The most glaring weakness in evaluation, however, was the complete neglect of one objective: to become fluent in spoken English. The teacher conducted no formal evaluation of students' oral English. Instead, he only gave informal, oral evaluations of their performances, with primary attention to pronunciation and intonation. Though the teacher cited "ability to talk" as the second most important objective of the course, he did not evaluate this objective in any systematic way, and therefore, it was not included in the overall grade assigned to students. Moreover, students were not given many opportunities to talk in class, which suggests that their ability to speak English did not increase very much in this course.

Grouping patterns and organization were other weaknesses. Students were always grouped for instruction in the same way, as a whole class, with all student responses processed back through the teacher. Students never worked in small groups, and only worked individually on tests, quizzes, dictations and written exercises. Of the three organizational principles identified by Tyler (continuity, sequence and integration), only continuity was apparent in this course. In fact, the teacher ran the class in virtually the same manner each week. He began every session by asking students to read the text aloud, one paragraph at a time. Then he asked for student questions, answering these one at a time until students stopped raising them. Next, he explained the text, going line by line. Finally, he gave sentences in Chinese to be translated into English. The teacher made so much use of continuity that he appeared to bore his students at times. After weeks and months of the same routine, students were observed gazing out the windows or reading other materials in class.

As for sequence, there was little evidence of this, either in the thematic content of the texts, the difficulty of vocabulary, or the presentation of grammar. Integration—the consolidation of knowledge horizontally across lessons, units and courses—was never evident. The teacher did not provide enough variety of activities to allow this, and did not review previous lessons to help students consolidate their knowledge. Instead, each lesson was treated as a discrete entity. Once it was finished, the teacher did not go back to it.

As for the integration of this course in the department's overall course offerings, department administrators and the Intensive Reading teaching group decided how many chapters teachers would cover each semester to ensure that students completed all the textbooks by the end of their fifth semester. Other than this, the department had no curricular plan for the two and a half years that students took Intensive Reading I, and had given no apparent thought to the way this course related to others students took during this time.

The use of classroom space did not vary from week to week. Students had their own desks, and sat in the same place each week. Since desks were arranged in pairs, students sitting next to each other became a kind of informal small group. They could often be seen sharing books and notes, and chatting with each other, either during class or at break time. The teacher also had a fixed position in the class, at the front on the podium behind the lectern. The teacher was never observed to leave the podium while teaching and only moved to turn around and write on the blackboard behind him or to direct comments to students on his right or left. At those times, he moved away from the lectern, but not down off the podium. In fact, the existence of a podium in a small classroom like this helped to create a physical barrier between the teacher and the students. The teacher stood above the students and was separated from them by the lectern. In a very concrete and yet symbolic way, the podium and lectern served to set the teacher apart from his students, and reinforced his social role as the source of knowledge and authority in the class.

Two other spatial elements deserve brief comments — heat and light. Observations of this class were conducted in March and April. During this time, the classroom had no heat, and temperatures ranged from a low of 56 degrees F. to a high of 63. During the coldest days, the room was quite uncomfortable, and students were observed rubbing their hands together, or even each other's hands, to stay warm. Regarding light, the room was equipped with four fluorescent bulbs hung from the ceiling, but only two of them worked. The major source of light was the south-facing windows, which admitted sunlight on clear days. When the weather was cloudy, however, the room was too dark to comfortably read in, although everyone did anyway.

The allocation and use of time in this course is difficult for me to specify exactly, because I was unable to observe all six hours of the course each week. But the teacher and students I interviewed gave their impressions of time use each week, and based on these, as well as my own observations, I arrived at the following breakdown of activities by average time spent:

Activity	Time	Percent
oral reading	15 mins.	4
student questions	30 mins.	8
explication of text	60 mins.	17
translation work	60 mins.	17
speaking practice	60 mins.	17
grammar exercises	60 mins.	17
quizzes/dictations	45 mins.	12
class routines	30 mins.	8

During the sessions I observed, a running chronology was kept. From this, I estimate that the average percentage of teacher talk was about 85 percent, while students talked only 15 percent. The percentage of student talk was probably higher on the day when students practiced oral English, but one student complained that he got few opportunities to speak in class.

Discourse Analysis

To explore the curriculum of this class in greater detail, especially the "hidden" or implicit curriculum, the last session I attended was recorded on videotape and subjected to discourse analysis. The first hour of the session was chosen for detailed analysis, since the activities during this hour formed one complete lesson. During this time, students read the text entitled "Albert Einstein," asked questions about words and grammatical forms, and listened to the teacher give answers to their questions and explain the text line by line.

The fact that this session was videotaped appears to have affected the outcome in two ways. First, since the teacher knew I was going to videotape that day, he appeared to be better prepared, and invited more student questions than usual. Second, since the teacher also informed the students beforehand that I would be videotaping, they, too, seemed better prepared and more active than usual. This was particularly evident in the amount of time devoted to student questions, which was far greater than in the other sessions I observed.

During the first hour of this session, the teacher appeared to be teaching five objectives, although he only explicitly mentioned one of them. These were:

> *Objective 1:* To read aloud from the text with correct pronunciation and intonation.
>
> *Objective 2:* To listen for mistakes in student pronunciation and intonation [mentioned by teacher].
>
> *Objective 3:* To ask questions about the syntax and semantics of the text.
>
> *Objective 4:* To identify grammatical functions and meanings of new words.
>
> *Objective 5:* To translate orally between Chinese and English.

The teacher offered a number of learning opportunities to students to achieve the objectives listed above. But some objectives received far more attention than others. Regarding objective 1 — reading aloud from the text — the teacher asked 12 students to read one paragraph each. After each student read, the teacher commented on their pronunciation and intonation. Objective 2, which the teacher specified at the beginning of the session, was to listen for student mistakes during oral reading. After six of the students had read, the teacher asked students if they had heard any mistakes. In four cases, students identified incorrectly pronounced words. The teacher confirmed these, and repeated the correct pronunciation. In the other cases, the teacher himself identified the mistakes in student pronunciation or intonation, but asked the class how the word or phrase should be pronounced. Most of the time, several students responded in chorus with the correct pronunciation or intonation.

Regarding objective 3 — asking questions about the text — students were unusually active during this session. The teacher encouraged student questions more than usual, waiting for them to ask and asserting twice, "You should have questions if you are well prepared." As a result of this encouragement, 10 students asked a total of 11 questions about the function and meaning of words and phrases in the text. The teacher responded with detailed explanations, often using examples or translation to help students understand. Among the questions asked by students were the following:

"What's the difference between 'knowledgeable' and 'intellectual'?" "Can you explain about clocks and theory of relativity?" "What is 'rate'?" "What's the difference between 'property' and 'possession'?"

Though students' questions tended to be about meanings, the teacher's answers usually focused on grammatical analysis. For example, in responding to the difference between "knowledgeable" and "intellectual," the teacher noted that the former was always an adjective, while the latter could be used as a noun. The teacher had far more difficulty explaining the theory of relativity, which should not be surprising. As he tried to explain how the rate of a clock decreases as it approaches the speed of light, he commented, "I'm a little bit confused on this point, too."

The fourth objective, to identify grammatical functions and meanings of new words, was presented in two ways. First, the questions raised by students, as discussed above, were an opportunity to clarify functions and meanings of words. Second, toward the end of the first hour, the teacher began his explication of the text, and continued this after the break for another 30 minutes. During this portion of class, the students' only learning opportunity was to listen to the teacher explain words and phrases. Some students took notes while listening to help them remember; others did not. It should be noted that the teacher actually did most of the identifying, not the students, and in this sense, the learning oportunity did not serve the objective.

Finally, regarding oral translation, the teacher asked one student to translate a phrase ("rate of speed") from English to Chinese, and one student asked the teacher if his Chinese translation of the word "regard" was correct. During the second hour, the teacher spent another 20 minutes of class time doing oral translation.

This class session was organized in three basic parts: oral reading, student questions and explication of text. During the oral reading section, the teacher called on a student to read, the student read aloud one paragraph, the teacher asked the class if there were any errors in pronunciation, and the teacher identified and corrected errors or commented on the lack of errors. During the student question section, the teacher invited questions, students asked them, and the teacher gave detailed answers. During the explication of text section, the teacher went back to the beginning of the text and read line by line, stopping to explain grammatical forms and meanings of new words. He also used oral translation during this time to check the students' ability to put Chinese sentences and phrases into correct English.

By failing to present grammar and vocabulary in some defensible sequence, the teacher made it more difficult for students to identify all the functions and meanings they encountered. He covered such a wide range of grammatical points and presented so many new words that it is doubtful whether students remembered very much of this. The lack of integration as an organizational element compounded the students' difficulty in mastering grammatical functions and vocabulary. Since the teacher provided no opportunities to consolidate knowledge from past lessons, students sometimes asked the same questions about words and grammar week after week, indicating they had not yet mastered these.

During the videotaped lesson, the teacher only made use of oral evaluation, and this was limited to three of the lesson's five objectives. Objectives 2 and 3 were not evaluated at all. The teacher evaluated objective 1—oral reading—more than any other. After each student read, the teacher commented on their performance. In two cases, he praised the students for the accuracy of their pronunciation and the native-like quality of their intonation, encouraging them to continue reading this way. He also corrected errors in the pronunciation and intonation of nine students. In one case, he insisted that a student had erred in the pronunciation of the word "France," though to my ear she had pronounced it in an acceptable American accent. The teacher, however, insisted the pronunciation of the vowel should be as the British say it (rhyming with "fonts").

The teacher's evaluation of students' ability to identify grammatical functions and meanings of words was limited to four questions he asked the class. Students answered three of them correctly, which the teacher acknowledged, and he gave the correct answer for the fourth question after students failed to respond. The teacher only evaluated the oral translations of students twice.

Except for the first objective, the teacher provided very little or no evaluation of students. This clearly was a major weakness of the lesson. Unless students have a chance to practice the objective in question and receive evaluation from the teacher about whether they are right or wrong, little learning can be expected to take place.

The statistics compiled from the discourse analysis reveal a number of important clues about the "hidden" curriculum. First, the teacher clearly dominated the class session, doing 78 percent of the talking, and initiating most messages. The teacher's domination is even more striking if one looks more closely at message forms. Of the 33 questions, the teacher posed 22. Of the 32 assertions, the teacher made 17. The only assertions made by students were those included in their reading from the text. Moreover, the teacher made all 16 explanations and all 19 directives during the hour. Even the response category was dominated by the teacher, who made 10 of 19 responses, including answers to some of his own questions. This is also reflected in the fact that students refused to answer the teacher's questions twice. Second, despite the teacher's overwhelming domination of the class, 14 of 16 students spoke at least once during the hour, and 12 of 16 students received messages from the teacher directed to them personally. Most of the student talk was confined to the first 14 minutes, when 12 students read aloud, and to the student question section, when 10 students asked questions. During this portion, though, student questions accounted for less than 10 percent of the total time. The remainder was occupied by the teacher's lengthy explanations to each question.

A third finding emerging from the discourse analysis is that students were actually more active during this hour than usual, primarily because they asked more questions than in previous weeks. I estimate that student talk occupied about 7 percent more time in this hour than in other observed sessions. Finally, it should be noted that this hour was marred by loud noises coming from the hallway which made it difficult to hear students as they read aloud. The noise reached such a level at one point that the teacher was compelled to step outside and ask students and workmen to quiet down. After this, it abated somewhat but continued to be a disrupting factor throughout the session.

Other insights about the "hidden" curriculum can be gained by looking at the tone, style and channel of the discourse. The tone was serious throughout the lesson except for one mock comment, made after the teacher had gone into the hallway to ask people to quiet down. Upon his return, he said, "They are repairing the toilets [located just across the hall]. I can stop the students from making noise, but I can't stop the workers." Students laughed heartily at that remark. Students also laughed twice more during the hour, but both times they were laughing at the teacher's apparent confusion in answering student questions, once on the topic of relativity and once when the teacher had trouble thinking of an example to explain a point of grammar. The tone of the lesson varied in two other ways also. The teacher switched to a serious, laudatory tone twice when he praised the correct oral reading of two students. He also switched to a serious, critical tone twice, both times to complain about the loud noises in the hallway. Regarding style, the teacher stuck to the formal throughout the lesson with only one exception. At the beginning of the lesson, when he asked for volunteers to read and no one responded, he said, "C'mon, Xiao Li, you first", a more informal remark than others he made. Finally, the channel of this lesson was oral throughout, except for two words written on the blackboard towards the end of the hour. Chinese was used twice, both times by students. In the second hour, however, the teacher used Chinese nine times as he conducted oral translation practice.

In addition to the discourse analysis, both the teacher and students were asked about their views of the class climate. During our interview, the teacher was asked to rate the class climate of the observed group on a scale of one to ten, with ten being best. He gave the class a five, but said the climate was "not very good" compared to other classes he has taught. When asked to elaborate on this, the teacher commented:

> The students get along well. They help each other. But the class atmosphere is not very active. I think there are too few boys, only four. And three of them are dull, not active. Among the girls, a few are active, but they are

usually more passive. Boys should take the lead in everything and be more active, but in this class, the boys are shy.

His theory that the lack of boys in class causes passivity seems indefensible. Certainly, the teacher did little to encourage more active participation on the part of students, and the few times he did solicit their involvement, students of both sexes generally responded well.

In interviews with two randomly selected students from this course, I asked them to identify the one thing they liked best and least about the class. For best thing, one student mentioned "learning the usage of new words". The other said, "I like to practice listening and writing." The one thing they liked least about the class also differed. One said, "I usually speak little in class. I would like to speak more." The other commented, "The teacher explains too much. Some things he says don't make sense, or we already know these things. There's no need to explain them."

The two students were also asked to comment on whether or not they could help decide what they learn or how they learn in class. Both agreed they could help decide some things. When asked to give examples, they cited: (1) bring up topics or questions about the text to discuss in class; (2) help decide whether the teacher should go over something in detail by telling the teacher that they already know it.

Despite these two examples, one student complained, "We have less freedom in class then when we study by ourselves. The teacher decides what we should learn or do next."

The student responses indicate mild dissatisfaction with the way they are being taught. They think the class is not well organized, and they think the teacher does too much talking and explaining, leaving little time for them to speak or practice other skills. Further, they believe they can help decide to some extent how they are taught, but have virtually no control over what they are taught.

Despite these complaints, the class climate during the sessions I observed was not tense or oppressive in any way. Students and teacher seemed to get along well and they frequently chatted cordially in Chinese during the break, which seemed to help develop a good personal relationship between them. The major problem I observed was the inactivity of students and their occasional boredom with the predictable class routine. While this class may have been more passive than others, I would primarily hold the teacher responsible for the lack of student participation. His teacher-centered approach to teaching, coupled with a commitment to the grammar-translation method, provided few opportunities for students to speak or otherwise actively engage in learning activities. Interestingly, when I asked the teacher whether students should help decide things in class, he immediately agreed they should, but then went on to contradict himself. I asked him to mention what kinds of things students should help decide, and he said:

> Sometimes we get student suggestions. But generally speaking, they just get what they are taught. It's necessary for students to help decide, but sometimes the students' point of view is narrow and incorrect. Sometimes, they are unsatisfied or angry, but they don't see things from a wider perspective.

Clearly, this teacher does not think much of student suggestions and opinions. Rather, he sees himself in a much better position to decide what and how they should learn. With such an attitude, it is unlikely that this teacher would seriously consider and act upon student suggestions.

In fact, I saw no direct evidence of student decision making during the five observed sessions. The only thing that students did to help shape the direction of activities was to raise questions of concern to them, but even this opportunity was not always available. During some weeks, the teacher allowed only a few questions or none at all. But during the videotaped lesson, the teacher encouraged student questions, and in this limited sense, students helped to decide how the course would be conducted that day.

It should not be inferred from the above remarks that the teacher exercises sole decision making power himself. In fact, the teacher reports quite the contrary when it comes to materials, content, activities and evaluation of the Intensive Reading I course. When I asked him to list the kinds of curricular decisions he typically makes, the teacher commented:

> I can make few decisions myself. I am a member of a small teaching group of first year [Intensive Reading] teachers. We often meet and decide on how much time to spend on each lesson, what we should emphasize, what activities we should do, etc., so that students in all three classes get to same level. We also decided to use the textbook, along with the department leaders.

From this, it is clear that curricular decision making in Intensive Reading is a collective matter, involving the three teachers of the course and the English Section Head. None of them has unlimited authority to make decisions. In fact, the teacher asserted later that if all three teachers opposed a textbook chosen by the department administration, they could insist on another. Into this equation must be added the students' opinions, suggestions and actions, which have indirect influence on the classroom curriculum, and occasional direct influence in the areas of activities and teaching strategies.

One final point about this course should be mentioned. From the teacher's answers on the questionnaire, I learned that he had only a bachelor's degree, has never studied abroad or taken graduate courses, and has taught for only five years. Further, the teacher cited, as the reason he entered teaching, "assigned to be a teacher by the government," and he felt his expectations of teaching had not been fulfilled. This background information reveals an inadequately educated teacher who did not choose his profession and does not generally find it satisfying. It helps to explain the old-fashioned teaching methods he employed, the meager cultural content of his lessons, and the errors he made in class, including both small things like incorrect pronunciations of words, and more serious errors or omissions he made while trying to answer student questions. While the teacher cannot be blamed for his lack of training and knowledge, since he has no choice over whether he will receive further education in China or abroad, this certainly illustrates one of the major problems confronting Chinese education, especially in the field of foreign languages. Too many college teachers have not received the kind of rigorous advanced education necessary to conduct their courses well.

Summary

Of the five objectives for this course identified at the outset, students appeared to be having the most success with two: translating between Chinese and English, and memorizing new words and portions of texts. They were also making progress in reading aloud, and recognizing grammatical functions and meanings of new words, but the limited or sometimes inappropriate nature of the learning activities for these two objectives made it difficult for students to make more rapid progress. Regarding the last objective—to become fluent in spoken English—the students appeared to be making the least progress. This is mostly due to their lack of opportunities to speak in class, and also partly due to the inherent limitations on speaking ability of an audio-lingual approach to English learning. Though students memorized dialogues and practiced numerous substitution and pattern drills, they had virtually no opportunity to use language in real-life situations or to create meaningful messages of their own.

This course is also weak for what it does not include. The most glaring omission is reading comprehension. Besides definitions of vocabulary, virtually no attention was given to the meanings of the texts read in class. Though comprehension questions of a factual nature were included in the textbook, the teacher only went over these once. Otherwise, he paid no attention to students' ability to identify factual details, summarize main ideas, draw logical conclusions or other higher level comprehension skills. This illustrates more clearly than anything else the absurdity of referring to the course as "Intensive Reading." Reading skills, except for correct oral pronunciation, simply are not an objective of this course as taught by this teacher.

One other serious omission is the lack of writing skills as a component of the course. Though students in the first year cannot be expected to write very well yet, they should begin to develop this skill through a carefully controlled writing program focused on the topic sentence and paragraph. But in this course, students only wrote short answers on exercises and translations, neither of which helps them to develop their ability to express written ideas in English.

In sum, I believe this course is not well designed for students in their first year of undergraduate English study. They would learn more if the course were broken up into four separate skills: speaking, listening, reading and writing, and if translation were postponed until it could be taught later as a separate, advanced skill. The advantages of this approach are numerous. Students could receive more appropriate and diverse practice in each of the four basic language skills, and they would tend to learn grammar in a more useful way as they tried to apply it to the four skills. Also, it would encourage teachers to give proper attention to those skills like speaking, reading and writing which are currently being ignored or underemphasized.

SECOND YEAR: INTENSIVE READING I

"All right, let's go on with our work," the teacher announced above the murmur of student conversation in Chinese. Students quickly retook their seats and opened their textbooks. A few students who had left class during the break straggled in just as the class resumed. The teacher, a woman in her early thirties, waited for everyone to take their seats. "Let's go over some words from the text," she began. "First, the word 'soothe'." She turned around and wrote the word on the blackboard, adding a 'v' after it to indicate it was a verb. "Who can tell me what 'soothe' means?" She paused for a moment, waiting for a volunteer to answer.

"Make calm," a student said.

The teacher repeated the definition and asked, "What else can it mean?"

"Make comfort" [sic], a second student offered.

"O.K. Or it can mean make less angry, less anxious. What situation would you use 'soothe'?"

After a brief pause, a boy in the back said, "Soothed by his words, I fell asleep."

"Good," the teacher commented. "There's also another meaning of 'soothe'—to make less painful, as in taking medicine to soothe a sore throat. Put this sentence into Chinese: Nothing the mother said could soothe her son's anger."

A girl in the first row translated the sentence into Chinese. The teacher said, "Right," when she finished and repeated the translation for the rest of the class to hear.

This excerpt was taken from a second year course in Intensive Reading I. As previously mentioned, students take this course for five semesters, starting in the first year. The course is a comprehensive introduction to English grammar with attention also given to reading, speaking, listening and translating. By the time they reach the fourth semester, students are supposed to have mastered basic grammatical structures of English, and should be able to read and comprehend intermediate texts and speak fluently on topics related to daily life.

I observed five two-hour sessions of this course in the spring semester over a seven week period. One of the sessions was taught by a different teacher. The class did not meet for two consecutive weeks due to a sports meet and physical labor, which students perform once a semester. Though this course meets six hours per week, I only observed two hours due to schedule conflicts.

When the teacher was asked to list the things she wanted students to learn, in rank order, she replied as follows:

(1). "vocabulary work, including usages and meanings"
(2). "increased ability to use the language"
(3). to make full use of dictionaries
(4). to read more easily, and with increasing comprehension and speed
(5). to take dictation as basic training to help students take notes from lectures

Two randomly selected students were also asked to state what they had learned in second year Intensive Reading I. One student mentioned two things: "I enlarged my vocabulary with new words and phrases, and learned some spoken English." This student could not name anything else learned in the class.

The second student commented, "This is a difficult question, because last term I think I learned more than this term. Last term, I learned to speak English fluently, and to write English letters to my friends and middle school teachers. But this term, I don't think I've learned something, at least not very much." When pressed to mention one thing learned in the second term, the student said, "I just listen to the teacher talk."

Based on my observations of this course and a discourse analysis of one recorded session, I identified seven important objectives of the course, listed in rank order:

Objective 1: To identify the meanings of vocabulary items in English
Objective 2: To use vocabulary items in English sentences
Objective 3: To identify factual details in short English texts
Objective 4: To translate between English and Chinese
Objective 5: To become fluent in spoken English
Objective 6: To use correct grammatical structures in English sentences
Objective 7: To write down material dictated in English

It is immediately apparent that the teacher, students and I have very different opinions about the objectives of this class. The two students were only able to identify four things they had learned in the second year course: vocabulary, spoken Enlgish, letter writing and listening. The teacher mentioned five things, but I only observed her teach four of the objectives week after week. Dictionary work, the teacher's third objective, was only observed to happen once for about 10 minutes. Thus, I do not include it in my list of the seven most important objectives. The teacher and I basically agree on the other four objectives she mentioned, although I stated them differently to conform to Ralph Tyler's definition of an educational objective.

Additionally, I identified three other objectives that the teacher appeared to be seeking in her conduct of the course: fluency in speaking, translating, and using grammatical structures. I cannot fully account for the teacher's failure to mention these, since she devoted time to them nearly every class session. Perhaps she simply forgot about them, or considered them less important then the five she mentioned. In an ill-defined course like Intensive Reading, which has diverse purposes but no specific objectives, it is easy to overlook or forget what one is teaching. I myself was unable to reduce the important objectives of this class to five or fewer, as I did for the other courses I observed.

The materials for this course consisted of a single textbook, entitled *First Certificate in English Course for Foreign Students* (by Ona Low; Great Britain: Edward Arnold Publishers, 1974). The book is a comprehensive intermediate text devoted to grammar, reading, vocabulary and speaking skills. It consists of 20 lessons, each of which contains a text and a wide variety of exercises. The lesson begins with a 400 to 800 word text, usually about life in Great Britain, and is followed by up to ten types of exercises on vocabulary, grammar, reading comprehension, dialogues, substitution and pattern drills. The textbook is primarily based on an audio-lingual approach to English language teaching, with extensive use of model dialogues, substitution and pattern drills, but also places greater stress on reading than most strictly audio-lingual textbooks do. Additionally, occasional use was made of notional-functional gambits, such as dialogues on offering, accepting and refusing invitations.

The content of the sessions I observed varied somewhat, because the teacher did not follow a rigid schedule in completing each week's lesson. Basically, the teacher covered one lesson per week, supplementing the textbook with translation exercises and dictations. The exact content of the sessions I observed is as follows:

> *Session One* [taught by a different teacher]: dictation exercise, vocabulary exercises, speaking practice (dialogue and pattern drills), and reading comprehension questions on a text entitled "Newly Arrived in Britain."
> *Session Two*: oral student report, dictation exercise, idiom practice, pronunciation practice, grammar exercises, speaking practice (dialogue, pattern drills, making sentences).
> *Session Three*: oral student report, oral spelling, vocabulary definitions, oral translation, vocabulary exercises, speaking practice (making questions), grammar exercises, and reading comprehension questions on a text entitled "An Irish Wedding."
> *Session Four*: oral student report, spelling quiz, reading comprehension ques-

tions on a text entitled "Shelter for the Night," vocabulary exercises and definitions, oral translation.

Session Five: oral student report, dictation exercise, oral translation, vocabulary definitions and exercises.

Each of the seven objectives I identified earlier was supported by at least one learning activity, usually more. The range of activities in this class was greater than that of most other courses I observed. As the content of each session shows, the teacher engaged students in four to eight different learning activities during each two hour session. To give a clear sense of the range of activities employed, they are listed by objective below:

Objective 1: To identify the meanings of vocabulary items in English
   1. giving definitions of new words
   2. multiple choice exercises on synonyms and idioms
   3. matching exercises (match vocabulary with correct definition)

Objective 2: To use vocabulary items in English sentences
   1. make sentences in English using vocabulary items
   2. fill in the blank and "cloze" exercises (to supply a missing word in context)

Objective 3: To identify factual details in short English texts
   1. answer factual detail questions about text orally
   2. multiple choice exercises on factual details in text

Objective 4: To translate between English and Chinese
   1. oral translation practice (both English to Chinese and vice versa)
   2. written translation practice (English to Chinese)

Objective 5: To become fluent in spoken English
   1. oral student reports
   2. make oral questions for given answers
   3. read dialogues aloud
   4. do substitution and pattern drills aloud
   5. ask the teacher questions

Objective 6: To use correct grammatical structures in English sentences
   1. fill in the blank exercises (students supply correct form of word or phrase to complete the sentences)

Objective 7: To write down material dictated in English
   1. dictate passages from the textbook
   2. dictate previously unseen passages
   3. spelling quiz

Three of the seven objectives were well-supported by a variety of learning activities. These included: identifying meanings of vocabulary, practicing speaking English, and writing down dictated material. It is probably not a coincidence that two of these were mentioned by students as things they had learned.

In some cases, though, one could question the appropriateness of the activities, given the objective sought. This is particularly true of objectives 2, 5 and 6. Objective 2—to use vocabulary items in English sentences—was primarily supported by various fill-in-the-blank exercises in the textbook. While these were useful in getting students to supply an appropriate word in a given context, they could not ensure, in and of themselves, that students could use the vocabulary to communicate original messages orally or in writing. The same criticism can be raised about most of the activities to support objective 5: to practice speaking English. Except for oral reports and questions, the activities involved speaking in a highly contrived environment. This in no way guarantees that students could create their own oral messages with any greater fluency than before. Objective 6—to use correct grammatical structures in English sentences—suffered from the same limiting activities. Students only used such grammatical structures as: verb tenses, prepositions, commands, subjunctives and passives in controlled exercises. They did no composition writing, and thus had no opportunity to use correct grammar in forming their own written messages. Also, the teacher was not observed devoting much attention to grammar usage in speaking. Moreover, the teacher made no distinction between correct grammar and appropriate grammar (given a particular context).

The teacher relied on four basic teaching strategies as she conducted the course. These were drill and practice, audio-lingual, translation and lecture. Of the four, drill and practice was by far the most commonly used. All exercises were done in this mode, including those for vocabulary, reading, grammar, and speaking. The teacher also combined this approach with oral translation practice. An example of drill and practice was given at the beginning of this section. The teacher poses questions, students give short answers, and the teacher evaluates them. Another example:

> T: What does "I've got to be up" mean [question]?
> S: I must get up from bed [response].
> T: Right. I must get up [evaluation].

A second teaching strategy, closely related to the first, was the audio-lingual approach. This was used primarily for speaking exercises and practice, but also occasionally occurred in grammatical exercises. The audio-lingual approach, as used by this teacher and textbook, consisted of model dialogues which were read aloud, substitution drills and pattern drills. An example of a pattern drill is given below:

> T: Look at the example [reads from text]: "Are you taking your exam next year?" We can answer [reads from text]:"I hope to, I intend to, I want to, I ought to." Here's the first question [from text]: "Are you going anywhere for the holidays?"
> S1: I want to.
> T: Any others?
> S2: I hope to, I intend to.

Later in the session, the audio-lingual approach was combined with a functional approach to present a series of short dialogues on giving, accepting and refusing invitations. Students read these aloud and did substitution drills using some of the phrases given.

Translation was a strategy used in several ways. The teacher gave written translation work, usually consisting of an English passage from the text that students had to translate into Chinese. She also used oral translation to check students' understanding of new vocabulary and their use of grammatical structures. Finally, she conducted oral translation practice as an end in itself at times. This was evident when the teacher asked students to translate a wide range of sentences with no immediate bearing to the text.

Teacher lectures were kept to a minimum in this course. The teacher rarely spoke for more than five minutes at a time without asking students a question. Occasionally, though, she would give an extended explanation of a vocabulary item, or a reference in the text. During these times, some students took notes of what the teacher said. One other teaching strategy—discussion—was observed to occur once for about ten minutes. The teacher asked a series of open-ended questions about travel that invited students to state opinions on the subject. This was prelude to the reading of a text about a traveler in the English countryside. Once the teacher turned to the text, however, she immediately resumed a drill and practice mode.

This teacher paid more attention to evaluation than most others I observed. Each objective was evaluated at least once during the five sessions I observed. The evaluation was of two types: oral and written. Oral evaluation was employed in drill and practice sessions, as I have already illustrated, and in oral translation and speaking practice. The teacher tended to evaluate each student answer, either by acknowledging its correctness, or by pointing out mistakes in pronunciation, grammar or word choice. Occasionally, the teacher praised a particularly clever answer by saying "good" or even "very good." Written evaluation was used for dictations, written translations, spelling quizzes, and periodic examiniations covering vocabulary and grammar. These were always graded by the teacher and formed the major part of a student's grade for the course. Because of this, students paid more attention to written evaluation than to the oral evaluation they received. The teacher also appeared to give greater credence to the written evaluations, thus elevating these activities and the objectives they were designed to evaluate to a higher plane. As a result, students were more likely to consider vocabulary, translation, grammar and dictation as the most important content of the course.

Despite the wide range of objectives sought, the teacher appeared to be well organized. She directed the class from one activity to the next without wasting a great deal of time on classroom routines. Students were always grouped for instruction as a whole class. They did no small group work during the sessions I observed, and only worked individually on quizzes and dictations.

Reflecting the variety of activities, time use also varied considerably from session to session. Overall, I estimate that the teacher talked about 75 percent of the time, while students talked about 25 percent. Silent work was almost nonexistent in this course. Taking average times devoted to various activities, I arrived at the following approximate breakdown of time allocation:

Activity	Percent Time
drill and practice	60
oral translation	15
speaking (other than drill)	10
written evaluation/quizzes	10
lecture	1
routines & discipline	4

According to the teacher, the activities of the other four hours per week that I did not observe were similar to those already described. If so, this breakdown of time use demonstrated the overwhelming role of drill and practice in this course. And of the drill and practice sessions I observed, the majority were devoted to vocabulary, either identifying meanings or using vocabulary in sentences. Thus, the two objectives related to vocabulary received far greater emphasis than the other five. Reading comprehension was the next most common objective stresseed in drill and practice sessions, followed by speaking drills and grammar. Furthermore, more time was devoted to oral translation than to speaking, grammar or written evaluations. Though the teacher failed to mention it in her list of important objectives, she certainly devoted an inordinate amount of time to translation, especially considering that Intensive Reading is supposed to be a course in basic English skills.

The spatial setting of this course was a small classroom with the usual bare concrete floor and whitewashed walls. The teacher stood on a podium behind a lectern and faced three rows of students seated at their desks. This room was better lit than most; it had four functioning fluorescent lights hung from the ceiling, and the south-facing windows admitted much natural light. Also, students had done a good job in decorating the classroom. Across the front, above the blackboard, a slogan was spelled out in large red letters: "KNOWLEDGE HAS NO LIMIT." Student writing, in both English and Chinese, was displayed on a bulletin board under the title, "Broaden Your Knowledge." Between the two windows on the south-facing wall was a poster depicting a famous photo of four Chinese revolutionaries: Mao Tse-tung, Chou En-lai, Zhu De and Liu Shao-ch'i. On the back wall, students had hung a map of China, a world map, two calendars and three class certificates: one for placing in a sports meet, one for winning an essay contest, and one entitled

"The Party Is in Our Hearts," given to acknowledge the class's mastery of Communist Party doctrine. All in all, the classroom environment was as pleasant as any of the classes I visited, and certainly cleaner than most.

Discourse Analysis

To examine the curriculum and class climate in greater detail, the fifth session was recorded on audio tape and a discourse analysis of the first hour was conducted. Audio taping was chosen over video because the teacher refused to allow me to video tape, saying it would make her too nervous. To compensate for the lack of video, I carefully recorded speaker changes in my notebook. The audio recording was an initial intrusion, but the teacher and students appeared to forget about it once the class session began in earnest.

After careful analysis, I arrived at the following objectives for this session, listed in the order in which they occurred:

> *Objective 1:* To deliver a short oral report in English
> *Objective 2:* To accurately write down a passage dictated in English
> *Objective 3:* To translate orally between English and Chinese
> *Objective 4:* To define new vocabulary words in English
> *Objective 5:* To use new vocabulary words to make sentences in English

The learning activities students engaged in are listed below according to the objective they were designed to support:

> *Objective 1:* To deliver an oral report
>   one student gave a three minute oral report on the weather, films currently showing and a planned bike trip to the suburbs
> *Objective 2:* To write down a dictated passage
>   all students wrote down a dictation of a previously unseen text entitled "Mice That Waltz"
> *Objective 3:* To translate between Chinese and English
>   four students translated seven sentences from Chinese into English
>   six students translated eight sentences from English into Chinese
> *Objective 4:* To define vocabulary
>   12 vocabulary items were defined by students in English
>   the teacher also gave definitions of 10 vocabulary items
> *Objective 5:* To use vocabulary to make sentences
>   three students made sentences using two vocabulary items

Of the five objectives, two were weakly supported by learning activities. The first, to deliver short oral reports in English, was accomplished by only one student. Of course, each session a different student had a chance to practice this objective, but the limited time devoted to it made it doubtful whether students were making great progress in giving oral reports. Secondly, the last objective, to use new vocabulary words to make sentences in English, was practiced by only three students. Again, the limited opportunities to practice this objective did not bode well for rapid student progress in using vocabulary. Objectives 2 and 3 were both supported by substantial appropriate practice, but objective 4, to define new vocabulary, suffered from one inappropriate activity, the propensity of the teacher to do the defining instead of asking students to do so. Still, students were asked to define 12 of the words discussed, and appeared to do so without great difficulty.

This session was organized into three distinct parts: oral report, dictation, and drill and practice. The time devoted to each is given below:

student report	3 minutes
dictation	16 minutes
drill and practice	28 minutes
Total	47 minutes

The drill and practice session consisted of a mixture of oral translation and vocabulary practice. The teacher appeared to use translation in this session primarily as a way to check student understanding of vocabulary items.

The teacher evaluated each of the objectives she taught during the session. Except for the dictation, which was corrected and graded, all evaluations were oral.

To examine the implicit curriculum and class climate in greater detail, the statistics generated by the discourse analysis will be presented. First, the teacher dominated the course, doing 78 percent of the talking, and initiating 68 percent of all messages. Student talk, in this session, was limited to short responses to teacher questions, except for the one student report at the beginning. This becomes even clearer when one looks at the message forms broken down by speaker. The teacher initiated 42 of 43 questions, 13 of 15 explanations, 37 of 42 assertions and all directives and suggestions. Students only dominated one category, responses; they made 38 of the total number of 42.

Despite teacher dominance, 12 of 17 students spoke during the hour, and 11 students received personal messages from the teacher. But the student talk was not equally distributed. Four students dominated, and these same students received 20 of 31 personal messages from the teacher. It is interesting that three of these four students were boys; the only girl to do much talking was the one who gave the oral report at the beginning. Though there were only six boys in the class of 17, three of them did far more talking than all the other girls combined. The skewed distribution of student talking time was primarily caused by the fact that the teacher allowed volunteers to answer most questions. Those who did not volunteer to answer were generally not called upon, and therefore did not speak. Of the five students who did not speak, four were girls.

Another important finding of the discourse analysis is the extent to which Chinese was used in this session. I estimate that 10 percent of the class session was conducted in Chinese, including eight of the 43 messages sent by individual students, and 15 of the 103 messages sent by the teacher. This is a lot of time to devote to Chinese, considering the many English language objectives sought in this course. Of course, most of these were uttered during the oral translation practice, which lasted 15 minutes. The teacher firmly believed that oral translation was an important objective of the course.

Further insights into the implicit curriculum can be gained from examining the style and tone of the discourse. The style was formal throughout. This provided no opportunity for students to hear and practice speaking in an informal style, which is far more common in American conversation than the formal. The lack of informal language seemed to stem from the teacher's preference for a serious, formal classroom style. In another session, for example, students began to give short, informal answers to teacher questions. The teacher informed the students she wanted them to answer in complete sentences instead. Though this teacher studied abroad in Canada for two years, she did not make use of the informal conversational style that she certainly was exposed to there.

The tone of the discourse was serious, except for one mock statement, made by the girl who gave an oral report. In discussing a planned bike trip to the suburbs, the girl proclaimed, "I'd like to go, but I'm not strong enough to ride that far." Students laughed softly at her remark. It was the only laughter during the 49 minute session. The teacher switched to a serious, laudatory tone three times, when she praised the answers of three students, informing them their answers were "very good." The teacher also switched to a critical tone once in evaluating a sentence made up by a boy. This exchange is given below:

> T: Make another sentence using "pull oneself together."
> S: I pull myself together to answer the teacher's question.
> T: That doesn't make sense. It means you don't want to answer the question.

There was a good deal of tension in the above exchange. The student's sentence certainly does make sense, and the teacher identified precisely the meaning the student intended. This illustrates an underlying climate of unease and hostility that existed in this class. I saw numerous examples of it during the sessions I observed, most dramatically of all in the very first session. Before coming to observe, both the English Section Head and I had spoken to the teacher, and she had reluctantly agreed to allow me to observe. The first day, I was taken to her class by the English Section Head. When we arrived, the teacher said I could not observe that day, because she had something private to talk over with the class. The English Head proceeded to explain to her in Chinese that we had already agreed I would begin observations, and that I had come to school that day for this express purpose. But the teacher was adamant. Nothing that the English Head or I said could alter her stand. So, the English Head took me across the hall to another second year Intensive Reading class and persuaded the teacher to allow me to observe unannounced. That is how I came to observe a different teacher for the first session.

Later, several students in the class told me what had happened. They said that this teacher had just been assigned to their class starting in the spring, and a number of students were unhappy about the change. Some of the boys, in particular, were bored with the class and didn't think the teacher was doing a very good job. As a result, they made a lot of trouble in class, and the teacher had decided to bawl them out during the first session I attempted to observe. Considering this a private matter, the teacher did not want me present while she criticized the students for their poor behavior.

Later, when I asked the teacher about the class climate, she described "an invisible wall between me and the students." When asked to explain the source of this barrier, the teacher commented:

> This group of students received too much criticism in the past one and a half years. They just gave up or don't want to behave in class, or they make silly jokes. I don't like it. They aren't used to my teaching style. My other class is more active and more fun. I haven't got to this stage yet in this class, but I imagine I will eventually.

When asked to rate the class climate on a scale of ten, with ten being best, the teacher gave this class a five. That seems overly generous, considering her remarks above. But, I did see some improvement in class climate as the weeks progressed. The first session I attended, the teacher and students argued three times about the correct answers to vocabulary and grammar exercises, and the climate was anything but amiable. By the last session (recorded on tape), though, I detected only the one tense moment described above.

When two students were asked to identify the one best and worst thing about the class, neither student could think of one best thing. One said in Chinese, "This class is just a task. It's not a question of liking or disliking it." The other student said, "I like an active class. I don't agree about being too strict. But we study in the Chinese way. Chinese teachers like to be strict."

Regarding the one worst thing, students mentioned the texts, and the lack of opportunity to speak in class. Regarding texts, one student said:

> I don't like the texts. If the texts are not interesting, then class is no good.

>   Some texts are too abstract, too hard to understand. If the teacher can ex-
>   plain clearly, then it's interesting. It depends on the teacher.

The other student complained about the teaching strategies employed,
saying:

>   I don't like the teacher just talk and the students just listen. Students will
>   be absent-minded. Make students active. We can concentrate our attention
>   that way.

Another source of student dissatisfaction was their lack of participation in
curricular decision making. During the sessions I observed, I saw no evidence,
either direct or indirect, of student decision making. Students did not even
have many opportunities to ask questions. During the recorded session, for example, only one student asked a question in the whole hour. The students I
interviewed both felt they had no say in what they were taught or how they
were taught. I asked them how they felt about having no say. One student said,
"I've gotten used to it. In middle school, they always do like that. You can't
change it." The other student was more equivocal: "Of course, I want to help
decide things. [Pause.] Sometimes, the teacher asks us to tell her our opinions
about how to teach, but how can we know what's best?"

When I asked the teacher whether students should participate in class decision making, she replied that they should help decide, but admitted that the
teachers had "slackened off" in their efforts to solicit student opinions. She did
give one example of student decision making, however. She said:

>   Once in a while, we have students come together to talk about what they
>   feel about teaching, pace, content and methods. We used to go over exercises
>   in great detail, trying to cover everything. Some students said the materials
>   were too easy, and it was a waste of time to go over everything. They pre-
>   ferred to take out unimportant things and have more discussion in class. We
>   took up that suggestion and it worked.

This is a curious statement, given what I observed happening in class. I saw
only one true discussion which lasted about ten minutes. The majority of class
time was devoted to going over exercises, precisely what the teacher claimed
had been changed. In fact, it is hard to imagine spending more time on exercises than students already were doing in this class. Perhaps the teacher was
referring more to the content and materials of Intensive Reading. In the fall
semester, the department made a significant change in materials, deciding to
complete the Chinese-compiled *English* series in three semesters, and adding
the British textbook to the curriculum in the fourth semester. In my discussion
of the *English* series (see Chapter 3), I noted that the series appeared to be too
easy, especially the first two volumes. Furthermore, test scores on the criterion-
referenced reading test revealed that first year students in their first semester
of study at Teachers University could successfully identify factual details
within the range of vocabulary included in *English*. In fact, these students
scored an average of 80 percent correct on this part of the test, again suggest-

ing that the materials were too easy. Apparently, the Intensive Reading teachers and the administration came to the same conclusion, and thus decided to add the British text to the second year Intensive Reading curriculum.

From what the teacher said, decisions about the Intensive Reading curriculum were made jointly by the English Section Head and the three second-year Intensive Reading teachers. Regarding the administration's decision-making role, the teacher commented, "They have a lot of power." Among things they decided were: the course offering for each year, the assignment of teachers and students to classes, and the resolution of classroom problems. The teaching group decided, with final approval from the department, to introduce the British textbook and reorganize the Intensive Reading materials. They also decide as a group on the teaching plan for each week to assure that students of the three classes all reach the same level by the end of the semester. The only thing the teacher decides herself is how to evaluate students, and what remedial work is required, based on the results of evaluation.

Summary

Of the seven objectives identified for this course, students appeared to be having the greatest success with three: to identify the meanings of vocabulary items in English, to identify factual details in short English texts, and to translate between English and Chinese. Their success on these three objectives stemmed in part from the variety of learning activities associated with them, but mostly was the result of the amount of time devoted to these objectives. Taken together, practice on these three objectives occupied about half of the class time in the sessions I observed. Furthermore, students were frequently evaluated on these objectives and received ample knowledge of results. Another factor which explains student progress on two of the objectives— identifying meanings of vocabulary and factual details—was the stress given to these two objectives in other courses, notably first year Intensive Reading I and II and Extensive Reading. The results of the criterion-referenced reading test I administered show that students were quite adept at identifying factual details when the vocabulary of the texts was within their range of understanding. Second year students scored an average of 83 percent on this subtest, but that was only 3 percent better than first year students, which suggests that students' abilities in this area are not improving very rapidly.

Students were having even greater difficulty with the other four objectives, for a variety of reasons. The two objectives related to using vocabulary and grammatical structures in English sentences suffered from inappropriate and limited opportunities to practice the skills implied in the objectives. Students were rarely asked to use vocabulary or grammar to create their own messages. Rather, they practiced these skills on fill-in-the-blank exercises whose relevance to real communication was slight. Their ability to write down material dictated in English suffered from poor listening skills, which did not receive much stress in the course. According to the teacher, students did fairly well on spelling tests, where the object is simply to memorize and spell words correctly, but they did worse on dictations, especially of previously unseen material, due to listening comprehension problems. Finally, the students' ability to speak English did not seem to increase much in Intensive Reading. Though the teacher employed a variety of learning activities for this objective, she devoted very little time to it, no more than 20 percent of the total course time. Even then, students spoke either in response to the teacher's questions, or in the format of substitution and pattern drills. They had only one opportunity to practice speaking English in the kind of real-life situations they would meet in the future.

In sum, the problems with Intensive Reading I become even more exacerbated by the second year. The number and range of objectives sought is too great, even in a course meeting six hours per week. The focus is decidedly on grammar-translation and rote drill and practice, with the limitations inherent in these approaches. To complicate matters further, students were bored with these activities and had grown disenchanted with the teacher and the course. This must have formed a powerful barrier against student learning, particularly for those who were most disillusioned and discontent.

LISTENING COMPREHENSION

I entered the cleanest, most modern room in the foreign languages department building. To help keep it that way, everyone took off their shoes and donned a pair of rubber slippers upon entering. Once inside the language laboratory, I was immediately impressed with the array of technology available, all of it imported from Japan. At the front was a master recording console where the teacher sat. From this position, she could play tapes for the students to hear, allow students to record portions of the class, listen in to what students said over their microphones, patch student microphones into the master console so that everyone could hear, and speak directly through her microphone to all students at once or to individual students. In addition, the room was equipped with two speakers mounted on the front wall that could be wired into the master console, a 25-inch color television, a video recorder and an overhead projector with a projection screen. At each of 36 listening booths, one pair of headphones with an attached microphone and one built-in tape recorder were provided. The large room had windows on three sides which were sealed with plastic to keep dust out and covered by heavy black drapes. Unlike the dull concrete of other classrooms, the language lab featured a spotless, red linoleum floor and was lit by 14 fluorescent lights hanging in pairs from the ceiling.

The teacher sat at the master console with her headphones on. Seventeen students gradually drifted into the room and took seats wherever they liked. Most chose seats towards the back of the room, but they were scattered around the lab. When everyone had arrived and put on their headphones, the teacher began to speak through the microphone: "Today, we are going to listen to a dictation of some numbers from lesson ten. Please dictate the numbers just as we did last time. Ready?"

She paused momentarily to survey the class. Then, she pushed a button on the console and an American woman's voice came over the headphones. The voice began, "What's your address? Where do you live? What's your house number? In the United States, the number is given first and is followed by the name of the street, avenue, boulevard or drive. Next, the names of the city and the state are written and are followed by the zip code number. Listen carefully. Write the addresses you hear, following this example: 1324 Main Street, Ann Arbor, Michigan 48105" [this was also printed on student worksheet]. The students listened to the female voice read a series of 12 addresses and wrote the house numbers and zip codes in the blank spaces provided on their worksheets.

This was a second year course in Listening Comprehension, offered in the spring semester. Students take this course 1.5 hours a week for the first four semesters of their undergraduate program. It is one of the newest courses offered in the department, dating back only four years. I observed five 1.5-hour sessions of this course over a six week period in March and April. Students took one week off to do physical labor. I also recorded the third session I observed on the audio recorder provided at my listening booth. Audio recording was chosen instead of video for two reasons. First, the teacher was reluctant to allow me to video tape. Second, audio taping was an easy and unobtrusive way to record this particular course because I could use the recorder at my booth without having students know the lesson was being taped. Also, though the teacher had to flip a switch to let me record, she never saw the tape recorder running and seemingly forgot about it as the session proceeded. Because of this, the recording was the most natural of all that I made while observing classes.

This course was designed to provide students with practice in various listening comprehension skills. The teacher of the course, a woman in her mid-forties, identified five major purposes she was trying to achieve, which are listed below in rank order:

(1). to "develop the ability to take notes"
(2). to "train the students' ears" by listening to gradually more difficult materials

(3). to improve performance on listening exams like the TOEFL test

(4). to hold class discussions on topics covered in listening lessons

(5). to listen to and understand interviews and conversations

When two randomly selected students were asked to list the most important things they had learned in their second year Listening Comprehension class, both cited two things: learning about foreign countries by listening to lectures and learning number training and about statistics. Additionally, one student mentioned the broad goal of "training our listening comprehension ability." The other student was unable to state anything else that had been learned in the class. Moreover, the first student, before stating what students had learned, said, "We have learned nothing important in this class, just common sense things."

Based on the five class sessions I observed, I identified five major objectives of the course, listed in rank order:

Objective 1: To follow oral directions given in English

Objective 2: To write down factual information while listening to lectures in English

Objective 3: To write down statistics and numbers dictated in English

Objective 4: To identify factual details and abbreviations from lectures in English

Objective 5: To write down abbreviations and acronyms dictated in English

In comparing the three lists of objectives given above, a number of differences stand out. First, students were only able to state two clear objectives that they were learning, and even these were identified only after some prodding by me. Though these were stated quite generally, they basically correspond to three of the objectives I identified and two provided by the teacher. This suggests that students are only learning some of the course objectives. Second, the teacher and I came up with significantly different objectives for the course. In fact, we agreed on only one: to write down factual information while listening to lectures in English. The teacher's second "objective" is so vague it is virtually useless as an educational objective.

The third and fifth objectives the teacher mentioned were not taught while I observed the class, but the teacher said that these would be covered later in the semester. The fourth objective she mentioned — to hold class discussions — was only observed occurring once for about ten minutes. The other class "discussions" I observed were really drill and practice sessions in which students were asked to identify factual details from their listening materials.

The other objectives I listed were identified in one of two ways. First, some of the listening materials presented on tape included statements of objectives. I relied on these to identify objectives 1, 3 and 5. The other two objectives were arrived at after carefully reviewing notes of the observed sessions and conducting a discourse analysis of the one session recorded on audio tape. The teacher had no formal objectives for the course and only thought about my question in terms of broad course purposes.

The materials used in this course were all taken from American ESL textbooks, and included prerecorded tapes. The teacher had gotten duplicated copies of these from various associates and acquaintances and then had these typed and mimeographed for students. Since she did not have an original copy of any of these textbooks, she was unable to furnish me with complete details on the sources for these books. Altogether, I saw three sets of materials being used. The first was entitled *Improving Aural Comprehension* and consisted of 20 lessons in total. Each lesson covered a different aspect of comprehending spoken numbers or statistics. Students were provided with a worksheet to accompany each lesson. They listened to a native American read a series of numbers or statistics on various topics and then wrote down the correct figures on their worksheets. The exercises were usually of a fill-in-the-blank nature, but multiple choice questions were also provided at times. Additionally, each lesson was followed by a short quiz designed to check students' comprehension of the details in the lesson.

The second group of materials was called *Spoken Abbreviations*, and consisted of ten lessons on abbreviations and acronyms. Again, students had a worksheet for each lesson, and listened on tape to a native American read a series of abbreviations and acronyms. Students had to write down next to the complete phrase on their sheets the correct abbreviation or acronym as they heard it read on the tape. Each of these lessons also had a brief aural comprehension check of some of the abbreviations presented in the lesson.

The last materials were used more extensively than the first two in the sessions I observed. Entitled *Advanced Listening Comprehension* (published by the University of Arizona, 1980), the textbook consisted of ten short lectures on a range of academic topics, including climatology, history, sociology, geography and linguistics. Each lesson began with a brief preview of the lecture's content, a preview of vocabulary and sentences included in the lecture, a note-taking model for students to refer to and emulate, an eight to ten minute lecture and a quiz on factual details presented in multiple choice and true-false formats.

All of these materials appeared to take a notional-functional approach to English language learning. This has been defined as "a curriculum whose aim is primarily to establish the communicative competence of individuals, [and which] may present a set of lessons organized around certain functions, acts, or rules of conversation."[107] In the case of these materials, the functions included are those related to college academic life in the United States, such as academic lectures, commonly used abbreviations in various academic fields, and numbers and statistics presented in a context in which an American college student might encounter them. It should be noted, however, that none of these materials had been adapted for use in China, and they often assumed cultural knowledge about the United States and other foreign countries which neither the students nor the teacher possessed.

The exact content of the lessons I observed varied considerably from week to week. During the first session, students listened to a tape recording from *Improving Aural Comprehension* covering eight lessons. The topics presented in these lessons are listed below:

Lesson 10: United States addresses
Lesson 11: Population of the world's largest metropolitan areas
Lesson 12: Statistics on languages of the world
Lesson 13: Statistics on popular magazines in the United States
Lesson 15: Page numbers of student reading assignments
Lesson 16: Dewey Decimal system of library classification
Lesson 17: Statistics on U.S. college degrees by major
Lesson 18: Statistics on U.S. college degrees by sex and major

During the second session, two sets of materials were used. First, students listened to lessons nine and ten of *Spoken Abbreviations* and wrote down the abbreviations and acronyms on their worksheets as they were dictated on the tape. Among the abbreviations and acronyms given were AAA, AD, BA, BC, FM, ID, IQ, PS, and VIP. A comprehension quiz followed each lesson, but the teacher did not have students complete it, citing lack of time. The rest of that session was devoted to lesson five from *Advanced Listening Comprehension*. Entitled "Kuwait: Pipeline of the Middle East," it presented a ten minute lecture on the geography, history, economy and political system of Kuwait. After going over a vocabulary exercise in class, students listened to the lecture twice, taking notes the second time. They also answered multiple choice and true-false questions about factual details in the lectures which were collected and graded by the teacher.

The third class session was devoted to lecture seven from *Advanced Listening Comprehension*. Entitled "Women's Liberation: The Search for Equality," it presented a ten minute lecture on the women's liberation movement in the United States, including its historical origins, major accomplishments, and current problems. The teacher went over previews of content, vocabulary, and sentences from the lecture, and students then listened to the taped lecture three times, taking notes of the lecture the last two times. They then completed a multiple choice and a true-false quiz on factual details from the lecture.

The fourth class session was held in the students' regular classroom. Billed by the teacher as a discussion of the lectures on Kuwait and women's liberation, it was in reality mostly a drill and practice session in which the teacher asked questions about factual details from both lectures and students offered short answers. Towards the end of the session, the class held a true discussion for about ten minutes on the topic of women's liberation.

The content of the fifth session was another lecture from *Advanced Listening Comprehension*, this one entitled "Languages in Conflict: Irish and English." Students listened to an eight minute lecture on the national language policy of Ireland which gave a brief review of the history of the Irish and English languages. They heard the lecture twice, took notes on it the second time, and completed a multiple choice and true-false quiz. Afterwards, the teacher asked students to identify the factual details of the lecture, and had them summarize some portions by retelling the lecture from their notes.

During the five sessions I observed, students engaged in a total of eight kinds of learning activities. Most of these involved listening to spoken English on tape and writing down information given. Occasionally, students did other kinds of written work, or had an opportunity to talk about what they had learned. The eight activities are listed below:

1. listen to tape recordings and write down numbers and statistics on a worksheet in a fill-in-the-blank format.
2. listen to tape recordings and write down abbreviations and acronyms as dictated on a worksheet.
3. listen to lectures and take notes.
4. mark written answers to questions about factual details from taped lectures.
5. write answers to vocabulary exercises with a fill-in-the-blank format.
6. answer the teacher's questions about factual details of lectures.
7. discuss major issues and ideas raised in a lecture.
8. retell portions of a lecture.

These eight activities gave practice in four of the five objectives I identified earlier. The only objective which was not directly supported by a learning activity was the first, to follow oral directions in English. But this objective was a prerequisite for the other four objectives, and students could not successfully engage in most of the learning activities unless they correctly followed instructions given on tape and often repeated by the teacher.

The teaching strategies employed in this course were of four basic types: drill and practice, lecture, translation, and discussion. Drill and practice was the most common teaching strategy used. It formed the basis for the listening activities from *Improving Aural Comprehension* and *Spoken Abbreviations*. It was also the mode employed by the teacher during the "discussion" session. The lecture mode was used in the three lessons from *Advanced Listening Comprehension*. In addition, the teacher made limited use of a lecture mode during the discussion session held in the regular classroom. Translation was a strategy the teacher relied on in each of the observed sessions. She used it in several ways.

First, she often translated new vocabulary into Chinese to help the students understand the meaning. Second, she frequently gave directions to students in Chinese, or used both English and Chinese to direct the class' attention to procedures they should follow. Third, much of the routine business of the class, such as giving homework assignments, correcting typographical errors on worksheets, etc., was conducted in Chinese. While the teacher appeared to use Chinese primarily to facilitate the students' understanding of the materials, she also gave many directions in Chinese. This contradicted one of the objectives identified by the authors of the materials, namely to follow oral directions in English. Since students could usually count on the teacher to repeat directions in Chinese, they did not need to pay as much attention to this objective as the textbooks' authors intended.

The organization of this course differed somewhat from week to week. Grouping patterns were of two types: individual work in the language laboratory, and large group work during the "discussion" session and the oral drill and practice sessions in the lab. During the four sessions held in the lab, students worked alone most of the time. No small group work occurred during the sessions I observed.

Besides grouping, each of Ralph Tyler's three organizational elements— continuity, sequence and integration—was evident to some degree in this course. Continuity, the vertical reiteration of curricular elements, was commonly used. Students had recurring and continual opportunities to learn most of the objectives of this course. They listened to and wrote down statistics and numbers from 20 different lessons. They wrote down abbreviations and acronyms as dictated in 10 lessons, and listened to a total of 10 lectures by the end of the semester. Each session, students also had opportunities to identify factual details given on tape.

The course not only displayed continuity, but also relied on sequence to gradually build upon students' previous learning experiences. Sequence was evident in several areas. First, the teacher organized the course so that students practiced writing down statistics and numbers first, then abbreviations and acronyms, and finally took notes from lectures which required them to write down statistics and abbreviations along with facts. In this way, students moved from easier to more difficult listening skills, although not as gradually as they might have.

Second, the lessons from *Advanced Listening Comprehension* were sequenced according to the length of the lectures presented, and the amount of aid given to the students in the form of notes and repetitions on tape. That is, the lectures gradually became longer and more complex, and students were gradually given less help in taking notes, so as to eventually approximate real-life conditions in college courses.

The third element identified by Tyler—integration—aims at the horizontal organization of curricular elements. It was not used as extensively as the vertical elements discussed above, but was apparent in the organization of activities designed to support objective 4: to identify factual details and abbreviations from lectures in English. Students were given several different kinds of activities related to this objective, and in this way, could get a more unified view of the things required to master it.

To evaluate the extent to which students were mastering the objectives, the teacher primarily relied on various homework exercises included in the materials for the course. For example, to evaluate students' ability to write down factual information from lectures, the teacher collected the students' notes from each of three lectures I observed and graded them as homework. To check students' ability to identify factual details and abbreviations, the teacher collected the multiple choice and true-false quizzes from each lecture and graded them. The teacher did not, however, give midterm or final examinations in the course. This was a weakness in evaluation because the teacher had no systematic way to judge student progress in learning the objectives over longer periods of time. A second weakness of the written evaluation is that the teacher never asked students to write summaries of lectures from their notes. Since the whole purpose of notetaking is to be able to reconstruct lecture material later, and thus reinforce long-term memory, the teacher neglected an excellent evaluation technique by not asking students to write up their lecture notes into summaries of the lectures they had heard.

In addition to the written evaluations mentioned above, the teacher employed oral evaluation to assess student progress in one objective: to identify factual details and abbreviations from lectures. The oral evaluation generally consisted of a drill and practice session, where the teacher posed questions about factual details and students gave short oral answers. An example of this type of evaluation is given below, taken from the session held in the regular classroom:

    T: Who can tell us about Kuwait?
    S1: It's a small country. Very rich.
    T: Where is it located?
    S2: Near the Persian Gulf.
    T: When was oil discovered?
    S3: 1938.
    S[chorus]: 1951.
    T: Yes, 1951. Before oil was discovered, what was the country like?
    S4: Little-known country.
    T: What about reserves?
    S[chorus]: 15 percent of world's reserves.

The only objective the teacher did not evaluate in any way was the first: to follow oral directions in English. In fact, as indicated above, the teacher's frequent use of Chinese to explain directions contradicted this objective and the intent of the authors of the textbooks. Nevertheless, an ability to follow directions in English was a prerequisite to student progress in the other four objectives, especially when they listened to the tapes. To some extent, the teacher appeared to use Chinese because she noticed that students had trouble following the directions in English. At one point, she commented that students were having trouble completing their exercises according to the directions. But she did not provide extra practice to help students master this, and did not directly evaluate their ability to do so, either in written or oral form.

The spatial elements of this course were quite different from others I observed becaue of the unique conditions in the language laboratory. As the most modern room in the building, the language lab offered a variety of features that regular classrooms lacked. But the teacher did not make full use of them. For example, she never used the overhead projector or the video recorder. Also, during the first two sessions I observed, students were not allowed to record the lectures or other listening materials they heard. Still, the advantages of the language lab were numerous. The individual listening booths enabled students to work alone, but not usually at their own pace, since the teacher determined when they would listen to tapes and for how long. In the last two sessions in the lab, the teacher began to allow students to record the lectures on their own tapes so that they could listen to them again. This enabled students to determine their own pace, and to review lectures outside of class, if they had a tape recorder. Another advantage of the lab was its cleanliness and good light, which both contributed to a pleasant environment in which to learn.

But the language lab had its drawbacks as well. Though the teacher could patch student microphones through the master console so that everyone could hear student comments, this did not provide a suitable environment for discussion. Students were isolated in their booths and directed any comments they made to the teacher, who reprocessed them back for other students to hear. This is the reason the teacher chose to hold the fourth session in a regular classroom. There, students could hear each other more easily, and large group work was thus facilitated. Also, the language lab did not receive any heat during the sessions I observed in March and April. Temperatures ranged from a low of 55 degrees F. to a high of 67 by late April. Thus, class sessions on the coldest days were no more comfortable in the lab than in any other classroom.

The use of time in this course varied considerably between sessions held in the lab, and the session held in the classroom. In the lab, time was divided into four basic elements, while in the classroom, time was divided into only two elements. Based on the chronology I kept while observing each session, I arrived at the following approximate breakdown of time allocation by speaker:

Language Lab	Percent Time	Classroom	Percent Time
Teacher talk =	25	Teacher talk =	83
Student talk =	5	Student talk =	17
Taped talk =	55		
Silent work =	15		

In the lab, the teacher talk usually occurred at the beginning of the lesson, when the teacher announced the day's agenda and sometimes went over preview exercises orally. The tape recorded talk dominated the middle of the lesson, when students listened to various taped materials and wrote down information they heard. Silent work usually occupied the last portion of the class, especially when students listened to lectures, because they were always asked to complete the true-false questions on their own. Student talk occurred sporadically throughout the session. Students usually spoke when asked a question by the teacher or when they were unsure of what they were supposed to do next. In the classroom, teacher talk predominated, much as it did in other courses I observed. Student talk was limited to short answers to the teacher's questions or an occasional question raised by a student.

Discourse Analysis

To examine the implicit curriculum in greater detail, the results of a discourse analysis of the third session will be presented. It will be recalled that this session was devoted to listening to a lecture entitled "Women's Liberation: The Search for Equality." This particular lesson appeared to have three objectives:

1. To follow oral directions given in English.
2. To write down factual information while listening to a lecture in English.
3. To identify factual details and abbreviations from the lecture.

The learning activities offered to students for each objective are as follows:

Objective 1: To follow oral directions
1. The teacher told the students in English to listen to the lecture the first time and then take notes while listening the second time.
2. A male voice on tape gave the same directions again to students.
3. The male voice gave detailed directions on how to take notes and what information to listen for.
4. The male voice gave directions to students on how to complete the multiple choice questions at the end of the lecture.

Objective 2: To write down information
1. Students took notes on the lecture the second time they heard it.
2. Students were allowed to record the lecture and listen to it a third time in order to check their notes for completeness.

Objective 3: To identify details
1. The teacher went over the preview of content, preview of vocabulary and preview of sentences orally before students listened to the lecture.
2. The students listened to the lecture the first time while looking at the notetaking model included on their worksheets.

This class session was organized in four distinct parts. First, the teacher went over the previews of content, vocabulary and sentences in a drill and practice format. Second, students completed the notetakng exercise by listening to the taped lecture three times. Third, students were evaluated on their ability to identify factual details by taking a multiple choice and true-false quiz on the content of the lecture. Fourth, the teacher conducted classroom routines three times, at the beginning, in the middle and at the end of the session. The routines consisted of the teacher explaining last week's homework results, correcting typographical errors on the students' worksheets, and announcing next week's class agenda and homework assignment.

The results of the discourse analysis reveal that the teaching role was divided between the teacher and the taped lecture. During most of the session, the "teacher" was actually the two native American voices on tape. The Chinese teacher dominated only one category of message: directives. The taped lecture dominated two categories: questions and suggestions, while explanations and assertions were nearly evenly split between teacher and tape. These results also demonstrate that students did almost no talking during the class. In fact, aside from one chorus response, only two students talked during the entire 80 minutes. The rest of the time, students listened and wrote down what they heard, or took quizzes.

Another interesting finding from the discourse analysis has to do with the differing styles of the teacher and the taped voices. While the teacher tended to use directives in getting the class to do or understand things, the tape relied more on suggestions. In fact, all three suggestions were made by voices on the tape. It was suggested that students speed up their note taking pace, that they write certain key words and numbers, and that they review their notes at the end of the lecture. In all the sessions I observed, I never heard the teacher offer a suggestion to students. If she wanted them to do or remember something, she always used a directive.

The style, tone and channel of the discourse reveal much about the implicit curriculum of the class. The style was formal throughout, with no switches to an informal style detected. This suggests a severe limitation on the listening comprehension of students. While most discourse in American English is in an informal style, students did not listen to this style at all. The teacher's mastery of English seemed limited to a formal style, since I never heard her switch to the informal, and the taped lectures were also delivered in a formal style, much as a professor would use if he or she were reading a paper at a conference. The fact is, though, that most academic lectures in American colleges are delivered in an informal style, with the lecturer making frequent use of idioms, pauses, false starts, etc. Yet the listening materials in *Advanced Listening Comprehension* were always delivered in the formal style of reading aloud from a set text. Thus, students were receiving listening training in a very limited and seldomly used style of discourse.

The tone of this class session reinforced this formal style. It was serious throughout, with no mock or humorous statements. In fact, students never laughed or even smiled throughout the 80 minute session. Again, this does not conform to the typical American college lecture, where humor is a device often used to create interest or relieve tension and boredom. Despite the serious tone, there were switches to laudatory and critical comments, all of them initiated by the teacher. At the beginning of the session, the teacher used a laudatory tone to praise one student by name who had done the best on the previous week's quizzes. She also made five critical remarks throughout the session. Two of the remarks were directed to unnamed students who had done poorly on their homework assignments. One critical remark was directed at a student who had forgotten to write his name on his homework paper. Later in the session, when a student asked for the meaning of "impact," the teacher remarked critically, "Impact? You've already had that word." After that critical remark, students did not ask another question for the rest of the session. The teacher's critical remarks appeared to demonstrate some exasperation with the class, and had the effect of dampening student participation, especially in asking questions.

Finally, the channel of the discourse reveals important elements of the class curriculum and climate. While the channel was primarily oral throughout, it was supplemented by written materials 15 times during the session. These occurred when students were asked to read materials from their worksheets, either while listening to the teacher or tape, or silently on their own. Also, more significantly, the teacher switched from English to Chinese 16 times. In fact, I estimate that 10 percent of the 80 minute class session was conducted in Chinese. Even more revealing, the teacher spoke in Chinese 47 percent of the total time she talked. This is a far higher proportion of Chinese than I observed in any other class. The teacher made extensive use of Chinese when going over the preview of content and vocabulary by translating words and phrases in Chinese. She also used Chinese almost exclusively in conducting routine business like correcting typographical errors and announcing the agenda and homework assignments. As I have already suggested, the teacher's use of Chinese to give directions contradicted the intent of the textbooks' authors to get students to follow directions in English. Further, such extensive use of Chinese in an English listening comprehension class runs counter to the larger purposes of the course. Finally, because the teacher used so much Chinese, students were also encouraged to do so. During the discussion session in the classroom, students were observed to give answers and ask questions in Chinese instead of English. Thus, the teacher's reliance on Chinese, which was a matter of convenience for her, actually had a negative impact on all of the objectives she was seeking to teach.

My overall impression of the class climate in this course is split. On the one hand, students appeared to enjoy some of the listening activities, especially the opportunities to hear lectures by native American speakers. On the other hand, students sometimes seemed displeased with the way the teacher conducted the course, and exhibited some boredom with drill and practice exercises. The lack of humor or demonstrable joy tended to create a rather flat, business-like atmosphere.

During interviews, the teacher and two students were asked to comment further on the class climate. On a scale of one to ten, with ten being best, the teacher rated the climate of this class at the midway point of five. She gave the following explanation for her rating:

> This is the second year for me to teach this course. Students like this kind of practice. They are interested in the class and most of them are satisfied. Some said they missed the class when we don't have it. But a few find it too difficult. They asked me to reproduce more tapes for them to listen to.

When students were asked to name the one best and worst thing about the class, they readily cited several things. For best thing, one student said, "I like listening to native speakers with American accents." The other said, "I like listening without doing exercises, especially listening to materials about the history, customs, and traditions of foreign countries, and lives of famous persons." As for one worst thing, the first student cited the time spent on operating tape recorders in the lab: "It's a waste of time. The teacher could use one big tape recorder and one tape. But it's okay for students to record tapes if they have a tape recorder. I don't have one, though, so it doesn't do me any good." The second student complained about "doing exercises continuously. It's very dull." This student also said that the teacher should always speak English in class. Despite these complaints, the results of the student surveys indicate that Listening Comprehension is one of the best liked courses in the department, and is considered second only to Intensive Reading in importance. Students rated interest in the course, usefulness of the course, and student decision making power above the average for all courses surveyed. The students' high ratings of Listening Comprehension appear to stem from their preferred learning styles. They like working alone best, which is the main way they work in this course, and they prefer aural/oral learning modes, the first of which receives major stress in the class.

The extent to which students can help make decisions in this course appeared to be somewhat higher than for other courses I observed. During the five sessions I attended, I saw several concrete instances of student decision making. At the end of the first session, for example, the following exchange took place:

> T: Any questions?
>
> S1: I have a suggestion. You should give us tapes with some numbers so we get more practice doing this.
>
> T: That's a good suggestion. Comrade Wang [the class monitor, a kind of student representative], do we have a cassette with number practice?
>
> Wang: No.
>
> T: I'll ask the technician to reproduce a tape for you. That's all for today.

In a later session, the teacher told students in Chinese that they should let her know what they thought of the exercises and the class. Though students did not respond to her at that time, they may have talked to her after class. The next week, the teacher announced that students could begin to tape the lectures on their own cassettes and listen to them later in their spare time. Also, during the session in the regular classroom, the students were active in decision making three times. Once a student asked the teacher again to provide them with more tapes of lectures so that they could listen on their own. The teacher agreed. Secondly, the teacher asked the class at one point whether she should write some abbreviations they were discussing on the blackboard. One student said, "You needn't," and so the teacher did not bother to do so. Finally, at the beginning of the session, the following exchange took place:

> T: Did you listen to the tape again out of class? [Students were being allowed to record lectures by then.]
>
> S1: I haven't got the tape.
>
> T: Did anyone listen to the tape? [Pause.] Yes or no?
>
> S2: Yes. [Long pause.]
>
> T: If the rest of you haven't listened, how can we go on with the discussion? What can we do? Comrade Wang [class monitor], what's your opinion?
>
> Wang: We can look at our notes and see what we remember.

The teacher appeared to accept the monitor's advice, because she then began to ask questions about the lectures.

A word about the class monitor is in order. All Chinese classes, from primary through college level, have a monitor appointed by the administration of the school, or in a few cases, elected by students of the class. The monitor is usually a male, even in this department where two-thirds of the students are female. The monitor is generally chosen for his political reliability, above all (he is often a member of the Communist Youth League), as well as his good academic record and maturity. The duties of the class monitor vary from class to class, but he is generally responsible for student behavior in class, for seeing that students turn in their homework, that their behavior conforms to political and social norms, and for representing student opinion when it is solicited by the administration. At Teachers University, for example, one monitor informed me that the monitors from each class meet about once a semester to discuss common problems and present opinions and suggestions to the administration. In this sense, they are class representatives, though those at Teachers University are not elected by their peers. The Listening Comprehension teacher relied more heavily on the class monitor than did other teachers I observed.

Besides the instances of student decision making I saw, the students I interviewed both said they could sometimes help to decide certain things. One student said, "Students give some suggestions, but the teacher decides [about] them." The other student said, "We can submit topics we'd like to listen to." Neither student reported suggesting anything to the teacher themselves, but said other students had.

Ironically, when I asked the teacher whether students should have any say in deciding what they learn or how they are taught, she replied in the negative. But when asked to explain this, she focused her attention on the materials of the course. In this area, she believed that students could not possibly know about state of the art listening materials, especially those from abroad. "If students knew some materials, I wouldn't use them, because they can only buy them in the bookstore." She said she was always on the lookout for new listening materials, and obtained the ones she was using from friends who had returned from abroad. Regarding the question of how students are taught, she allowed that she occasionally asked for their opinions, and cited the example of providing more listening tapes when students requested them.

Still, student decision making was limited to the curricular areas of activities and content. Objectives, materials, strategies, organization and evaluation were all the prerogative of the teacher. In the case of this course, the teacher exercised considerable decision making on her own. She indicated that the administration did not oversee or intervene in her conduct of the course or the materials and content she chose to use. The only curricular force other than herself to influence the course was the State Education Commission, which conducts tests of college students periodically, including listening comprehension tests. The teacher allowed that she sometimes taught toward these examinations in the hope of seeing student scores go up. Otherwise, she was limited only by the difficulty of acquiring suitable listening materials in China.

One other aspect of the class climate must be discussed. That is my presence as a participant-observer. I appeared to have had a dichotomous impact on the class. On the one hand, students were barely cognizant of my presence in the back of the language lab, and did not know I recorded one session of the course. But the teacher, on the other hand, was always acutely aware of my presence. More than any other teacher I observed, she sought to involve me directly in the class. After each session I observed, she asked me for my opinions and suggestions about how to teach the materials. I politely put her off at first, telling her that we would talk at length once I had completed my observations. But, during the fourth session in the regular classroom, towards the end of class, the teacher called on me to say a few words about how students should study listening comprehension. I declined to become involved, saying, "I really can't add anything to what's already been said."

Afterwards, though, the teacher insisted that I give her some advice about how to teach the listening materials. She indicated that students were not doing very well on their note taking and she didn't know what to do about it. At this point, I did not feel I could continue to avoid her questions. So, I suggested that students seemed to need practice identifying main ideas of lectures and summarizing what they had heard. Two ways to do that, I continued, were to ask students to orally summarize the lecture after listening to it, and to ask students to write written summaries based on their notes. She thanked me and we parted. The next week, after students listened to the lecture on Ireland, she asked them to retell portions of the lecture from their notes, one of the activities I had recommended. So, in this way, I became largely responsible for one of the course's learning activities.

Summary

Of the five objectives of the Listening Comprehension course I listed at the beginning of this discussion, students appeared to have the most success with two: to identify factual details and abbreviations from lectures in English, and to write down abbreviations and acronyms dictated in English. Their relative success with these two objectives was reflected in higher homework scores on these items than on others the teacher collected and graded. The first of these objectives was also mentioned by both students who were interviewed as one of the things they had learned in the course. They had success in identifying factual details and abbreviations, I believe, largely due to the variety of learning activities devoted to this objective, and the weekly evaluations of their ability to perform these skills. They were doing well on the other objective primarily because they had already spent a great deal of time on abbreviations and acronyms in the fall semester, and because they found these far easier to write down accurately than numbers and statistics.

Their progress in two other objectives was much slower. These were to write down factual information while listening to lectures in English, and to write down statistics and numbers dictated orally in English. They did poorly on these exercises and asked the teacher to provide more listening practice on these two objectives. Their difficulties seemed to stem from several factors.

First, they did not fully understand the cultural context of the lectures and the contexts in which statistics were given. Further, the teacher, who has never been abroad, was unable to provide them with the necessary cultural background to make the lectures fully understandable. As a result, much of the practice they engaged in had little meaning for students, and they quickly become bored with it.

Second, they did not receive sufficient practice in recognizing main ideas and key facts, which is a prerequisite skill to successful note taking. Without such skill, they were often confused about what they should write down. Some students simply tried to write everything, but they found that the voices on tape spoke too quickly for that.

Third, the statistics practice was made difficult by the fact that students did not know anything about the subjects they listened to and had little idea what key terms like "rate," "rank," and "mean" meant. The teacher did little to clarify the exercises and only defined terms by translating them into Chinese. Given the students' limited math backgrounds, the translations they received from the teacher did not appear to help them very much. Also, large numbers above 10,000 are always difficult for Chinese, because they use a different counting system than English speakers do. Chinese has no equivalent category for "hundred thousand," "million," or "billion." Instead, these numbers are counted in multiples of "ten thousand." Knowing this, the teacher should have given special attention to this problem, but did not.

The fifth objective – to follow oral directions given in English – is impossible to judge, since the teacher did not evaluate students' ability to do this, and frequently gave directions in Chinese. In fact, inability to follow directions in English may have been a root cause of problems with the two objectives mentioned above, but it is impossible for me to factor this out. Certainly, the teacher's extensive use of Chinese did not help students increase their English listening comprehension and is totally inappropriate in a course of this nature.

The other major problem of this course was the overemphasis on drill and practice and identifying factual details at the expense of discussing lecture content and recognizing main ideas. With so little attention to content and ideas, and no attempt to see implications or draw conclusions, students quickly became bored with the listening exercises. This problem was partly due to the materials themselves, which were preoccupied with facts, statistics and abbreviations, and was compounded by the teacher's conduct of the course. Even when she attempted to hold discussions or get students to retell lectures, the stress was always on identifying facts and statistics, not recognizing important ideas, drawing conclusions or formulating opinions. The results of the criterion-referenced test revealed that students were good at identifying facts but poor at drawing inferences. Students only averaged 48 percent on the inference sub-test, and they showed no gain whatsoever in this reading skill after six months of instruction.

Most of the time, the teacher simply handed out worksheets, played tapes and collected worksheets, in a never-ending cycle. She did virtually no "teaching" per se, except for the one "discussion" session. While this approach resulted in student progress in some basic listening skills, it left out some of the most important aspects of comprehending aural communication. Considering that this was the last semester students would study Listening Comprehension, I was left wondering when, if ever, students would learn other important listening skills.

5

Learning from Abroad
in Advanced English Courses

Introduction

One of the most significant developments in the English language curriculum of universities in China over the past decade has been the introduction of foreign teachers in large numbers. Before 1976, the number of foreign
English teachers in China was exceedingly small, probably less than 100 or so
in the whole country. Most of these were long-time residents of China who
had come in the thirties and never left. After the death of Mao, however, the
number of foreign teachers grew rapidly. By 1979, there were about 500 foreign
teachers in Beijing alone. Five years later, that number had more than
doubled.

An equally important change occurring at the same time was the growing
number of Chinese teachers of English who were allowed to go abroad to
study. While no precise figures on English teachers are available, an estimated
40,000 Chinese have gone abroad to study since 1979,[108] the largest number
since the Communists came to power in 1949.

Still, the number of Chinese English teachers who get to go abroad is tiny.
At Teachers University, less than 10 percent of the English faculty had ever
been abroad. For those who never get the chance, the government has recently
begun to import materials, audio-visual equipment and teachers from abroad.

This chapter describes two advanced English literature courses taken by
juniors or seniors which are designed to provide them with an understanding
of foreign literature and culture. One was taught by a senior Chinese professor
who had spent two years in Great Britain; the other by a visiting American
professor of English literature.

FOURTH YEAR: STYLISTICS

The classroom was overcrowded but functional. It had an unpainted concrete floor and white, chalky paint on the concrete walls that came off if you

rubbed against them. The room contained 28 desks which were lined up in pairs to form three rows stretching from the lectern to the back wall. Two narrow aisles separated the desks and were the only way for students to reach their seats. One door led out of the room into a long corridor and two windows faced south onto a small courtyard. At the front, a large blackboard occupied about two-thirds of the wall's length. Immediately in front of the blackboard stood a large wooden podium raised about 6 inches off the floor. In the middle of the podium was a lectern behind which the teacher stood. Above the blackboard on the front wall, spelled out in large red letters, was the slogan: "THE PATH IS BENEATH YOUR FEET."

Twenty-five students crowded into this small room along with two observers, an older Chinese teacher auditing the class and myself. The teacher stood behind the lectern and talked about poetry, occasionally turning around to write on the blackboard behind her. As she talked, most students looked down at the open textbooks on their desk. A few took notes. Others simply stared out the window or whispered to the student sitting next to them.

At one point, after a break, the Chinese teacher, who spoke slowly in a British accent, told the students: "Some of you think poetry is over your head. It's too difficult. Others think, 'I'm not going to be a student of literature. I'm going to be an English teacher or an interpreter.' But poetry is based on ordinary language. They are close. Also, poetry influences ordinary language. So, if you understand poetry, you'll understand ordinary language better. Five or six years ago, I myself would never have dreamed to teach poetry, but I see a use for it now. Poetry is accessible to all, not only the literary minded. I'm trying to show you a way to approach a poem so that you can analyze and understand it."

This was a fourth year course in Stylistics, with an emphasis on poetic style. The teacher combined traditional poetic analysis based on rhyme, rhythm and imagery with elements of structural linguistics, especially phonology and syntax, to fashion an elective course for students interested in literary analysis.

The teacher described the purposes of the course as follows: "I want to get them interested in poetry and acquaint them with a model that can help them analyze and understand English poetry." One student from the course described what she had learned as follows: "Now I know the general rules of poetry, the meter, rhythm, sound patterns, etc. I learned a little about the way to analyze a poem." Another student commented, "I have learned some skills, such as how to derive the meter and stress patterns of poems, the diction, and what some poems mean."

I observed two versions of this course, one in the fall semester and one in the spring. The fall semester course was the more ambitious of the two, since it was taught over a 20 week period. The spring semester course lasted only six weeks, and was therefore a truncated version of the earlier course. After observing two hour sessions for seven weeks, and interviewing the teacher and two students, I derived the following two objectives of the course:

> *Objective 1:* To examine how linguistics contributes to an understanding of the English language
>
> *Objective 2:* To analyze British and American poetry in terms of its phonology, syntax, lexicon and semantics.

The course materials consisted of a teacher compiled "textbook" which was mimeographed and distributed to students free of charge. The teacher reported that the materials were based primarily on research in stylistics and structural linguistics conducted during her two year stay in England as a visiting Chinese scholar. In addition to her own research, she drew heavily upon the work of various British professors of literature that she had met. The material was organized into three main parts: presentation in narrative form of major elements of poetry, analysis of selected poems in terms of the major elements described, and samples of British and American poems drawn primarily from the nineteenth and twentieth centuries. Among the poets included were Shakespeare, Wordsworth, Shelley, Hardy, Whitman, Dickinson, T.S. Eliot, D.H. Lawrence, Frost, Gwendolyn Brooks, and Langston Hughes.

The content of the class sessions observed fell broadly into two categories. The first was lectures on linguistic and stylistic elements of poetry such as rhythm, rhyme, sound patterns, syntax, diction and imagery. The second was analysis of selected poems in terms of the above elements, usually conducted in a drill and practice format in which the teacher posed factual questions and students responded with short answers. On rare occasions, real discussions ensued, with teacher and students engaged in free-form debate of the correct analysis and meaning of poems. During the sessions observed, the content of lectures included the following topics: poetry and rhythm, especially meter, sound patterns of poetry like alliteration, assonance, rhyme, etc., functions of sound patterns, syntax and diction, the role of tone, style, imagery and figurative language, and syntax of free verse.

The most common teaching strategy employed was the lecture. The teacher invariably began each session with a brief review of the previous class's content and then presented new information either by directly reading from the textbook, lecturing from notes or writing examples on the board and explaining them in detail. Later in the session, the teacher employed a kind of drill and practice in which students were asked to look at a sample poem and answer oral questions involving its linguistic analysis. An example of this technique is given below:

> T: Look at stanza A on page 15 taken from a poem by Shelley. [Students turn to page 15.]
>
> T: Could you tell me the meter?

S[chorus]: Iambic.

T: How many feet?

S1: Five.

T: Yes. Iambic pentameter. Any variations in the first line?

S2: No.

T: Second line?

S3: No.

T: No?

S1: Yes. "Winds."

T: Right. Tell me, can you find falling rhythm?

S[chorus]: Curfew...parting...slowly...darkness.

T: Yes. [Repeats these words again.]

In contrast, a discussion of the poems, when it occurred, involved conflicting interpretations of a poem's meaning, and always included questions initiated by students and/or much longer student answers to questions posed by the teacher. An example of discussion is taken from a class in which the poem "We Real Cool" by Gwendolyn Brooks was presented.

T: What is the relationship between the title "We Real Cool" and the last line, "We die soon"?

S1: I think it indicates their fighting spirit.

T: What are they doing? Making revolution? [Laughter.]

S2: No, they do empty things.

T: That's right. They are frustrated, without hope.

S2: Does the title form a contrast?

T: Do you mean they really think they're great?

S2: No, they really know they are going to die soon.

T: Yes. They don't really think they're cool at all.

S3: I'm still not sure what the author is trying to say. Does he [sic] protest the way blacks live or the society that treats blacks badly?

T: I think the author is trying to show the despair and hopelessness of life for young blacks in America.

Here, the questions are more open-ended, leading to differing interpretations of the author's intent. Students raise questions themselves and try to reconcile their impressions of black America with what the author is saying in the poem. The teacher plays a more facilitating role than in the drill and practice mode, where the teacher is the sole judge of the correctness of student answers.

Learning activities in this course consisted of four types: listening to lectures, taking notes while listening to lectures, answering the teacher's questions and asking the teacher questions. Of these four, the first was the most common activity. As for the second, less than half the students were observed to take notes during lectures. The others watched the teacher and listened or looked at their textbooks while listening. Only once did the teacher direct students to take notes, but there was no indication that students were required to do anything with their notes later. The next most common activity was answering questions posed by the teacher, either in the drill and practice or discussion modes of the course. Least common was students asking questions of the teacher. Except for procedural questions about homework and the like, students only raised questions during the rare occasions when a discussion was held.

The course was organized around related topics and presented sequentially to students. The fall semester course, spanning twenty weeks, had the following topic sequence: styles of English discourse, dialects in English, including various regional British dialects and black American English, and poetic stylistics, including rhythm, meter, sound patterns, rhyme, syntax, diction, tone, imagery, and figurative language like metaphor and simile. The shorter spring semester course concentrated solely on poetic stylistics, with no attention to discourse or dialectology. Basically, the poetic section of the course began with phonology, then syntax, lexicon and finally some attention to semantics, although the latter received little stress.

The course also displayed some aspects of continuity and integration. Continuity was evident in the fact that the teacher usually reviewed the previous class content and asked students each session to analyze poems, often using the same elements. Integration was not a regular organizing criteria, but at the end of both the fall and spring courses, the teacher asked students to combine all the stylistic elements they had learned in analyzing several poems. In this sense, the students' knowledge of various poetic elements became more unified in an overall system of analysis.

Evaluation of students was handled differently in the fall and spring semester courses. The fall course included evaluation of student writing, while the spring course did not. In the fall, students were assigned homework in which they had to write analyses of poems according to various stylistic elements. These were sometimes collected and graded by the teacher. Also, students took a final examination in this course. On the exam, they were given a previously unseen poem and asked to write an analysis of it using all the elements they had learned. In addition, as the teacher conducted drill and practice or discussions, she evaluated individual student responses, generally by saying, "good," "yes," "right," and so on after correct answers, and by saying, "No," "Is that correct?" or some similar follow-up question after incorrect answers.

The spring course, which lasted only six weeks, contained no evaluation of student writing. Though homework was assigned, it was never collected and students took no examinations. Everyone who attended the course automatically passed it. The only evaluation in the spring was the verbal kind described above.

Students were always grouped for instruction in the same way—as a whole class—but the spatial constraints of three different classrooms used for the course helped to create different grouping patterns. The fall semester course was held in the classroom described in detail at the beginning of this section. Owing to its small space, students were tightly bunched together, with pairs of students sharing contiguous desks. Though the class was always conducted with the teacher at the front and students in rows facing her, the proximity of pairs of students sometimes gave rise to informal small groupings. Students were observed talking to their partner, either about the lecture or unrelated topics, and they often shared books, notes, dictionaries, etc. Furthermore, students sat in the same seats each session, since they kept materials in their desks.

The spring course was held in two different rooms, both of them far larger than the fall semester classroom. As a result, students tended to be more spread out, and some changed seats frequently. One observed session was held in the department's auditorium, a 205 seat room with a stage at the front and a sloping incline towards the rear to afford better views of the stage. Since only 28 students attended the class, they were scattered around the front half of the auditorium and separated from the teacher by the stage. In this setting, students were very inactive, and the teacher lectured almost the whole time. Even when she asked questions, student responses were inaudible in the cavernous auditorium and discussion was out of the question.

The other four observed sessions of the spring course were held in a large classroom with 36 desks and ample room in the back for more. Like the smaller classroom, this one had a blackboard, podium and lectern at the front where the teacher stood. Desks were also arranged in three rows, but the middle row had four desks across rather than two. This spatial arrangement permitted students to sit together if they chose, and most did. A few students sat alone, or in pairs far in the back of the room, but most tended to sit toward the front or in a row of desks near the windows. The teacher made no effort to seat students in any particular fashion, and the fact that they were scattered around an oversize room resulted in some students being isolated from the learning activities going on, while others frequently whispered to students sitting next to them.

Heat and light were both inadequate in the foreign languages department building. Classroom temperatures in January ranged between 45 and 55 degrees F. By mid–March, the heat was turned off and classrooms did not warm up to over 60 degrees until April. The lack of good light is also endemic, and directly related to inadequate supplies of electricity. During one Stylistics session, electricity was lost in the building, and the classroom was literally plunged into darkness for 15 minutes. The larger classroom used in the spring session had no functioning lights during three of four sessions observed. This made it extremely difficult to read the blackboard. I found it difficult to see my notes unless I sat next to a window.

One other point worth noting about classroom space was the filthy condition of some classrooms, particularly the two used in the spring semester. The auditorium had paint peeling off the walls, large water stains around windows, and a floor littered with papers, food, dust, etc. In the large classroom, nothing hung on the bare walls and the floor was strewn with old newspapers and dirt. This room was cleaned only once in four weeks.

Such things as heat, electricity and cleanliness are luxuries in China, and their absence is an expected part of life. As an American, I found the poor physical conditions far more objectionable than Chinese teachers and students seemed to. But these conditions certainly do not make for a pleasant learning environment.

The final curricular element to be discussed is time. During both naturalistic and recorded observations, a running chronology of the session was kept. On average, the teacher talked about 95 percent of the time. Of the remaining 5 percent of student talk, most of it was dominated by a handful of students. About half the students never spoke during class. Time spent on the three major learning activities of the class reinforce the fact that teacher talk predominated. About 70 percent of class time involved teacher lectures, about 25 was devoted to drill and practice, about 3 to classroom routines, and only 2 percent to discussion.

One other important time period was the break taken in the middle of each two hour session. Though some students got up and left class during the break, most stayed. During break, the teacher also stayed in the room, and either answered students' questions or approached groups of students to talk. The teacher always switched into Chinese during break and became far more animated in conversations with students. During these times, students were overheard commenting about the course. They complained about the difficulty of poetry, they told the teacher where they were having trouble understanding her lectures or material, and even ventured to say at one point that the classroom was too large for effective discussions. During these conversations, teacher and students often laughed or held heated discussions. Once break ended, the teacher immediately remounted the podium and a solemn silence fell over the classroom. The teacher occasionally commented about what had been discussed during the break, as the example given above in the section on objectives illustrates. I concluded that the break time was important to establishing teacher-student relationships, and represented the only visible opportunity for students to express opinions about the course.

The overall class climate prevailing in the fall and spring semesters was markedly different. The fall course featured more active student participation, including student-initiated questions during discussions, and the students appeared to be following the lectures more intently. About half were observed taking notes. During drill and practice sessions, students answered most questions without hesitation, and at least half the class spoke. In the spring, student participation was markedly lower, and only about one-third of the students ever spoke on any given day. Furthermore, the teacher often had to answer her own questions when students failed to respond. Student enthusiasm and interest in the course were most dramatically revealed by attendance patterns. In the fall, all 25 students enrolled in the course attended both sessions observed. In the spring, attendance fell precipitously toward the end of the course, from a beginning enrollment of 28 to a low of 13. Moreover, only about six students in the spring actively participated and took notes during lectures. The rest either stared at their textbooks, gazed out the windows, or whispered to students sitting next to them.

When asked to comment on the class climate of the spring course, the teacher remarked:

> I'm not very happy with this class. I feel disappointed or depressed after class. They are passive, and there's a gap between us. They aren't interested and are complacent about their lack of knowledge of literature and poetry.

When asked to rate the climate of the two classes on a ten point scale, with ten being best, the teacher gave the fall course a seven, but the spring course only rated a four. Interviews with two students from the spring course also revealed dissatisfaction with the course. One student, when asked to name the thing she liked least about the course, cited the lack of discussion and lack of teacher clarity during lectures. The other student complained that the course was too short, and the classroom was too big for the small number of students. This student also admitted that she hadn't spent much time preparing for the class, and cited the lack of homework and exams as the main reason she hadn't devoted more time to it. The other student, who stated that she had reviewed the textbook before each class, nevertheless also felt that the lack of tests or grades was a disincentive to devoting more time to the course.

As for the one best thing about the course, students cited the teacher's skillful oral reading of poems and opportunities to answer questions and discuss poems. But one student noted that the latter occurred too infrequently. Both students also said they felt they could help decide some things about the course, especially regarding the way the teacher conducted it. One student reported that during break time, students told the teacher that the classroom was too big for discussions and that she should assign more homework. The other student noted that the teacher asked students for their opinions at times, and that the students raised a number of questions about the lectures that were still puzzling them. Student opinions appeared to have had some impact in two areas. First, the teacher changed classrooms after the second week, from the auditorium to the large classroom. This helped somewhat to create a better climate for discussion. Second, the teacher often commented about student questions after the break, sometimes devoting more time to areas where students were having trouble. But the teacher never did collect homework or give exams, one change that could have encouraged students to prepare better and provided them with a sense of how they were doing in the course.

Discourse Analysis

To explore the class climate and the curriculum in greater detail, especially the "hidden" curriculum, the last session of the spring course was recorded on videotape and studied in detail using discourse analysis. The first hour of the session was chosen for discourse analysis, because it was representative of other sessions I had observed. During this time, the teacher summarized the poetic elements that had been presented during the course, explained the syntax of free verse, used an example of free verse from Walt Whitman to illustrate several points, and finally presented four poems for analysis.

The statistics showed that the teacher dominated the class, doing about 95 percent of the talking and initiating all questions, directives, explanations and assertions.The students' role was limited to answering questions. Only 5 out of 16 students spoke during the hour. Moreover, one student spoke 11 times, more than the other four combined. Those students who did not participate were recorded talking with classmates seated nearby, gazing out the window, or in one case, simply putting their heads down on the desk and closing their eyes.

For this session, the results of the discourse analysis were used to identify four curricular elements: objectives, learning activities, organization and evaluation. The session had the following objectives (with time devoted to each given in parentheses):

> *Objective 1*: To review previously presented material on meter, sound patterning and imagery in poetry (15 minutes).
> *Objective 2*: To recognize elements of the syntax of free verse poetry (7 minutes).
> *Objective 3*: To analyze selected poems in terms of their syntax, diction, sound patterns, style, imagery and semantic meaning (38 minutes).

The learning activites for each of the objectives were divided into two types: lecture, and drill and practice. Regarding objective 1, the teacher lectured on the topic, and posed seven questions to the class, five of which were answered by students, and two of which the teacher answered herself after failing to draw a response from the class. As for objective 2, the teacher lectured on the topic, using a poem by Walt Whitman to illustrate certain points, and asked two questions, both of which were answered by students. For the third objective, the teacher presented four poems for analysis. Most of the analysis was done by the teacher herself, but she asked students 40 questions related to this objective and got 30 responses. She answered the other ten questions herself after failing to elicit student responses.

For each of the objectives listed above, the teacher followed a similar organizational approach, which can be divided into three parts. First, the teacher asserted something about the topic or read directly from the text. Second, the teacher explained the topic in greater detail, often using examples from the text or some written on the blackboard. Third, the teacher asked students questions about the topic or sample poems, and attempted to elicit responses.

Evaluation of students during this session was limited to verbal responses or assertions made by the teacher after student responses to questions. Typically, the teacher evaluated each student response, saying things like "good," and "yes" for correct answers, and formulating follow-up questions to incorrect or incomplete answers along the lines of "What else?" or "Why do you say so?" Additionally, the teacher frequently expanded upon student responses, either by repeating them for the whole class to hear, or by elaborating upon them with examples drawn from the poem. Aside from evaluations of individual students, the teacher made a critical evaluation of the whole class after she had posed three consecutive questions about the meaning of a word without eliciting a response. At that point, she told the class, "You don't know this word, and didn't bother to look it up."

Aside from this one critical remark, the tone of the class was serious nearly all the time. Students laughed only twice during the hour, once when the teacher gave an example of deviation of register in Chinese, and once when the teacher explained the relationship between two lovers in a poem. The style of language used was formal throughout the session. The oral channel was employed throughout, and supplemented 11 times by messages written on the blackboard. The teacher used Chinese once in the example cited above, and one student used Chinese to give a translation of a word.

Summary

The two Stylistics courses I observed were only partially successful. The content was fairly ambitious in the context of the students' other course, because this is the only course that presents information about linguistics. In both versions of the course, students sometimes seemed confused, and had difficulty answering the teacher's questions, but this was far more apparent in the spring course. This stems in part from the fact that the subject matter was so new to students, and also because they did not appear to prepare very well for the class. The lack of preparation can be traced to disinterest in poetry, the teacher's failure to insist that students do homework, especially in the spring semester, and the limited use of evaluation to inform students about their progress. A factor cited by the teacher to explain the lack of student interest in the class was that it was an elective course, and therefore not considered important in relation to other mandatory courses.

Though the teacher always apeared well prepared and often used cogent examples to illustrate major points in her lectures, she made little attempt to engage students in discussions of the more interesting aspects of the course. She did not encourage student questions, nor involve them in other ways, such as asking them to prepare oral reports on analyses of poems, or inviting them to offer interpretations which differed from her own. As a result, students spent most of their time listening to the teacher and got few opportunities to practice the skills being taught. The extent to which the fall semester course was more successful can be attributed to the fact that the teacher held more discussions, evaluated student writing, and took more time to explain important points than in the shorter six week course. Still, given the limited opportunities for active participation and the meagerness of evaluative feedback, it is impossible to say how much students learned from either of these courses. When asked about this, students of the spring semester were able to cite only a few examples of things they had learned, most of which involved identifying poetic forms rather than analyzing poetry or understanding its meanings.

SELECTED READINGS OF
AMERICAN AND BRITISH LITERATURE

An American teacher in his late thirties entered the classroom and took his place behind the lectern at the front. "Good morning," the students greeted him in unison.

He looked up from his textbook. "Well, good morning." He scanned the room with a wry smile. "You made my day." The class burst into laughter. After they had quieted down, the teacher said, "Today, let's turn to Stephen Crane's 'The Blue Hotel.' You saw the film version of this story on Tuesday and I hope you've all read the story." He paused again to survey the students. "Are there any differences between the film and the story?"

A girl in the front said, "In the film, the man was killed in the hotel. In the story, he's killed in another place."

"That's right. Why?"

"Maybe the film wants to concentrate on one place," the girl offered.

"He didn't wish to be killed in that house," another girl added.

"So, the irony is greater," the teacher responded. "The Swede says he won't leave the hotel alive, and in the film, he doesn't." He stepped down off the podium and stood in front of the first row of desks. "What about the killing? Is the Swede's murder the result of others' actions or an accident brought about by the Swede himself?"

The first girl spoke up again. "Swede was afraid of everyone. Others are aggressive and offensive."

"So you think the others are directly responsible?" the teacher asked.

"Yes. Johnny and gambler are most responsible."

"Do the rest of you agree?," the teacher asked.

"I agree in part," a girl in the back said. "The change in the film at the end is the final touch to show how helpless everyone is. The Swede offended others. Cowboy is simpleminded, wants revenge. The Easterner feels grief and sympathy, but knows the Swede was wrong. But after the death, his conscience was disturbed."

"You said a couple of interesting things. First, the Swede's death is almost inevitable. Second the Easterner has a conscience. He's bothered by the death. Right?"

"Yes," the girl said, nodding her head.

"Now, put the two together," the teacher suggested. "Here we have literary naturalism combined with elements of determinism. Remember, we talked about this last time." The teacher walked back to the lectern and began to talk at length about naturalism and determinism.

The preceding is an example of the kind of activities which went on in Selected Readings of American and British Literature, a required course for seniors that was usually taught by a foreign teacher. It was an advanced literature course covering major American and British authors of the last two centuries. I observed five consecutive sessions of this course in March and April and recorded the last one on videotape. Each of the sessions involved one group of 16 to 18 students and an American visiting professor of literature.

When I asked the teacher what he thought the objectives of the course were, he cited three:

> First, what questions to ask themselves about a work of literature. Second, some sense of basic literary history and also some acquaintance with major authors of the nineteenth and twentieth centuries. Finally, how to express their ideas orally and in written form.

Two randomly selected students from the course were asked to state the things they had learned in the course. Both of them mentioned learning about literature and about authors, and also learning how to analyze literary works. Additionally, one told me, "Before in other classes taught by Chinese, we had no habit of talking. Now, I've formed this habit, thanks to our American teacher."

Based on these comments and my own observations, I identified three important objectives of this course, listed in rank order as follows:

Objective 1: To analyze Western literature in terms of its plot, characters, theme, style, tone, imagery, language, etc.

Objective 2: To read important writers and works of literature of the
past two centuries
Objective 3: To express oral and written ideas clearly in English

Though we state the objectives differently, there is agreement in this
course about what the major objectives are. In fact, this was the only course
I observed where the teacher, students and myself were in complete agreement
about the objectives. This is true because the teacher communicated objectives
to students and conducted the course with his objectives in mind.

The materials of this course consisted of short stories and poetry written
by major English writers of the last two centuries, mostly drawn from *Norton
Anthology of English Literature.* Since the teacher had the only copy of this
textbook, student copies were typed and mimeographed from the teacher's
book and formed the "textbook" of the course. To supplement the textbook,
the teacher showed filmed versions of some of the short stories and biographies
of some of the authors, which the teacher borrowed from consular or embassy
libraries, an important source of materials in China, since books and
audiovisual materials are in chronic short supply.

The precise content of the five sessions I observed included three short
stories, six poems, and three films. These are listed below:

Lesson One: "The Jolly Corner" by Henry James, a short story and film
about a man who returns to the United States after many years abroad
in Europe.
Lesson Two: "The Blue Hotel" by Stephen Crane, a short story and film
about life in the old American west.
Lesson Three: "The Secret Sharer" by Joseph Conrad, a short novel
about life at sea.
Lesson Four: poetry by William Yeats, including "Prayer," "Byzantium,"
"September 13th" and "Easter, 1916."
Lesson Five: "Four Quartets" by T.S. Eliot, a film about his life, and
"The Path Not Taken" by Robert Frost.

Since observations were conducted in the early part of the second semester
of this course and the teacher presented literature chronologically, the content
consisted of late nineteenth and early twentieth century authors only. There
was greater stress on American writers during the weeks I observed, but the
teacher stated that he also included works by the major British and Irish
writers elsewhere in the year-long course.

The learning activities of this course were fairly numerous and diverse,
especially in comparison to other classes I observed in the department. Activities that I observed are listed below along with the objective they were
perceived to support:

Objective 1: To analyze Western literature
  1. Students orally answer questions posed by the teacher about plot, characters, themes, styles, etc.
  2. Students ask questions about elements of literature and the teacher answers them.
  3. Students discuss issues raised by the teacher.
Objective 2: To read important works of English literature
  1. Students read major works of fiction and poetry outside class.
  2. Students listen to teacher lectures about the lives of authors and the cultural context of their works.
Objective 3: To express oral and written ideas clearly
  1. Students discuss literature they have read.
  2. Students present oral summaries of literature in class.
  3. Students write a monthly paper on a work of literature.

Each of the objectives was supported by at least two learning activities, and more importantly, each of the activities was appropriate for the objective being sought. In particular, the teacher encouraged students to actively participate by talking and writing about the literature they read.

Students were more active in this course because of the teaching strategies employed to instruct them. The teacher used two strategies that were rarely seen in other courses I observed: discussion and question-answer. During discussions, the teacher posed open-ended or controversial questions about literary works and encouraged students to talk about them. This was most commonly used during sessions in which short stories were presented, as the example at the beginning of this section illustrates. During sessions on poetry, the teacher sometimes tried to initiate discussions, but students were too confused about the poems' meaning and did not generally respond well to this strategy.

A second inhibiting factor was that the class was not well-suited spatially for discussion. Though the number of students was small enough, their seating arrangements were such that students could not see or hear each other well, and most of their comments were processed back through the teacher, who had to constantly intervene to keep discussions going. A third factor inhibited discussion as well—students were clearly not used to such a strategy and sometimes resisted assuming the active role that the teacher encouraged them to take. As a result, a core group of about eight students tended to be active participants while others simply sat and listened to the proceedings.

A second strategy virtually unique to this course was question-answer. In this strategy, the teacher encouraged students to ask questions about things they did not understand and then provided answers for them. This should not be confused with drill and practice, a common strategy in other courses I observed, where the teacher asked questions and students gave short answers.

By using question-answer frequently, the teacher was able to see how well students understood the lesson. Equally important, he also provided them with an opportunity to steer the course in directions of interest to them. This strategy seemed to suit students well, because they always asked questions when the teacher invited them to do so. It was easier for students unused to speaking to formulate questions than to participate in the less-structured environment of a discussion, and as a result, more students became involved when this strategy was employed. The teacher used it in every session I observed, but seemed to resort to it particularly when discussion stalled or went flat, as was the case during the two sessions on poetry.

Two other teaching strategies were also employed: lecture and explication of text. Teacher lectures were used to present information about authors and the historical and cultural context of literature that students could not get elsewhere. During lectures, students listened and most were observed to take notes. The teacher made frequent use of the blackboard to write key words or even draw or diagram concepts he wanted students to remember. Lectures were most commonly used during poetry lessons, since students had difficulty understanding the context and meaning of the poems they read. Finally, explication of text was a strategy used sparingly by the teacher when students were having difficulty, as with poetry, or when he wanted them to clearly understand key passages of short stories. Typically, the teacher would read a passage aloud from the text, and stop to explain vocabulary, implied meaning and literary elements such as theme, style and tone. Once again, this strategy was most often used for poetry, but occurred in some other sessions as well.

It should be noted that the teacher always relied on a direct method of instruction, since he did not know Chinese. This meant that students got direct practice listening and talking in English and that they could not rely on translation to help them understand. Consequently, the course was more difficult for those students who were unaccustomed to listening and talking in English. And the teacher did not deliberately slow down or alter his choice of vocabulary (the so-called sheltered approach) to accommodate less proficient students. As a result, the course was definitely challenging to students. Several told me that they enjoyed having a native speaker for a teacher, but also found it more difficult than courses taught by Chinese instructors. Some of the less proficient students, however, appeared to find the course too difficult and were bored or frustrated by their lack of understanding.

To evaluate student learning, the teacher relied on both oral and written evaluations. During class, the teacher frequently evaluated student answers and comments for their factual accuracy. When students clearly misunderstood something, the teacher would correct them, but usually did so without criticizing them. When students expressed an opinion, however, the teacher did not generally evaluate it, preferring instead to ask other students what they thought about it. In this way, he encouraged further discussion. The teacher also appeared adept at sensing when students were having difficulty understanding a point he was trying to make. He sometimes would stop and ask a student with a puzzled expression on his face what the difficulty was. In this way, he was able to pinpoint problems that required further elucidation.

Written evaluations were conducted once a month. Students were asked to select one work they had read and write a paper about some aspect of it, either its characters, plot, theme, style, tone, imagery, etc. These essays were collected and graded by the teacher. Additionally, students took a final examination in the course consisting of several essay questions covering some of the important works and themes presented. Both the written and oral evaluations were effective means of finding out what students were learning and provided useful information to students about their progress in the course.

The course was characterized by generally effective organization. Students were grouped for instruction in two ways. When films were shown, the entire senior class met together to view them in the department auditorium. During these sessions, the teacher usually did not talk except to briefly introduce the film. Secondly, when the class met to discuss films and literature, they were in smaller groups of 15 to 20 students. They always worked as a whole group, however. No small group or individual work occurred during class sessions I observed. Of course, students worked alone outside of class, especially in preparing their papers and examinations. Also, the teacher maintained regular weekly office hours so that students could come and talk to him individually about difficulties or particular questions they had.

When this course is considered in terms of Ralph Tyler's three principles of organization—continuity, sequence and integration—it emerges as one of the best organized courses in the department. Continuity was evident in that similar activities and strategies were employed from week to week, providing students with repeated opportunities to learn the objectives. Sequence was apparent in the fact that materials and content were organized chronologically, from early nineteenth century writers like Hawthorne up to contemporary writers like Updike and Bellow. In addition, the teacher alternated between fiction and poetry, and insisted that students write at least one paper on each so that they could practice analyzing these two types of literature. The chronological approach did not, however, result in sequencing content by difficulty level. Within one literary period, students encountered authors who were easy to understand along with those who were not. For example, students found Stephen Crane and Joseph Conrad to be readily accessible, but had great difficulty with Henry James, Yeats and Eliot.

Finally, integration was an important organizational principle of this course. In fact, it was one of the few course I observed that paid attention to the horizontal integration of knowledge from many sources. The teacher often reviewed previous lessons, and more importantly, compared texts under discussion which others students had read or heard about. He also frequently pointed out the relationship between literature and the cultural and historical context in which it was created to help students gain a greater appreciation of the forces which impel writers to create. Through these efforts, students had opportunities to broaden their understanding of the role literature has played in the development of Western society. This was something unique to this teacher's course.

The allocation of time varied from week to week, but the percentage of time devoted to each of the three objectives was estimated as follows:

Objective	Percent Time (%)
Analyze literature	65
Read authors	20
Express ideas	15

These time estimates do not include student homework assignments, done outside of class, which required heavy reading and some writing.

The percentage of teacher and student talk ranged considerably depending on the content of each session. Teacher talk reached a high of 94 percent during the last poetry session on Eliot and Frost, while student talk was highest during the lesson on Conrad, occupying about 20 percent of all talk that day. The amount of student talk appeared to be a direct function of the difficulty level of the materials. When materials were accessible, student talk averaged around 15 to 20 percent, but for difficult material like poetry, student talk dropped to 6–10 percent, with the teacher doing a lot more lecturing.

The spatial elements of this course did not differ significantly from others I have described. The classroom was crowded, as all were, but had a few more desks than usual. Students sat in four rows of six desks each, lined up in pairs from the podium to the back wall, leaving two narrow aisles for students to reach their seats. Because students could not see or hear each other well, especially across the room, student talk was usually processed back through the teacher. He often repeated student comments so that others could hear them. One thing the teacher did to facilitate discussion was to come down off the podium and walk up and down the aisles. In this way, he encouraged students to talk more to each other, and became more the facilitator instead of the authority figure. This helped to some extent, but he did not really have room to maneuver much.

As for heat and light, both were more plentiful in this room than in others I visited, primarily because of a late morning time slot and south-facing windows along one wall which let a lot of natural light into the room. Classroom temperatures in March and April varied from a low of 54 F. to a high of 68.

The room had four working fluorescent lights which helped to create adequate light for reading and writing.

Discourse Analysis

To get a better sense of the implicit curriculum, the final session I observed was recorded on videotape and 76 minutes of the 105 minute session were subjected to discourse analysis. The video recording in this course was the most natural of the four I did. The teacher had never been taped before, but viewed the prospect with interest. Students also acted quite naturally during the session. The only change I noticed was that the teacher dressed better that day, choosing to wear a sport coat over a sweater, instead of his usual winter overcoat.

The topic of the session I videotaped was T.S. Eliot's "Four Quartets," probably the most difficult poem students encountered in this course. With numerous references to Christianity and European history, the poem required knowledge of these fields to be fully appreciated. Since students had little idea about Christian doctrine, the teacher spent a good deal of time lecturing on the topic, and answering student questions about it. He also used explication of text more often in this session to help students grasp Eliot's often obtuse meanings. Because the material was so difficult, there was less student talk this day than in other sessions I observed.

The results of the discourse analysis reveal the extent to which the teacher dominated the talking time in this lesson. He not only talked 94 percent of the time, but made most of the explanations and all the directives and assertions. Only 7 of 18 students spoke, and 5 received a message from the teacher directed to them. This indicates that less than half the students were actively involved in the lesson. The rest were either passive listeners, or did not pay attention at all. Several students in the back were observed to read Chinese books during part of the lesson.

Some interesting findings emerged from this analysis. Unlike other classes I observed, student talk in this session mostly consisted of questions asked of the teacher. Students asked 13 questions and the teacher made 15 responses. This was the main way students actively participated in the lesson on this day.

Differences with other courses also emerge when the tone, style and channel of the lesson are considered. The teacher used a serious tone most of the time, but made five mock statements, more than Chinese teachers did. Students laughed 15 times during the session, mostly during the teacher's lecture on Christianity. They laughed at things which were meant to be serious, but struck them as funny because they seemed so strange. For example, when the teacher tried to explain the Christian notion of the Second Coming, some students found this humorous. The teacher clearly tried to spice up his lectures with humor as well, which students appeared to appreciate. Additionally, the teacher made one critical comment to a girl seated in the front row. At one point, he paused in his lecture, came up to this girl, who had a puzzled look on her face, and exclaimed, "Is this too much for you?" The girl smiled nervously and shook her head.

The style of language was formal most of the time, but the teacher occasionally lapsed into an informal style when relating an anecdote or joke. In addition to the oral channel, which the teacher used throughout, he also wrote ten key words on the blackboard and drew a time line of Christian history during his lecture. This teacher used the blackboard more often than others I observed, which seemed to help students grasp some of the points he was making. This session was unique in one other way. It was the only one I observed that contained no Chinese, since the teacher did not speak any, and the students did not use Chinese while class was in session. Interestingly, though, during break time, students invariably reverted back to Chinese unless they were talking to the teacher.

The discourse analysis provides insight into the class climate of this course. The teacher maintained friendly relations with students and entertained them with jokes and anecdotes. About half the class actively participated and took notes as the teacher lectured. For these students, the course was meaningful and enjoyable. The other half of the class did not participate. Some appeared to be following the lesson, but others were not. One student told me he didn't like poetry, finding it too difficult to be enjoyable. For students like him, the class was probably more a source of frustration than joy.

When I asked the teacher to characterize the quality of this class, he rated it a seven on a scale of one to ten. In explaining this rating, he said:

> The feelings we have for each other are basically good. I like this class and their feelings toward me are good. They probably think I'm doing a good job. On the whole, they are doing better this semester than last. They're interested, but not necessarily enthusiastic. For many, this will have little to do with their future job. It's tangential. Regarding their feelings toward each other, I have a hard time gauging this. Males and females are separated. The guys are on the fringe, participate less and occupy the bottom academically. I sense undercurrents, but no open hostility. Some girls are cliquish. One guy has been a real loner. Other students make fun of him.

When two randomly selected students were asked to rate the course, they both cited the teacher's methodology as the best thing. One student said, "The teacher is important for students to learn lesson well. We've had several foreign teachers, and sometimes we get bored. But this teacher's class is interesting. Even students who don't like literature enjoy the class. We go deeper into the meaning of works."

The second student echoed this sentiment, saying, "I like the method used by the teacher. His lectures are clear. He guides us to discuss the writer's works in class."

Regarding the one thing they didn't like, the two students had different answers. One cited the difficulty of reading some of the materials, especially James, Yeats, and Eliot. The other student thought that some classmates asked silly questions that were not worth asking and took up valuable class time.

These responses reveal basic agreement between the teacher and students about the class climate. Both rate it positively, but also indicate some areas where improvements could be made. Though the climate was not always ideal, the participants had managed to create a climate that was conducive to learning, and occasionally characterized by real joy and satisfaction.

Both students I interviewed felt that they could help decide how to learn in this class. They indicated that the teacher chose materials and content, but left it up to students to read and interpret the meaning. One student cited the example of Melville's *Billy Budd*. "When we discussed that story, students had different opinions. The teacher let us think what we wanted. He never approved or disapproved of our ideas and seldom gave a simple answer."

The teacher stated that he thought students should have some freedom of choice in class. He noted that students were allowed to choose the topics they wrote about for their monthly paper and could raise any questions they liked in class. As for the materials and content, he stated that he chose these himself, partly because he knew what students had read in previous literature courses, and partly due to the logistical problem of choosing materials well in advance to allow time for typing and duplicating.

Summary

This course appears to have been successful for most students. They were learning the rudiments of literary analysis, were reading important works of English literature, and making progress in expressing ideas orally and in writing. Their success is directly attributable to the teaching strategies and learning activities employed in the course, which encouraged active student participation. Additionally, the course had clear objectives, which were regularly evaluated and presented with effective organization. Finally, the teacher, the only Ph.D. I observed, demonstrated a breadth of knowledge about his subject which was impressive.

The one problem which emerged was the difficulty level of some materials, which made it frustrating for less proficient students. The teacher was aware of this, and showed films whenever he could get them to help students understand the content. But he also defended his choice of materials by pointing out that this was probably the only chance these students would ever have to read the classics of English literature. If they were exposed to them now, they might return to them at some later date when their English level was sufficient to fully understand them. Given what I saw in other courses, the teacher had a point here. If students were to gain exposure to English literature, including the cultural and historical context in which it was written, they would probably only do so under a foreign teacher. None of the Chinese teachers I observed spent a significant amount of time on these topics.

And yet, I was left wondering whether the teacher's commitment to presenting a literary heritage could be justified when half the students found some of the materials too difficult to enjoy. There is a fine line between challenging students and frustrating them. By insisting that students read poets like Yeats and Eliot, who have baffled native speakers for decades, the teacher was in constant danger of crossing this line. Personally, I found I learned a great deal from the sessions I attended, and I minored in English literature. But perhaps this was the course's weakness. It was better suited to native or near-native speakers than to the Chinese students of English in this class. Still, there was a group of students whose proficiency level was high enough to benefit from the course. Since the students had fairly disparate proficiencies in English, the teacher had a tough decision to make regarding which group of students to teach to. By choosing to focus on the higher group, the teacher challenged the students to stretch themselves to the limit. Some would argue that this is what quality education is all about.

6
Learning to Teach English in Teaching Methodology Courses

Introduction

With the tremendous interest in studying English, the demand for English teachers in China has skyrocketed. To fill the need, the government is training teachers of English in growing numbers. Of the students at Teachers University who participated in this study, about 90 percent will become English teachers. Roughly two-thirds will be assigned to middle (high) schools in the surrounding area, while the other third will be given positions at the college or adult level.

Since Chinese teachers of English handle the bulk of teaching, the nature and quality of their pedagogical training is an important topic, both to Chinese educational officials and to the roughly 250 million Chinese students of English. Accordingly, this chapter describes the results of observations of a third year Teaching Methodology class that is required of all students. It is the first of two semesters of teacher training that students receive before doing six weeks of practice teaching in a nearby middle school.

THIRD YEAR: TEACHING METHODOLOGY

A young teacher in his late twenties mounted the podium and began to address a group of 11 third year students. "Today, some of you will present practice lessons from the middle school English textbook. Before you begin, let's review the principles of English language teaching that we have learned." The teacher turned around and pointed at five statements he had written on the blackboard. "First, teach with the purpose of communication. Second, teach directly in English. Third, teach all four language skills. Fourth, use visual aids and gestures to help students understand. Finally, your teaching should be student-centered, not teacher-centered. Make sure students get chances to practice."

The teacher paused briefly. "Any questions?" No one said a word. "All right, who would like to go first?" The teacher paused again, surveying the class. No one stirred. "Let's have a volunteer," the teacher reiterated. After another long pause, a boy in the back finally stood up and said, "I'll have a try."

The student came to the podium and wrote the words "window," "on," and "near" on the blackboard. Using a box and a book, he demonstrated the meanings of "on" and "near." Walking to the window, he informed students what the English word was, and pointed to its spelling on the blackboard. Then, to make sure students knew the meanings of these three words, he translated them into Chinese. Later, he read a short dialogue from the middle school textbook aloud, asking students to repeat each sentence after him. Finally, students did a substitution drill in which the word "door" was substituted for "window." Before sitting down, the student teacher reminded the class to memorize the three new words they had learned and to read the text over and over until they could recite it from memory.

These students were teaching their very first English lesson as part of their first semester of Teaching Methodology, a required course for all undergraduates taught over two semesters in the third and fourth years. I observed five sessions of this course in the spring semester over an eight week period. The course did not have three of its weekly meetings, once due to student physical labor, and twice due to teacher commitments elsewhere.

The setting, content and activities of the five sessions varied markedly, more so than any other course I observed. Two of the five sessions were devoted exclusively to watching videotapes of model lessons taught by experienced Chinese secondary teachers of English. These were held in the department auditorium and were attended by all three classes of the third year. One session, held in a smaller classroom, was devoted entirely to student minilessons of the type described above. The remaining two sessions were split into different parts: student minilessons and a teacher lecture in one session, and videotaped model lessons and a written assignment in the other.

Besides these variations, I also observed three different teachers at work in this course. The video lessons were introduced and briefly evaluated by an elderly Chinese teacher of Russian, who was in overall charge of the third year Teaching Methodology course. Since he didn't know English, he conducted his portion of the class in Chinese. The session which was entirely devoted to student minilessons was taught by another Russian professor, a woman in her fifties. Like her colleague, she used Chinese as the medium of instruction. The lecture, second minilesson, and written assignment were conducted by a young Chinese teacher of English who had just completed his M.A. in teaching methods at Teachers University. Originally, I had intended to observe the senior Russian teacher exclusively, but his section did not always meet and he was extremely reluctant to allow me to observe. So, I chose to attend the other Russian teacher's section instead. Then, she too, objected to my presence in her class, apparently finding it too embarrassing to be teaching English language teaching methods in Chinese in the presence of a native speaker of English. So, after one session in her class, she asked me to observe the young teacher of English instead, which I did during the last two sessions. Furthermore, neither of the Russian teachers completed the teacher survey I gave them (translated into Chinese), and both declined to be interviewed.

Though the frequent changes in schedule, setting and teachers presented a problem of continuity, I was rewarded with a greater breadth of understanding regarding the conduct of this course by the three teachers responsible for it. To help compensate for the incongruities in my observations, I recorded two sessions of this course on audio tape, each conducted by a different teacher, and will present the results of both of these later in this discussion.

When I asked the younger English teacher to state the goals of Teaching Methodology in rank order, he listed them as follows:

(1). To learn and apply the principles of foreign language teaching as formulated in the textbook
(2). To "learn some specific methods and ways to teach the traditional four language skills and organize lessons"
(3). To write clear teaching plans
(4). To "know some recent developments in our country and abroad in the field of applied linguistics"
(5). To "combine theory and practice"

When two randomly selected students were asked to state the important things they had learned in the course thus far, both mentioned learning "rules and principles" and "some theories" of English language teaching. One student also mentioned that "we practice teaching," but the other said, "practice is limited so far. We must remember all the rules without much practice." Neither student was able to mention anything else learned in the course.

From my observations and discussions with teachers and several students, I arrived at the following four objectives of the course, listed in rank order:

Objective 1: To recognize teaching methods and strategies employed by others while teaching English
Objective 2: To memorize principles and theories of foreign language teaching
Objective 3: To prepare teaching plans for middle school English lessons
Objective 4: To apply principles of foreign language teaching in practice lessons

Though the teacher and students stated their objectives quite generally, they basically correspond to the second and fourth ones that I identified.

Additionally, the teacher and I agreed that preparing teaching plans was an important objective of the course. But neither the teacher nor the students mentioned my most important objective. At first glance, this seems strange. How could I come up with one most important objective that neither the teacher nor students mentioned? I did so by pondering the teacher's objective: to "learn some methods...to teach...and organize lessons," and the purposes of devoting two and a half sessions to the watching of videos of model lessons. From what teachers said about this and the types of evaluation they employed after students watched the lessons, I concluded that the major purpose of these model lessons was to help students recognize "good" teaching methods as practiced by the teachers of these lessons. Also, during the student minilessons, students were instructed to observe their peers and identify the types of methods they were using. Since these two activities occupied more than 80 percent of the sessions I observed, I concluded that objective 1—to recognize teaching methods and strategies employed by others while teaching English— was the most important objective taught in this course. At the same time, I must admit that "memorizing principles and theories of foreign language teaching" was a very high priority in the course, and may well have eclipsed the first objective in sessions I did not observe.

The materials used in this course were of two types: textbooks and videotapes. The major textbook of the course was a Chinese language book entitled *Wai Yu Jiao Xue Fa* [Foreign Language Teaching Methodology], written by a committee of Chinese educational experts and published by People's Educational Publishing Company, Beijing, in 1980. The book is designated by the State Education Commission as one to be used throughout the country in colleges and universities that train foreign language teachers, and presents major principles, theories and reserarch findings in the area of foreign language teaching, with examples drawn from English, French, Japanese and Russian. Students eventually read the whole book and were sometimes given written assignments based on various topics covered. Additionally, students were assigned Volume 1 of the middle school English textbook used throughout the country. Entitled *English* (Beijing: People's Educational Publishing Company, Secondary English Language Section, 1982), this text was used primarily as a source for student minilessons and teaching plans. The text was based primarily on an audiolingual approach to English learning, but also incorporated some elements of the grammar-translation approach, particularly in the use of Chinese to translate definitions of English vocabulary.

The videotapes consisted of model lessons performed by veteran teachers in various middle schools across China. Students viewed a total of six videotapes during the sessions I observed, ranging in length from 30 to 90 minutes. Two of the tapes were prepared at Wuhan Teachers College, and the other four were prepared by various educational institutes and bureaus in Beijing. The videotaped lessons were based on a number of foreign language teaching methods, including grammar-translation, direct, audiolingual and communicative competence.

As noted, the content of the sessions I observed varied considerably. In the first session, students spent two hours watching two videotapes prepared by Wuhan Teachers College. These were shown in the department auditorium on two 25-inch color monitors and were viewed by all three sections of the third year student body. The videos were briefly introduced by the head teacher in Chinese and he also offered some comments on them at the end. Students saw two teachers demonstrate model lessons devoted to speaking and reading skills. One teacher made extensive use of grammar-translation to teach a short text about a Chinese peasant family. The second teacher made extensive use of the audiolingual approach by having students practice a series of pattern drills and read aloud a short dialogue on planting trees. This teacher also used oral translation drills, and had students sing songs. After viewing the two videos, the teacher commented on them, generally praising the methods employed, especially the use of visual aids, and pointing out the planning that had gone into the lessons. Students were asked to compare their own teaching experience in minilessons to what they had seen in the videos.

During the second session, all three classes were again brought together in the auditorium to watch videos for two hours. These featured a teacher from a keypoint middle school in Beijing. (A keypoint school is one in which the best students and teachers are concentrated.) These videos were the newest ones seen by students, having been made in 1984 by the Beijing Central Education Research Institute. The first one showed portions of an experimental course taught by a veteran teacher of English who used her own materials, rather than the national middle school textbook. Unlike the other videos, the teacher conducted the class entirely in English and made use of various strategies collectively referred to as the communicative approach. She began by teaching a dialogue about asking permission to change seats, an approach associated with the notional-functional branch of communicative teaching. Students learned phrases like "May I change seats with – –?" and acted out the dialogue in class. They also listened to a tape recording of the dialogue made by two native Americans. Later, the teacher practiced what she called "meaningful drills," which were a series of chain dialogues in which each student, in turn, had to add something to a dialogue begun by the teacher. In the second video, the same teacher taught a short dialogue between two boys who were discussing how to read a new book.

The third session I observed was held in a regular classroom, and included only the 15 students in section two of the course. This section was taught by the female Russian teacher. During this two and a half hour session, six students presented their first minilessons to the class, based on one lesson from the middle school English textbook. Students made exclusive use of grammar-translation or audiolingual approaches in teaching the lesson. The teacher offered an evaluation of the students' performances and held a discussion of the methods employed. Both of these activities were conducted in Chinese.

The fourth session was also held in a regular classroom and included 11 students in section three of the course, which was taught by the English-speaking teacher. During this three hour session, students spent two hours presenting their first minilessons from the middle school English textbook, engaged in a discussion of the student performances and listened to the teacher evaluate their performances. In the third hour, the teacher gave a lecture on teaching listening comprehension skills. This session was conducted almost entirely in English.

The last session I observed was divided into two parts. For the first two hours, students watched two more videos in the auditorium, and in the third hour, they went back to their classrooms and wrote answers to several questions posed by their teachers. The videos in this session were older than the others, having been made in 1979 and 1980 in Beijing by the Municipal Education Bureau. Both were based on an outdated version of the national middle school English textbook, which was thoroughly revised in 1982.

In the first video, an older female teacher presented a story about two middle school students who visit an art exhibition. The students, who were equivalent to American seventh graders, listened to the teacher tell the story with the aid of drawings shown on an overhead projector. Students then repeated the story line by line and answered factual detail questions about it. Later in the lesson, students orally translated sentences from English into Chinese. The teacher made extensive use of Chinese to explain grammatical points in a detailed explication of the text. The second video featured a young woman teaching another group of junior high school students. In this lesson, the teacher demonstrated possessive adjectives and verb tenses in English by using hats as props. Students also recited a dialogue in unison and acted out the dialogue. After these videos, the head teacher talked about how both teachers taught verbs in English and asked students to think about methods they might use in teaching English verbs, typically a difficult point for Chinese students due to major differences between English and Chinese in expressing tense.

In the third hour of this session, students split up into sections and wrote an evaluation of the videos they had just seen. The English teacher, who I observed that day, gave students four questions and asked them to write a composition in English answering these. These were handed in at the end of the hour and graded.

Reflecting the wide variety of content in this course, learning activities were also diverse. The activities students were observed engaging in are listed below according to the objective they were perceived to support:

> *Objective 1:* To recognize teaching methods and strategies employed by others while teaching English

1. Watch videos and discuss later in class
2. Watch videos and write answers to questions about them
3. Watch fellow students teach minilessons and discuss them

Objective 2: To memorize principles and theories of foreign language teaching

1. Read the textbook and write summaries of principles and theories enunciated therein
2. Listen to lectures on applied linguistics and take notes
3. Write a paper on an assigned topic relating to principles and theories of English language teaching

Objective 3: To prepare teaching plans for middle school English lessons

1. Write up teaching plans for lessons assigned from the middle school textbook
2. Prepare a minilesson for presentation in class

Objective 4: To apply principles of foreign language teaching in practice lessons

1. Teach a minilesson from the middle school textbook

Of the four objectives for this course, the first two were supported by the largest number of learning activities, but the time devoted to some activities was limited. All of the activities were appropriate for the objectives sought and their diversity provided numerous opportunities for students to master the objective in question. But the limited time allocated to some activities made it doubtful whether students were making significant progress on objectives 1 and 4.

The teaching strategies employed to conduct this course were of four types: demonstration, performance, lecture and discussion. Demonstration was exemplified by the video lessons, which were intended to demonstrate various teaching methods used in middle school English classes. Performance was in evidence when students were asked to get up and teach a minilesson to the class. Here, the strategy was to give students actual practice in conducting an English lesson. Lectures were used extensively by all three teachers to present principles and theories of foreign language teaching and applied linguistics. The two Russian teachers lectured in Chinese, while the one English teacher lectured directly in English. Finally, discussions were occasionally held in which teachers invited student opinions and comments on the methods used in videos or the performance of their peers during the minilessons.

The use of demonstration, performance and discussion as major teaching strategies made this course unique. No other course I observed used videos for demonstration or incorporated student performances, and only one other course taught by an American made extensive use of discussion. Thus, teaching strategies were one of the strongest curricular elements of this course.

To evaluate the extent to which students were mastering the objectives, teachers made use of both oral and written evaluation. Oral evaluation was used to rate the performance of teachers in the video lessons and student minilessons. After student minilessons, for example, the English teacher told the class that they should not use unknown words or complicated structures in teaching beginners, that they should avoid using translation and that they should ask students questions to determine whether they understood the lesson.

The Russian teacher, in her evaluation of student minilessons, also stressed using English as the medium of instruction, but said she thought some translation of vocabulary and grammatical terms was all right. She also stressed the need for students to practice and said students should talk about 70 to 80 percent of the time. Finally, she urged students to think about the purposes and objectives they were seeking in their lessons and to organize and present them accordingly.

Written evaluation was extensively employed in this course. Students were asked to write teaching plans, summaries of chapters in the textbook, evaluations of videos and one major paper which served as the final exam for the course. The students in two sections did all their writing in Chinese, however, since their teachers did not know English. All writing assignments were collected and graded. In addition, the teachers also counted class attendance and participation as elements in the students' final grades.

Both kinds of evaluation gave students useful feedback in judging their progress in the course. But weaknesses in evaluation were also present. The oral evaluations of videos and minilessons were fairly general and did not usually refer to specific individuals. Thus, students did not get as much knowledge of their own progress in applying teaching principles in their practice lessons as they might have. The written evaluation in two sections suffered from the fact that it was conducted entirely in Chinese. Not only did students get no practice writing in English, but they tended to focus much more on translation than did students in the one section who wrote in English. During minilessons in the second and third sessions, I noticed that students taught by a Chinese-speaking teacher were far more likely to use Chinese in their English lessons than those taught by the English-speaking teacher.

The organization of this course exhibited all three of Ralph Tyler's principles for curricular organization — continuity, sequence and integration. Yet, organization was marred by the fact that the class did not meet for three weeks, and that frequent schedule and agenda changes took place. These were reflected in the discontinuity of my observations. On several occasions, I was told that the course would meet at a specified time, only to learn later that the schedule had been changed at the last moment. Once, I was told that students would present minilessons in the next session, but when I arrived, the teacher announced a change in agenda. This created confusion for me as a participant-observer, and probably had the same effect on students in the course. Beyond this, the cancellations and schedule changes revealed a lack of seriousness on the part of those responsible for the course.

Having said that, I should hasten to add that the sessions I observed did incorporate elements of curricular organization, especially sequence, which was the strongest of the three curricular organizational principles in this course. The teachers hoped to move students through four distinct phases of teacher preparation, organized in a hierarchy of increasing difficulty. These are listed below in the order they were presented:

(1). Students read about principles and theories of foreign language teaching and listen to lectures on these subjects

(2). Students view video tapes of model middle school lessons

(3). Students perform minilessons in class

(4). Students engage in practice teaching for six weeks in a nearby middle school (in the first semester of the fourth year)

This sequence was apparently designed to familiarize students with principles and theories first, and then gradually encourage them to apply these in increasingly real-life situations. The only problem in this sequence was that students were not always clear about the relationships among the various activities they were engaging in. Most notably, they watched videos in three of the five sessions I observed, and performed minilessons in two of the five sessions. The relationship between these two activities, however, which constituted the bulk of the sessions I attended, was never made explicit. Were students expected to emulate the teaching methods they saw in the videos? If so, which methods? And which of these methods was most likely to bring about desired outcomes? I saw little evidence that teachers devoted time to these questions. In lieu of this, students appeared to base their methodology strictly on that implied in the middle school textbook, a combination of the grammar-translation and audiolingual approaches. They were never encouraged to experiment with other methods or materials in their minilessons. In short, the course lacked sufficient integration.

The only evidence of integration I observed was the variety of activities devoted to objectives one and two. For objective 1—to recognize teaching methods and strategies employed by others while teaching English—students engaged in three kinds of activities, including watching videos and watching their peers teach minilessons. But the behavior implied in this objective, recognizing, was not accorded sufficient attention. In particular, discussion, an effective means of recognizing teaching methods, was limited to a small percentage of class time. Most of the time students spent watching videos, they had no clear instructions as to what they should look for or why they were engaging in this activity. Objective 2—to memorize principles and theories of foreign language teaching — exhibited the most integration of all the objectives. Students read their textbook and wrote summaries of it, listened to lectures and took notes, and wrote a term paper on some aspect of foreign language teaching. Through these three activities, students had a variety of ways to master this objective and gain a better overall understanding of the complexity of the theories involved.

The other two objectives, however, did not appear to benefit from integration. Students prepared one lesson which was taught in their minilesson, but the relationship between planning and performance received little stress in the sessions I observed. Finally, the fourth objective — to apply principles of foreign language teaching in practice lessons — was supported by only one opportunity to teach a minilesson, and this lesson was the same for all students. Since the lesson had to be based on the middle school textbook, students were limited in the number and range of teaching principles they could bring to bear in their minilessons. In particular, principles based on communicative competence were difficult to apply to a lesson based on grammar-translation and audiolingual approaches to English language learning.

Grouping patterns in Teaching Methodology were of two types. For videos, students of the third year met in one large group in the auditorium. This larger setting was chosen so that everyone could view the videos at once, eliminating the need to show the videos three separate times. In contrast, minilessons, lectures, discussions and evaluations were conducted in smaller groups of 11 to 15 students, each conducted by a different teacher. During these times, students usually worked as a whole group, but some individual work also occurred, especially during written evaluations. Students were never observed to work in pairs or other small groupings.

The grouping patterns employed in this course tended to reinforce the traditional Chinese notion that the teacher is the center of authority and wisdom in the classroom. Except when they were performing, students were generally passive listeners or viewers in activities arranged and directed by their teachers. It is not surprising, then, that when students were asked to perform minilessons, they tended to rely on the same teacher-centered approaches that they saw their own teachers use. Though two of the teachers espoused the principle that English lessons should be student-centered, they never indicated how students could accomplish this, and did not apply the principle themselves in their own teaching.

The spatial elements of this course tended to reinforce a teacher-centered approach. The department auditorium where the videos were shown is a large, 205 seat hall with a stage at the front where the two television monitors were placed. During these sessions, students tended to sit towards the front, but were sufficiently scattered to make discussion virtually impossible. The teacher stood at the front when introducing and commenting on the videos, and did not encourage students to talk. While the videos were showing, however, students frequently talked among themselves, and they often laughed at what they saw. Many students were observed to sneak out early and attendance at the videos dropped from a high of 60 at the first session to a low of 36 by the fifth session. Falling attendance at the video sessions prompted one teacher to remind students that attendance was compulsory and that they should ask for permission to be absent from these sessions.

The other sessions I observed took place in two regular classrooms. Both were medium sized, with 18 desks arranged in pairs to form three rows, and a podium and lectern at the front for the teacher. The classroom used by the Russian teacher featured a world map, a map of China and a small calendar on the walls. This room also had a bookcase full of newspapers, a hot water table and an old reel-to-reel tape recorder. The room was well-lit by natural light coming in through two south-facing windows and supplemented by four fluorescent lights hung from the ceiling. The temperature on the day I attended in late April was a pleasant 70 degrees F. The second classroom I visited was about the same size as the other, but better decorated. On one wall, students had made a bulletin board with the title (in Chinese) "Our Rich Daily Life," featuring pictures and newspaper articles in English and Chinese from the local press. The back wall was decorated with a world map and five small calendars, and a third wall featured three awards, one for winning a speech contest, one for a sports meet and the third for mastering communist doctrine ("The Party in Our Hearts" award). Above the blackboard at the front, the following slogan was spelled out in red letters: NOTHING VENTURE NOTHING HAVE, apparently an attempt at the English idiom: Nothing ventured, nothing gained. Though the temperature in this room was a comfortable 72 degrees on the two days I observed in late April and early May, the room suffered from poor light, owing to its north-facing windows and the fact that only two of three fluorescent lights worked.

The allocation and use of time in this course varied considerably from week to week. As previously noted, the course did not meet for three of the eight weeks I observed, which meant 15 percent of the total time available for this course had already been lost by the end of the second month. Of the 12.5 hours I observed, time was allocated by activity as follows:

Activity	Time
watching videos	6 hours
mini-lessons	4.5 hours
lectures	1 hour
evaluation	1 hour

From this, it can be seen that videos occupied the majority of time, with minilessons a close second. Of the time devoted to minilessons, however, most of it involved watching someone else perform. Each student had only 15 to 25 minutes to perform their own lesson.

Regarding the distribution of talking time, students did virtually no talking except when they were performing their minilessons. I estimate that student talk occupied only about 2 percent of the total time during videos, lectures and evaluations. In the two sessions in which minilessons were performed and discussions were held, however, student talk occupied about 70 percent of the time, the highest figure for student talk of any of the courses I observed.

Discourse Analyses

To explore the operational curriculum and class climate in more detail, the results of two discourse analyses will be presented and discussed. The first discourse analysis to be presented consisted of a 46 minute lecture on listening comprehension skills delivered by the English-speaking teacher to his section. A total of 13 students attended. The setting was the second classroom described on page 153. This lecture was part of an on-going series that the teacher had prepared to supplement the class textbook. He explained that he felt the Chinese text did not present sufficient information on research findings in applied linguistics from abroad, especially those published in the past decade in the United States and Great Britain. The lecture I taped was a continuation of one begun two weeks earlier, in which the teacher had described some of the elements involved in comprehending aural messages, including decoding, selection, prediction and storage in memory. He continued to talk about selection and prediction and then turned his attention to listening materials and activities in the EFL and ESL classroom, drawing the distinction between artificial and authentic listening materials, propounding criteria for preparing and selecting listening materials and illustrating this with examples of listening activities students might wish to incorporate in their teaching.

This lecture was clearly dominated by the teacher. In fact, I estimate that the teacher talked 99 percent of the time. Only one student spoke in answer to a question from the teacher, and several students asked one question in unison, when the teacher made a mistake in writing one of his points on the board. Otherwise, students simply listened and took notes on what they heard and what the teacher wrote on the blackboard. To supplement his lecture, the teacher wrote a total of 23 messages on the blackboard, and numbered these to help students see the order in which points were being developed. He used a formal style of English in delivering his lecture, sometimes reading directly from his notes. His tone was serious throughout. Students only laughed once, when the teacher made a mistake in numbering the points he was writing on the blackboard.

This lecture appeared aimed at one objective: to memorize principles and theories of teaching listening comprehension. The teacher offered three learning activities in support of this objective, but the first one occupied 99 percent of the time:

(1). Listen to the lecture and take notes (most students did this)
(2). Answer the teacher's questions (one student answered one question, two other teacher questions were answered by the teacher himself)
(3). Ask the teacher questions (the teacher offered this opportunity, but students did not make use of it)

Clearly, of the three activities, the first was the most passive, and yet the most utilized. If one believes that people learn by doing, then students learned little from this lecture. By taking notes, though, students at least had an opportunity to write down some of the key points of the lecture, which undoubtedly would help them in memorizing the principles and theories presented.

As a pure lecture, this session was organized around the content the teacher presented. Typcially, he asserted something about a topic like selection, by defining it and stating its role and importance in listening comprehension. He then explained the topic further through examples drawn from research or listening materials. He continued in this way through the topics of the lecture, alternating between assertions and explanations of each topic.

It was difficult to see what students were supposed to do with the information they received in the lecture. While some very good ideas were presented, students were not given many clues about how to apply these ideas to their own teaching. For example, at one point the teacher criticized the middle school textbook for the artificiality of the language used in dialogues and recommended that students use authentic listening materials instead. This is excellent advice, but it was contradicted by the minilessons, in which students were instructed to teach the lesson as presented in the middle school textbook, artificial language and all. In other words, the teacher was presenting information to students that they never applied in practice and that they could never apply, given the fact that all middle school teachers must use the same flawed textbook.

Aside from this major weakness, the lecture also suffered in that the teacher did not evaluate students to see if they had, in fact, memorized the principles he presented. He asked only three questions, and answered two of them himself without stopping to give students a chance to answer. He did evaluate the one student response by saying, "That's a good guess, but not right here." Otherwise, though, students received no evaluation. Furthermore, since students did not take examinations in this course, it was unlikely whether they would ever be evaluated on their memorization of the content of this lecture. If they were assigned a topic for their term paper on listening comprehension, they might be able to demonstrate their understanding of this lecture; if not, they never would be asked to. It is no wonder that one student, in commenting about lectures in this course, said, "We must remember rules we can't use."

The second session I recorded on audio tape consisted of the presentation of student minilessons, a discussion about them and the teacher's evaluation of the performances. In this case, the teacher was the Russian expert, and she conducted her portion of the class in Chinese. Fifteen students, eight females and seven males, and two observers in addition to myself were present. The setting was the classroom I described on page 153 above. I chose 80 minutes of the 140 minute class session for detailed analysis. The 80 minutes consisted of the teacher's opening lecture, the first two student minilessons, the last student minilesson, the discussion and the teacher's closing lecture in which she evaluated the performances. I eliminated from the discourse analysis three of the student minilessons, since these were basically repetitions of the three I did include.

The most noteworthy thing about the results of this discourse analysis is the fact that students were more active in this session than in any of the others I recorded at Teachers University. This was due to the fact that student performances were the main activity of the day. Consequently, student talk occupied 67 percent of the discourse, nearly triple the average for other courses I observed. Moreover, the total proportion of student talk for the entire 140 minute class was nearly 80 percent. Despite the large amount of time occupied by student talk, the distribution of time among students was skewed in favor of those who presented minilessons. For the discourse analysis, the three students who presented lessons did 43 percent of the talking in the 80 minute session. Another 18 percent of the student talk consisted of chorus repetitions of words and phrases which were taught during the minilessons. Besides these responses, the other students only talked 6 percent of the time, usually in response to questions during the minilessons. Also, only five minutes was devoted to discussion, but students did most of the talking during this time. In sum, while students did a great deal of talking in this session, the quality of their talk, except when acting as a teacher, was low, generally consisting of chorus repetitions and short answers to questions. Furthermore, 51 percent of the talk of this class was in Chinese, including the teacher's comments, the discussion and a large portion of the third student's English lesson.

There were two sets of objectives in this session, those related to teaching methodology, and those taught in the minilessons. The objectives are presented below:

> *Teaching Methods:*
> (1). To apply principles of foreign language teaching in practice lessons
> (2). To offer opinions and criticisms of the methods used in students' practice lessons

Minilessons:
  (1). To memorize new words, phrases and sentences (S1, S2, S4)
  (2). To translate between Chinese and English (S4)

The learning activities presented in support of the objectives are given below:

Objective 1: To apply principles of foreign language teaching in practice lessons
  1. Six students were asked to present a minilesson based on lesson 15 of the middle school English textbook, volume one
  2. All students were asked to prepare such a minilesson
Objective 2: To offer opinions and criticisms of the methods used in students' practice lessons
  1. Students discussed minilessons for five minutes, offering opinions about methods used and making one criticism of the grammar-translation method used by two of the six students
  2. The teacher evaluated the minilessons, giving criticisms and suggestions for 14 minutes
Objective 3: To memorize new words, phrases and sentences
  1. Student-teachers asked the class to repeat words and phrases up to 20 times each (especially student 1)
  2. One student-teacher (S2) had students do substitution drills
  3. Two student-teachers (S2, S4) had the class spell new words from memory
  4. All student-teachers had the class read aloud
Objective 4: To translate between Chinese and English
  1. One student-teacher (S4) had the class translate the text of the lesson from English to Chinese
  2. S4 also had students translate words and phrases from English into Chinese

Of the two objectives aimed at teaching methodology, the first was best supported by appropriate learning activities. Though only six of the students actually got to practice in this session, the other nine eventually got to practice this objective in later sessions. The second objective was weakened by two factors. First, a limited amount of time was devoted to the activities, especially discussion. Second, the teacher raised far more of the opinions and criticisms than students did, which directly contradicts the objective, since students are the ones who are supposed to be practicing the behavior.

The two objectives of the minilessons were supported by numerous activities, but one could question the appropriateness of some of them. In particular, the strategy adopted by the first student to have the class repeat words and phrases up to 20 times each had already demonstrated its limitations by the time he completed his 16 minute lesson. At first, the students willingly obliged their classmate and repeated everything he said with great gusto and humor. But after about 10 minutes of parroting such phrases as "The book is on the desk," even the tolerance of this amiable group had been stretched to the point of exhaustion. By the end, only a few students continued to repeat after the teacher. As a teaching strategy, mindless repetition is definitely not a winner. But the teacher never pointed this out in her evaluation of the student performances. In fact, she praised this student for using English exclusively to teach the lesson. While it is true that he was the only student to avoid using any Chinese, and he managed to get students to talk about 45 percent of the time, he accomplished this through one of the dullest teaching strategies imaginable.

As for the other activities employed by student-teachers, these were more appropriate, given the objectives being sought. The only question is: were these the right objectives? Are memorization and translation the two most important behaviors in learning basic English skills? While memorization of vocabulary and grammatical forms is indispensable, it is insufficient to ensure mastery of the language. And translation at the beginning levels of language study only presents one more barrier between the student and the target language.

Of course, these student-teachers, who were conducting their first English lesson ever, cannot be judged too harshly for the inadequacies of their objectives and methods. After all, they were simply following the lesson they were told to teach, which made extensive use of memorization and translation to present the content of the lesson, whose primary objectives appeared to be memorization of the two prepositions "near" and "on." Thus, the problem was less with the students' methods, which at least had the virtue of getting the class to practice, than with the material and content students were asked to teach, which relied exclusively on grammar-translation and audiolingual approaches. Inexcusably, the teacher, in her evaluation, did not point out the limitations of the middle school textbook, nor the methods on which it was based, leaving students with no alternative but to search for better methods to teach poor content.

The organization of the session was divided into three main parts: an opening lecture by the teacher in which she reminded the class of the purposes of the minilessons, the six student minilessons, and a closing part in which students discussed the lessons and the teacher evaluated them. Continuity, sequence and integration were all evident in this session.

Continuity was present in that each student was asked to teach the same lesson from the textbook. This enabled students to see six different classmates teaching the same basic lesson and to compare the methods they used to teach it. Sequence was evident in the role that performance played in the overall course design. After reading the textbook, listening to lectures, watching videos of model lessons, and preparing one lesson plan, students were asked to take the next step and actually practice teaching in front of the class. This is clearly a more difficult task than watching someone else teach, and it comes closer to the actual teaching situations for which students were being trained.

Finally, integration, while weaker than other elements, was apparent in the teacher's evaluation at the end of the class. During this time, the teacher reminded students of some of the principles they had learned and stressed the need to apply them in beginning middle school English lessons. In this sense, the teacher was trying to help students see the overall purposes of the class and to get a more unified view of how the various elements of theory and practice fit together. Among the points raised by the teacher were the following:

(1). Teach with the purpose of communication
(2). Stress speaking and listening skills in beginning lessons
(3). Use visual aids, gestures, etc. to help students understand the content
(4). Avoid translation if possible, but it's all right to use it for new vocabulary
(5). Allow students to talk more in class, at least 70 percent of the time (but the teacher did not say how this could be accomplished)
(6). Be well-prepared and make detailed teaching plans of everything you plan to do and say during class

Aside from these general comments, the teacher also briefly evaluated most of the students after they finished their minilessons. Basically, she commented favorably on the performances of two students, but raised some criticisms of the other four students. She told one student her lesson had been too long (25 minutes) and that she should define all new words she used. She told another student that he had forgotten to teach the text of the lesson, and criticized two other students for using too much Chinese to explain grammar and do translation exercises.

During the discussion, a rather heated exchange took place between two boys, who argued about the merits of translation as a teaching strategy. One student criticized the grammar-translation approach used by another, and the second student proceeded to defend its use, claiming it made learning easier by helping students to immediately understand the meanings of new vocabulary and their parts of speech. Other students joined in this debate, some arguing that translation prevented students from learning English while others thought it facilitated the language learning process. Though this debate was brief, it was the liveliest discussion I saw in more than 70 hours of classroom observation, and certainly focused on one of the major controversies surrounding foreign language teaching in China.

Whenever I talked with Chinese teachers of English, one of the first things they asked me was whether I though translation was a good or bad thing. The teacher's answer to this question was to take a position somewhere in the middle. While supporting the idea that English should be used as the medium of instruction, she allowed that some translation of terms was also acceptable.

Besides the evaluation discussed above, two of the three student teachers made substantial use of oral evaluation in their minilessons. Both tended to evaluate the answers they received to questions about the text, either by saying "Right" for correct answers or by asking the class "Correct?" after wrong answers. The third student did almost no evaluation of student answers.

To explore the class climate of this course in greater detail, it is useful to consider the tone and style of the two discourses presented above. The lecture delivered in English was characterized by a serious tone and a formal style throughout. Laughter occurred only once. By contrast, the minilessons were characterized by much laughter, which was mostly prompted by nervousness rather than humorous comments. Altogether, I counted 13 loud laughs in 80 minutes and numerous other chuckles. Clearly, students enjoyed watching their peers perform, though they were not anxious to actually get up and perform themselves. Another difference between the two sessions was the style of the discourse. When speaking in Chinese, both the teacher and the students made use of informal speaking styles, especially during the discussion and other spontaneous exchanges. In contrast, all English utterances were in a formal style, as was the English lecture delivered in the other class. I observed virtually no use of an informal style of English in any course taught by a Chinese teacher. It appeared that they were not familiar with or refused to use an informal style in class. As far as I could tell, students did not use informal English because they had never been taught such language.

Overall, the class climate prevailing during the minilessons was very positive, with much laughter and participation by students, and an amiable relationship between the teachers and their students in both sections I observed. The climate of other sections I observed was markedly different, though. The video sessions, as I indicated, prompted student laughter, and they occasionally made fun of the teachers, students and activities they saw. But students were also observed to whisper throughout the videos, and even did a lot of side talking while the Russian teacher spoke about the videos. Further, as indicated, the attendance dropped from 60 at the first video session to 36 at the last one. A number of students volunteered to me that they thought the videos were a waste of time and that the methods used were out of date. Thus, the climate in the video sessions was generally characterized by student boredom, which they relieved by skipping class, talking with their friends or making jokes about what they were seeing. I couldn't help laughing myself at one point when a teacher in the first video session tried teaching students the four "tones" of English. While Mandarin certainly has four tones, English most decidedly does not, although no one had convinced the teacher in the video of that fact.

When I asked the English-speaking teacher to rate the class climate of his section, he gave it an eight on a scale of one to ten, with ten being best. He explained:

> The atmosphere is pretty good so far. What I've been teaching is a new subject, so they are interested. . . . When I lecture, most are interested, ask questions after class, and request more reading materials on the subjects, which I try to find for them. Students are learning in my class, so I feel glad about this. Generally, I'm satisfied with their work and cooperation, but we do have some problems in class. For some, I am to blame. It's my first time teaching. Some activities are not well-organized. But some problems are due to student motivation. Some students don't want to be English teachers, so sometimes they aren't eager to attend videos or are not fully prepared in class. I need to adjust my teaching to make it more interesting and make students more eager to learn.

When two students of this section were asked to name the one best and worst thing about Teaching Methodology, one of them was unable to name one best thing, despite prodding from me. The other cited the minilessons as the one best thing, saying, "that was useful." Both students readily named things they disliked about the class. One said, "I hate the teacher listing rules and making us remember. The teacher should be an actor, and make students feel class is interesting."

The second student echoed these sentiments, saying, "Some points should be improved. Then I would like the class. The teacher just stands on the platform and writes on the blackboard, giving us rules we can't use. If we only take notes and memorize, we will be bored."

Clearly, the teacher and students have very different views of the climate of this course. The teacher tends to rate the climate favorably, the students, unfavorably. The teacher felt students were learning, but the students said they were only learning "empty" things. The teacher thought his lectures were the most important aspect, but students felt the minilessons were far more useful. The mismatch in their views goes a long way toward explaining student disenchantment with Teaching Methodology. The other major reason was expressed by one student who told me during a video session, "students are not interested in class because they don't want to be teachers."

Student discontent with Teaching Methodology was clearly evident in their responses in the student survey. Of all the subjects they study, Teaching Methodology received one of the lowest ratings for enjoyment and importance. For example, only 10 percent of the students said they liked Teaching Methodology very much, the lowest rating for any course. Further, only 12 percent said it was "very important" to them, also the lowest rating for any course.

A fourth year class who completed their class-specific surveys about Teaching Methodology rated the course as "boring." Further, they rated teacher concern for students, class organization, and knowledge of results as lower, on average, than students of other courses. Unquestionably, Teaching Methodology is not a popular course, both because of the way it is conducted and also because students are generally uninterested in becoming middle school teachers.

Another contributing factor to student dissatisfaction is the limited role they play in making decisions about the course. I saw no evidence of student decision making in the sessions I observed. When I asked the two students about this, they disagreed. One said that students could sometimes help decide things by making suggestions to the teacher, but went on to say, "I haven't made any before." The other student said students had no say in what they were taught or how they were taught. When asked how it felt having no say, the student replied, "It's very difficult in China. Even teachers can't decide. The authorities make all decisions."

When I asked the teacher about decision making, he verified that some decisions were outside his power to make, but others were made by him alone or in conjunction with the other two teachers of the course. Among decisions that were made by others was the choice of textbooks. The teacher said the Chinese textbook was designated by the State Education Commission as one which had to be used in teaching methodology courses for foreign languages, and was used by colleges all over the country. He defended this by saying the book had been "generalized from many years of experience and was suited to the unique situation of China," but he also complained that the book contained much information that was out of date. Besides materials, the State Education Commission also specified minimum requirements for the course, including the requirement that students complete two semesters of the course and engage in practice teaching before they could become middle school teachers. There was no syllabus or list of objectives for the course, but a general course description in Chinese was provided by the Commission.

The teacher also indicated that department administrators decided who would teach the course, and how many hours per week should be devoted to it. Also, he said that it was up to the administration to act on student suggestions and proposals to change the course. The teaching group decided collectively which activities to offer, what objectives and content to emphasize and what methods of evaluation should be used. Other matters related to teaching strategies, grouping, organization and use of time and space were left to the individual teacher to decide.

The teacher indicated he thought students should help decide some of these things, but in explaining his answer, he only mentioned activities as one curricular area where students should help decide. He noted:

> Students have their own interests. We would consider what students are

most interested in. If they want to see videos, we'll let them see more videos. If they want discussions, we'll give more of them.

When pressed to give a concrete example of something students had helped to decide, however, the teacher was unable to mention anything except that students had requested more reading materials on applied linguistics and he had provided these.

From the evidence above, I conclude that student decision making played virtually no role in the conduct of this course. Theoretically, students and teachers agreed students could raise suggestions about materials, activities, and strategies, but in practice, this rarely happened. Instead, students simply got what they got, like it or not. It is hard to judge the extent to which this contributed to student dissatisfaction. The two I interviewed were pretty much inured to the notion that they had little right to decide what they learned or how they were taught. Though they both expressed displeasure with the current state of affairs, the students held out little hope for dramatic change. But one of them urged me to make my suggestions and criticisms known to the administration, saying, "They'll listen to you, but they won't listen to us."

Summary

Of the four objectives identified in the beginning of this section, students appeared to be having the greatest success with objective 2: to memorize principles and theories of foreign language teaching. Both students I interviewed mentioned learning this, and the teacher also felt students were learning this. The amount of time spent on it, the variety of activities and the evaluation methods used to judge student progress on this objective all contributed to student learning. By the end of the second month of the course, students could readily tick off four or five principles they had learned.

Secondly, students were making progress in preparing teaching plans, objective 3. They prepared three of them during the time I observed and the teacher told them they had made significant progress over their first efforts. Considering the stress teachers gave to planning, and the number of opportunities to practice this skill, students could be expected to write detailed lessons plans by the end of the semester. In their minilessons, most students were well-prepared. But what exactly were students learning about preparing lesson plans? So far as I could tell, they were learning to write down detailed notes of all the activities they would ask students to do, and that's about the extent of it.

While clearly specified learning activities are certainly crucial to good teaching, so are objectives, organization and evaluation. These appeared to get next to no attention, at least during sessions I observed. Thus, though students were learning to write detailed learning activities, they were not learning to specify their objectives, or to carefully organize their activities to build up students' knowledge, or to evaluate students frequently, using various methods, so as to determine student progress. Without attention to these fundamental elements of the teaching process, let alone such subtleties as motivation, students could hardly be said to be fully prepared to write effective teaching plans.

On the other two objectives, it appeared students were faring even worse. Both suffered largely because the teachers never specified exactly what it was they wanted students to learn. Objective 1 – to recognize teaching methods employed by others – was particularly weak in this regard. Though students watched six hours of videos, and over four hours of their peers' teaching, it was never clear what they were supposed to learn from these. The teachers seemed to believe that students could sit and watch videos and somehow willy-nilly absorb the methods being demonstrated. In fact, the occasional discussions and written evaluations of teaching methods were far more effective strategies to get students to recognize the methods being used and see the advantages and disadvantages of each. But precious little time was devoted to such activities. The teachers might well have cut down on the number of hours devoted to watching videos and increased the time devoted to discussing them. In this way, students would have had a better opportunity to master the objective. Instead, students came to believe that the videos were a waste of time or at best, an amusing diversion. As a result, they lost their effectiveness as a teaching device.

The last objective – to apply principles and theories of foreign language teaching in practice lessons – was arguably the most important one being sought, because of its direct relevance to the ultimate purposes of teacher training. But it, too, suffered from a lack of focus and limited time for each student to perform. While teachers specified the principles students should apply, they did not generally indicate how students could apply these principles in effective ways.

After watching a total of 12 students perform minilessons in two sections, I was struck by the extent to which students did *not* apply the principles specified by their teachers. They did not teach English with the purpose of getting students to communicate, they did not always teach directly in English, they did not avoid translation, and they did not take a student-centered approach. Instead, they used grammar-translation or audiolingual approaches which focused attention on translation and memorization. This was largely due to the orientation of the materials they were assigned to teach, but nothing was done to change this.

Moreover, the teachers, in their evaluations, did not do enough to help students see the limitations of the methods they were using or demonstrate how they could employ other strategies with better effects. Without this kind of guidance, students were already beginning to form some very bad teaching habits which they might well carry with them through a lifetime of teaching. In short, students' ability to combine theory and practice, so valued in socialist China, was the most glaring weakness of this course.

7
Toward the Reform
of English Language Programs
in China: Future Prospects

During the Chinese lunar new year celebrations in 1985, an extraordinary event took place at the Great Hall of the People in Beijing. More than 25,000 teachers, the largest such gathering since 1949, were assembled to demonstrate China's determination to raise the social status of teachers. Participants heard Bo Yibo, Vice Chairman of the Communist Party Central Advisory Committee, make the following statement[109]:

> If we hope to promote our production and make our people more prosperous in the next 10 or 20 years, or even in the next century, we must launch two battles: one to improve technology and the other to revitalize education. Unless we fight and win these two battles, all our efforts to revitalize our economy will turn out a failure.

Problems Facing Chinese Education

Nearly four decades after the founding of the People's Republic, the Chinese educational system is in trouble. Although impressive gains in basic literacy have been achieved since 1949, the quality and efficiency of a system serving 200 million full-time students is now under attack from a number of sources. In recent years, hardly a week has gone by without a major article in the Chinese press about the problems of education, and the steps being taken to solve them. In early 1987 a wave of student demonstrations swept 11 Chinese cities, motivated in part by student complaints about the quality of their education. As the quote of Vice Chairman Bo implies, the rationale for the recent spate of criticism is the realization that China's educational needs, in light of its modernization drive, are rapidly changing. Today, China needs creative problem solvers and technical experts to transform agriculture and industry into competitive forces on the world market. Instead, what it now gets from its educational system are people skillful at rote learning who may know a little about several subjects, but lack specialization in any.

Though critics of education have raised a host of issues, most fall within four broad areas: curriculum, teacher education, educational management and physical resources. Complaints about curriculum include outdated textbooks currently used in primary and secondary schools, scarcity of vocational education at the secondary level, limited course offerings and specializations available at the college level, and the overall lack of "academic freedom" for teachers and students at all levels of education, but most noticeably at the college level. The latter is cited as one reason why Chinese researchers lag behind the world in many academic fields.[110]

Teacher education has also drawn the attention of many critics in China. The root problem, most agree, is the poor quality of teacher training programs, coupled with the low pay and social status of teachers. The problem is particularly acute at the elementary level. Many of these teachers have no more than a high school education and know nothing about pedagogy. Their teacher-centered methods of instruction encourage mindless imitation and rote memorization. For their efforts, they receive salaries that are far below those of factory workers and often cannot get decent housing. As a result, teachers are leaving education in alarming numbers.[111] They are being recruited to work in the burgeoning tourist industry, in factories and offices, and in trade and commerce. Unless something is done to curb this trend, experts predict that China will face a severe teacher shortage in the near future.

A third ailing area is educational management. Critics repeatedly have denounced the inefficient use of teachers and physical resources. This is blamed on the so-called "big pot" system of management, popularized by Mao Tse-tung, in which everyone shares equally in the distribution of wages and benefits, regardless of the quality of their performance.[112] Deng Xiaoping and like-minded critics claim this system does not reward initiative, provides no incentive for good teachers to put forth their best effort, and actually encourages incompetent teachers in the ranks.

Compounding this problem is a management system in which decision making is concentrated at the top, overburdening a few key educational administrators with an enormous work load, while many teachers have little to do. An additional hindrance is the propensity for school administrators to behave as though they were overseeing a feudal fiefdom accountable only to central authorities in Beijing. This encourages compartmentalization and turf wars among schools and departments, rather than cooperation and multidisciplinary solutions to problems.

Finally, critics point to the poor physical condition of schools, especially primary schools in the countryside, and the complete lack of schools in some remote areas as major stumbling blocks to educational progress.[113] Even in urban areas, schools often lack libraries, laboratories and equipment. In a related area, housing for teachers and students is in chronic short supply. Many schools lost significant parts of their physical plant during the anarchy of the Cultural Revolution, and have yet to recoup their losses. This leaves some teachers without a place to live while others must share dormitory rooms that cannot accommodate their families. Students are even worse off. If they can get a place to live at all, it is at best a cramped dormitory room housing six to eight students.

Conclusions of This Study

While the reports in the Chinese press cited above give an overall impression of the problems confronting Chinese educators, they do not go into sufficient detail or provide enough concrete evidence to give readers a clear picture of what is wrong, and more importantly, why things are wrong. A second weakness of these reports is that they reflect almost exclusively the views of government officials and educational experts. There is little evidence that educational leaders have conducted systematic research into the views of on-site administrators, teachers and students to determine what they think the problems are.

The results reported in this book, though based on the conditions at a single university, confirm many of the criticisms cited in the Chinese press, and also raise a number of important issues that have heretofore been overlooked, especially regarding the sources of problems and the difficulties facing reformers. Among the problem areas confirmed by this study are: outdated textbooks, lack of course offerings, lack of academic freedom, poorly trained teachers, ineffective teaching methods, low social status of teachers, inefficient management, top-heavy decision making, and poor physical conditions.

Curricular Problems

When one inquires about curricular problems in China, the usual response is that textbooks and teaching materials are outdated and in short supply. Among teachers and students in my sample, this was a common complaint. Teachers reported having great difficulty finding appropriate materials in English; books from abroad were especially scarce. Students rated textbooks among their least favorite sources for learning English.

The reason outdated textbooks are used is quite simply because better ones are not available. This has much to do with the state of the publishing industry in China, which is a subsidized government monopoly that finds itself unable to keep up with the demand for books in a society of avid readers. Adding to this problem is the bureaucratic way many textbooks are written and published. The ones used in an English grammar course are a good example. Written by a committee of experts at a leading university, the textbooks took nearly five years from conception to publication. By that time, the books were already out of date, but were expected to meet educational needs for another five years before the whole process would be repeated again.

Obviously, the publishing industry in China is antiquated and inadequate to meet current educational needs. Presently, books are cheap but scarce. One way to increase the supply would be to pump more government funds into publishing; another would be to decentralize publication by breaking up the present monopoly and allowing market forces to encourage growth. Of course, these reforms face stiff economic and political opposition. The government is already strapped for cash and does not view textbooks as a high enough priority to provide additional funds. Allowing market forces to stimulate the publishing industry would result in more books, but at higher prices that might cause hardship for schools. More importantly, it would also incense Communist Party conservatives who fear the spread of ideas different from their own. So, decision makers in China have shown little inclination to adopt either approach. In fact, since Hu Yao-bang was removed as Party Chairman, the government has announced tighter controls over the publishing industry to ensure that views contrary to party dogma do not find a publishing outlet.

A second major curricular problem identified by my study is the lack of course offerings and specializations. In the department I studied, students took a common core curriculum throughout the first three years of their undergraduate program. Only in the senior year did students get a few electives, and these were limited to literature courses only. Worse yet, students at Teachers University could not take courses outside their department. Students expressed deep dissatisfaction with this state of affairs. In fact, of all the complaints they made about the curriculum, the most common was the lack of choice in course offerings and majors.

The root cause of this problem is the way students are grouped for instruction. Even at the university level, students in China are assigned to fixed groups who take all their courses together. This means that no individualization is allowed. Courses are scheduled for a given group of students and all must take them whether they want to or not. To change this arrangement, Chinese universities must be willing to allow students to choose their own courses and specializations from a scheduled list. This requires a much wider variety of courses from which to choose. Though some commentators have called for more breadth in course offerings, none has yet seen the need to group students differently. Even if they did, school administrators whom I talked with oppose this idea on the grounds that it would create more work for them.

A third problem discussed in the press is the lack of academic freedom.

This is a controversial topic, to be sure. Not everyone I spoke with thought that academic freedom was relevant to China. And most doubted it could ever become a reality, at least in the sense that Westerners talk of academic freedom. Still, several administrators and teachers voiced the desire to see more discussion and debate in the department, and half the students expressed the hope that they would be given more freedom to learn. In fact, academic freedom was circumscribed in several ways. First, administrators reserved the right to censor teaching materials with "romantic" or "politically and ideologically suspect" content, as one administrator put it. Second, students generally did not have the freedom to choose their own research topics, even at the graduate level; instead, these were chosen for them by their instructors. Third, both teachers and students were observed to avoid discussions that called into question Marxist ideology or the Chinese political system. Despite these limits on academic freedom, a majority of students believed that they could talk in class about anything they wanted, and teachers reported that they felt free to conduct their courses as they saw fit.

Teaching and Learning

Turning now to teacher education problems, this study found that these are at the core of China's educational woes. To be certified as a teacher in the department I studied, students merely took two methods courses and did six weeks of practice teaching. Some university instructors in the department had even less training, used ineffective teaching methods, and suffered from low social status. Of the 13 Chinese teachers in my sample, only one had completed an M.A. The rest of the faculty had B.A. degrees. Considering that they were teaching students with virtually the same educational level as themselves, university instructors were clearly undereducated for their work. Perhaps more alarming, only 19 percent of the faculty had specialized in education or English teaching methods. The rest had majored in literature or grammar, with little or no emphasis in pedagogy. As a result, their teaching methods left much to be desired. Teachers relied on four strategies for the bulk of their instruction: drill and practice, explication of text, lecture, and translation. On average, teachers talked about 80 percent of class time. Students were mostly passive listeners in class.

One of the questions I sought to answer in this study was: What curricular and instructional practices have been imployed to teach English in China? Historically, two methods have wielded the greatest influence: the grammar-translation approach and the direct method. Both these methods were introduced from abroad in the late nineteenth century. The former, with its emphasis on memorization of rules and translation between Chinese and English, appealed to Chinese teachers because it did not require native fluency and did not contradict traditional Confucian notions about teaching, in which the teacher and the text were taken to be the highest authority. The direct method, on the other hand, was primarily used by foreign teachers of English, because it required fluency in the language. Only in the last 20 years has the direct method become widely used by Chinese teachers of English, primarily because teachers have better English skills themselves and also because of the increasing importance of oral skills.

In the last two decades, the audiolingual method, developed abroad during World War II, has come to exercise greater influence on language teaching in China. Most English curriculum development in recent years has taken an audiolingual approach, with greater attention to oral skills and memorization of sentence patterns and structures, rather than simply memorizing grammatical rules. Despite this, in the department I studied, more teachers were using the direct method combined with elements of grammar-translation than were using the audiolingual approach. Many teachers did not fully understand the rationale behind audiolingual teaching and some found that students got bored with this approach.

One other approach to language learning has just begun to influence Chinese educators—the communicative approach. Those who have been abroad or had graduate study in applied linguistics are aware of this new approach, and some advocated its adoption in China. Still, I found little evidence that this approach is being used by Chinese teachers.[114] To work effectively, it requires not only native fluency in English, but also native-like knowledge of the culture and society of English-speaking countries, knowledge that Chinese teachers gain only when they go abroad. Since few have this opportunity, the number of Chinese teachers of English qualified to use communicative methods is small.

Another major obstacle to the adoption of communicative methods is the requirement that students be active participants in class. This runs counter to everything that Chinese teachers know and believe about teaching. In China, teachers are still in loco parentis, even in college. To most, students are best seen and not heard. The effective class is one in which the teacher demonstrates his knowledge of the subject and students passively soak it up. Clearly, communicative activities like role-playing and discussion require the teacher to play a facilitating role, not a dominating one. I believe this fact, more than any other, explains why Chinese teachers are reluctant to try out this approach in practice, even when they are outspoken advocates of it.

Because of the methods teachers used, I found that students were making the greatest progress in basic skills, particularly in listening and reading English. They were doing less well in speaking and writing because they did not get enough appropriate opportunities to practice these two skills. Students spoke only about 10 to 20 percent of the time they spent in class, and had even fewer opportunities to speak English outside of class. Even in reading, arguably students' best English skill, students were skillful only at lower level tasks like identifying factual details. When asked to make inferences, students did not perform satisfactorily, even after three years of instruction. Furthermore, students showed no significant gain in either reading skill after six months of instruction. As for literature, students read the classic works of major British and American authors and learned something about literary history. But they did not fully understand the cultural context in which literature developed nor the role that culture plays in the use of English because Chinese teachers did not devote enough time to these topics or understood them poorly themselves. Finally, regarding teacher training, students learned some basic principles of foreign language teaching, especially those associated with the audiolingual school. They had less success in applying these principles because they did not always know how to apply them in China and their instructors provided insufficient guidance in this all-important area. Plus, students were apt to mimic the teaching methods they saw their teachers using, which consisted primarily of a combination of the direct and grammar-translation approaches.

I found in the courses I observed that events tended to follow certain predictable patterns. Though objectives and content varied, teachers used surprisingly similar activities, strategies, grouping patterns and methods of evaluation, with few exceptions. Listening activities, for example, predominated all other types. Students listened anywhere from 75 to 95 percent of the time. When they weren't listening, they usually answered the teacher's questions or wrote something. Grouping patterns invariably involved all students working as a whole class; only the sizes of classes varied. Students worked alone only when doing written work, and were never observed to work in small groups or pairs under the teacher's direction. Evaluation consisted of various pencil and paper tests and whatever oral feedback a teacher provided to evaluate student talk. In most courses, evaluation received less attention that it deserves.

In sum, the undergraduate curriculum is terribly predictable. Only two courses really stand out in my mind as being significantly different. One was Listening Comprehension, which had the unique setting of the language laboratory and relied more on audiovisual materials than other courses. The other was Selected Readings of American and British Literature, which was different because it was taught by an American who relied on strategies and activities which encouraged student participation.

In the end, I was struck most by the inefficiency I saw. Teachers and students spent an enormous amount of time on materials and activities that did not seem to be well organized or thoughtfully presented with a clear objective in mind. Certain basic skills in reading and grammar got an inordinate amount of attention while speaking, writing and more advanced analytical skills were virtually ignored. And all of this took place in an environment which was about as far removed from real communication as one could get. Despite these problems, students were learning English. There were clear differences in the proficiency of first and fourth year students which can be attributed to the instruction they received. Yet, I kept thinking about how much more students might have learned if they had had better trained teachers and a more effective curriculum.

Class climates were quite mixed. In no class I observed was the climate consistently ideal, but it was sufficiently good in a majority of courses to be conducive to learning. In three courses, however, the class climate was marred by ill will or chronic boredom. In these courses—second year Intensive Reading, Teaching Methodology, and Stylistics—learning was definitely impeded by the poor climate. Classes were generally serious and business-like, but there were rare moments of laughter and joy in a few courses. I will never forget the excited energy and raucous laughter during students' first minilessons in Teaching Methodology, for example. They were alive that day, and it was clear what they were doing mattered to them. Unfortunately, too many of the sessions I observed were dull and listless. Both teachers and students sometimes seemed to be sleepwalking through the lesson, doing things because it was a task to be done, without joy or obvious commitment.

The root cause of the inefficiency and ineffectiveness I saw is to be found in the nature of the teacher-student relationship. At core, it remains a Confucian one—the master and his disciple. If instructional practices are to change in China, it appears that the social roles of teachers and students will have to be redefined. And the historical record shows that this is a truly enormous task. For over a century now, Chinese teachers have resolutely refused to adopt new methods of instruction, whether they were advocated by foreigners or by Chinese communists. Despite sometimes brutal attempts to remake the outlook of teachers, they still feel most comfortable when they are in control of the class, do most of the talking and are seen by students as the sole authority and source of knowledge.

The student's role continues as it has in China for centuries: to be a passive receptacle for the wisdom of the ages as transmitted by the teacher. This role is deeply rooted in the Confucian ethic of respect for one's elders and superiors. Young people in China do not have an innovative role to play in the Confucian cosmos. Their task is to learn the ancient wisdom of their ancestors and to perpetuate Chinese civilization through emulation of this long tradition. It is a role which has served China ably in keeping its cultural tradition alive, but it is also an enormous impediment to change when that becomes necessary. In fact, tradition is so strong in China that 40 years of communism has not yet been able to overcome it.

Another tradition that has resisted change is the low social status of teachers. Though press accounts usually blame this problem on the Cultural Revolution, when teachers came under attack from radical students, the roots of this problem also stretch back into antiquity. Traditionally, intellectuals coveted jobs in the Chinese civil service. Only failing that did they turn to teaching as a profession. Today, teachers and students are keenly aware of the low social status of the teaching profession. Even at the university level, 30 percent of the teachers I surveyed did not feel their career expectations had been fulfilled. Among students, less than half expressed the desire to become English teachers, and they rated their Teaching Methodology courses as the least interesting and least useful of those they took.

To improve teaching, a two-pronged approach has been adopted. On the one hand, symbolic efforts to raise the status of teachers have been made, such as designating a national holiday for teachers (September 10), and requiring primary students to salute their teachers. On the other hand, material benefits are being improved. Pay raises, postponed for many years, have been awarded and new housing has been built in some places. Still, most teachers have seen more symbolism than concrete progress.[115] While the government promises more training and higher standards in the future, it currently forbids teachers to quit their jobs, which only increases resentment and job dissatisfaction.

Management of Education

The third area of concern for Chinese educators is management. Reformers are determined to overturn the Maoist "big pot" system and replace it with one based on incentives and individual responsibility. Before considering the merits of this reform, it is important to understand what the "big pot" really means. The 39 Chinese faculty in the English department were divided into just two ranks: junior and senior instructor. Everyone within the same rank received the same salary, regardless of teaching load, years of experience or qualifications. Furthermore, the year I conducted this study, nine of the faculty were not teaching for various reasons, although they continued to draw their full salary. Once assigned to the department, teachers enjoyed tenure for life; they could neither be dismissed nor transferred easily. On the other hand, they were not free to quit the position, either. Thus, teachers in China have the security of lifetime employment and the certainty that their peers will earn exactly what they do, regardless of the extent or quality of their effort. Critics charge this has led to teacher complacency.

Besides the effect on teachers, the "big pot" has also taken its toll on administrators. Like teachers, administrators receive the same pay for the same rank, and are rewarded very little for the extra administrative chores they perform. Second, the system encourages the concentration of authority in a few key people, who find themselves inundated in paperwork. The "big pot" requires the state to meet everyone's needs. In the department I studied, the English Section Head handled all academic affairs, plus the housing and daily schedules of students, without any full-time help. Nearly everything had to be approved and arranged by this one administrator, who was so overwhelmed that delays and cancellations occurred regularly. Meanwhile, two other department administrators had little to do with daily academic affairs in the English section, busying themselves instead with university-wide issues.

The cure for these problems, according to Chinese experts, is to institute a contract system in the universities.[116] Under this system, teachers are contracted to teach a certain number of courses per semester. Those who teach more hours receive more pay, while those who teach fewer hours get less. Additionally, bonuses may be rewarded for outstanding effort, although the criteria for determining who will receive bonuses are unclear. Finally, those who teach poorly may be transferred to another job.

This reform, which has already been tried out at a number of universities, offers some incentive to teachers willing to work hard and cuts down on the number of teachers who receive salaries without teaching. But it hardly addresses all the problems identified in the press and in my study. For example, who will decide which teachers will receive bonuses and on what basis? How does one determine who is teaching well and who is not? How will the work load of key administrators be reduced by these reforms? And ultimately, will this result in a better education for students?

The Decision Making Process

Investigation of educational decision making at Teachers University revealed that defects exist which have contributed to management problems. Although all the key groups involved in education—the government, educational officials, on-site administrators, teachers and students—each had some role to play in decision making, the process is decidedly top-heavy. As one moves from the State Education Commission to the classroom and the student dormitory, decision making power decreases dramatically.

The government, represented by the State Education Commission, other central government organs and provincial and local officials, exercised the widest decision making power. Theoretically, they claimed the right to make virtually any decisions they wanted. But that didn't mean these were always implemented as planned. Practically speaking, government decisions about education tended to define general parameters rather than specific details. For example, governmental agencies set overall purposes for educational institutions, minimum graduation requirements for various degrees, and funding levels, which determined student enrollment and staff levels. These were the most important decisions made by the government, and they created the environment in which all other curricular decisions were made. The State Education Commission was critical in one other area as well: the reform of education. The government insisted on its right to oversee and direct the reform process. Without its approval, reforms have little chance to succeed.

Otherwise, the government was active in decisions about only two of the curricular components I investigated: materials and evaluation. At Teachers University, materials for Intensive Reading and Teaching Methodology were decided in part by the State Education Commission, which compiled a list of approved texts from which administrators and teachers had to choose. The Commission's direct involvement in these two courses illustrates the importance placed on them by the government, and its determination to control the content of these courses. Regarding evaluation, the Education Commission tests students at Teachers University about every two years to determine their English and Chinese proficiency. These test results were very important to the department, because they were used to judge the effectiveness of the curriculum and instruction at universities throughout China. Those institutions scoring higher on tests were more likely to receive additional funds and get favorable attention in the press, while institutions which consistently performed poorly were subject to outside scrutiny which could lead to loss of funding or even people's jobs.

The university's administration played a more active role in the curriculum than the government, but its scope of authority was more limited. It made decisions regarding course offerings and schedules, grouping patterns, materials and the way time and space were utilized. At Teachers University, decision making was divided into four distinct levels of management: the president's office, the dean's office, the foreign languages department and the English section. The president's office can be best thought of as the liaison between the government and the university community. Most government decisions were transmitted to university presidents, who were required to implement them according to the conditions at their institutions. For example, the president's office largely decided how much money each department would receive, dispersing the overall university funding amount decided by the State Education Commission.

The dean's office of each of the major schools within the university gave final approval to course offerings drawn up by department administrators, and also had final say regarding the recruitment of staff and the enrollment level of students. In each of these areas, though, the dean's office worked closely with and relied upon department officials.

At the department level, decision making was in the hands of the Chairperson, Vice-Chair and English Section Head. Of the three, the Section Head was the most active in decision making, especially with regard to the materials, content and organization of the curriculum. The department-level administrators were more concerned with overall questions of funding, staff and enrollment, and they were critical if changes were initiated. In fact, what made department administrators a unique group from teachers was not so much their views of curriculum and instruction as their power to make curricular decisions. They decided which courses would be offered in the department, who would teach them, how many hours would be devoted to each, and when they would be taught. In some courses, they also determined the materials and content. In Intensive and Extensive Reading, for example, the Section Head sometimes chose materials directly or was consulted by teachers before materials were chosen. In other courses, administrators had the power to insist that teachers use other materials if they objected to the moral or political content of those chosen. Since materials are always scarce in China, and administrators had access to most of the ones available, they were able to exercise considerable influence over materials when they desired to do so.

Teachers were rarely consulted about department decisions, but they did make many kinds of decisions about the curriculum of their own courses. These included the exact objectives they sought, the content and topics they covered, the learning activities and teaching strategies they used, the organization of content and the evaluation of students. Among junior level faculty (those who taught courses in the first two years), decisions about these matters were often made jointly by the teaching group in charge of that course. These decisions were also more often scrutinized by administrators, who sometimes participated directly in the process. The senior level faculty, including veteran Chinese and most American faculty, usually made curricular decisions alone, because they taught a unique course offered by no one else. Moreover, their decisions were less subject to department approval, giving them considerably more decision making power than junior faculty had.

Student decision making authority was the weakest of all the groups investigated. Their decision making was primarily limited to making suggestions and raising complaints about materials, content and learning activities. In only one course that I observed—Listening Comprehension—did students participate directly in curricular decisions about materials and learning activities. In other courses, students occasionally made their opinions known to teachers and administrators, who might take them into account in making decisions, but students did not get to decide anything for themselves.

Barred from direct participation in decisions regarding their education, students had to resort to other means to make themselves heard. When students were unhappy about a class and dissatisfied with the teacher, they were observed to resort to passive resistance in class, that is they simply refused to participate. Quite often, students openly whispered among themselves while the teacher lectured; in a few cases, they were observed to fall asleep.

At one point during the year of my study, students turned to a more direct form of action. In early 1985, the university decided to reduce subsidies given to most students to support them in school, including elimination of vacation-time support. This decision, made without prior consultation, galvanized students into action. They quickly made their views known to the administration during several heated meetings held to discuss the decision. When they were rebuffed, they escalated the issue by writing big character posters which suddenly appeared around campus, denouncing the decision and calling for a reversal. For students to resort to this method of protest in 1985 was a bold move that invited political criticism. At the same time, it generated considerble attention at higher levels of authority, and eventually resulted in university officials postponing their decision. This incident, a prelude to much larger student demonstrations that came a year or so later, shows that students had considerable power when they were sufficiently motivated and unified by an important issue to exercise it.

Physical Resources

One final area which has drawn the attention of educational critics is physical resources. Given that China is a developing third world nation, one cannot expect lavish physical resources for education. The question critics have raised, though, is whether the current resources are minimally adequate to meet the need. Clearly, the answer is no. At Teachers University, for example, the English department was so strapped for space that faculty could not get offices on campus. Instead, the department had two small common rooms, one for Chinese and one for foreign faculty. Classroom space was also at a premium, especially during the morning, when most courses met. Campus housing for teachers and students was cramped and uncomfortable. Campus buildings were like refrigerators in winter and saunas in summer. Lighting was inadequate for comfortable reading in most rooms.

Most seriously of all, however, was the woefully inadequate department library. It was housed in such a tiny room, and contained so few books, that the department only allowed seniors and graduate students to use it. The university's main library was much larger, but its books did not circulate, and its English language collection was smaller than that of a typical middle class American family. Without reference books, scholarly research was out of the question for undergraduates.

Dissatisfaction

All the problems mentioned in the press and documented in this book are most acutely felt by those who must live with them every day. Thus, it is not surprising that dissatisfaction was widespread at Teachers University. I found that no group was completely satisfied with the curriculum. Of the groups I investigated, however, Chinese teachers seemed more satisfied with more curricular components than others. Close to teachers in outlook, administrators nevertheless identified more curricular problems, especially in the organization of the department and its course offerings.

Students, on the other hand, were clearly the least satisfied group of all. They often disliked the courses they took and the teachers who taught them, but they were most displeased about the lack of control over their lives.

In fact, Chinese university students have less say about their education than high school students in the United States. They cannot choose their own major, or the courses they take, or the teachers who instruct them, or the topics of their research. All of these things, as well as their living arrangements and even their future employment, are decided for them by university or government officials. In interviews, students repeatedly complained about their lack of decision making power, saying things like, "The authorities make all decisions" and "The officials won't listen to us." One summed up student life by saying, "They treat us like children."

It would appear that the recent student protests are a signal that university students in China are tired of being treated like children. Above all, students want the power to decide for themselves what they will learn and how they will use their knowledge.

The American teachers, like students, did not think much of the education being provided at Teachers University. To them, the department was bureaucratic, slow to act, and cautious in relations with foreigners. None of the five chose to remain another year.

Moreover, a direct relationship existed between areas of satisfaction and the extent to which individuals of that group exercised decision making power. Teachers, for example, were most satisfied with objectives, content, teaching strategies, evaluation and time use, all areas where they exercised the greatest decision making. Administrators were most satisfied with goals, class schedules, and use of space, three areas where they exercised considerable decision making power. Students were not satisfied with very much of the curriculum, and had little control over it. Like students, the Americans felt that they exercised little control over their lives in China, a major source of dissatisfaction.

Overall, I would say student dissatisfaction with the department's curriculum is the one most critical problem facing the department. It has reached the point where it is impeding student learning in some classes. Unless something is done to make learning more rewarding and satisfying for students, the department is not likely to improve in other areas where changes are needed.

Purposes of Learning English

One of the questions that prompted this book was: For what purposes has English been taught in China over the last two centuries? In examining the historical record, the most important purpose which emerges is to use English as a tool to modernize China. Beginning with the earliest government English language school in China, the *Tong Wen Guan*, and continuing up to the present time, this purpose has justified the teaching and learning of English more than any other. In the nineteenth century, Chinese leaders hoped that the study of English would enable China to learn advanced knowledge from the West which could be applied to strengthening China, so as to better resist foreign imperialism. For this reason, English was taught to diplomats and military officers in numerous government schools.

Later, in the first decades of the twentieth century, English became even more widespread, as urban Chinese studied the language for use in business, commerce, medicine and the sciences. By this time, modernization had been expanded in scope from the military to all aspects of Chinese society. Since this purpose sometimes conflicted with the religious goals of foreign schools in China, who did most of the English teaching, these schools were gradually taken over by the government and became wholly secular in purpose.

With the advent to power of the Chinese communists, the overall goal of modernizing China remained, but the means to reach this goal changed dramatically. Instead of following a capitalist model, the Chinese under Mao sought to build socialist-style modernization along the lines of the Soviet Union. During the 1950s, when Soviet influence reached its apex, the study of English was no longer viewed as valuable. The Chinese thought there was little they could learn about modernization from English-speaking countries, and relations between China and these countries reached a low point.

Starting again in the 1960s, and gaining rapid momentum after 1976, the Chinese government changed its mind about the value of English. Communist leaders, while continuing to oppose adoption of the Western model of modernization, realized that much of the world's advanced technology was accessible only in English. So, they began to give greater stress to study of the language again. After diplomatic relations between China and the United States were reestablished in 1979, English study saw its greatest resurgence in China since the 1940s. Today, more Chinese study English than all other foreign languages combined. And they do so with one overriding purpose: to help China realize the four modernizations in agriculture, industry, defense, and science and technology.

The role that Teachers University plays in this mission is to prepare English teachers for the secondary and collegiate level. These teachers will instruct students in basic English skills, with particular attention to achieving fluency in reading English so that English language books and materials can be understood in their original form and translated into Chinese for wider dissemination. Increasingly, English teachers are also asked to train fluent speakers of English to serve as interpreters and tour guides for the growing number of English-speakers who come to China for business or travel. In the department I studied, the learning of basic English skills was combined with study of literature and teacher training. The department believed that Chinese speakers of English should not only know the language, but also something about the history, literature and way of life of English-speaking countries so that students would be able to understand the context in which English is spoken and written. Moreover, the department wanted students to study basic principles of foreign language teaching so that they would be effective instructors of English upon graduation.

Besides these major purposes, I discovered that students in the department had a number of other important motives for learning English. Two of the most common were integrative motives, that is, learning English to become a part of English-speaking culture. Specifically, students reported that they had interest in the literature and culture of English-speaking countries and wanted to understand foreigners better. Nearly two-thirds of the students were also learning English to go abroad to study or work, though few of them actually get a chance to do so. Among the least important reasons students cited was to become an English teacher, a career that many consider unattractive because of low pay and low social status. Since students have little say about the jobs they are assigned after graduation, many become English teachers unwillingly.

Future Prospects

Some of the reforms discussed above have had little time to show results, but it is fair to ask whether they have the potential to make education in China more effective and efficient. At Teachers University, the only change actually implemented while I was there was a department decision that all teachers hired in the future must have at least an M.A. degree. Some of the proposals listed above were under administrative discussion, but no decisions had yet been reached.

Particularly interesting are the suggestions to improve teaching methods, clearly the weakest link in the instructional curriculum. Greater use of discussion as a teaching strategy was one idea promulgated frequently in the press. Yet, I saw no attention given to how this was supposed to come about. I presume that decision makers in the State Education Commission believed they could decree that teachers engage students in more discussion, and it would automatically happen. In fact, from what I saw of teaching in the department, there was little likelihood that Chinese teachers would suddenly begin holding discussions. Most probably did not know how, for one thing, and were certainly not convinced that it would work with Chinese students. I observed one teacher hold a discussion which was really a glorified drill and practice session in which she did more than 75 percent of the talking. If that is teachers' idea of discussion, it clearly will not represent much improvement over the methods currently in use.

The major obstacle to discussion, once again, is the perceived roles of teachers and students in China. In a true discussion, it is likely that there is no single answer to the question at hand. It is also possible that students might have better answers than their teachers. Both are anathema to the Chinese teachers I observed. They felt most comfortable, it seemed, when they were dealing with topics and questions that had clear-cut answers which they possessed but students did not. To teacher attitudes like these, we must adjoin student attitudes, which would obviously also affect the possibilities of discussion.

From what I discovered, less than half the students were willing to actively participate in the few class discussions that took place. The rest seemed content to assume a passive listening role, unless called upon to participate. This would not provide much of an impetus for discussion from students, and could prove frustrating to teachers, as some foreign teachers readily admitted.

On the other hand, students preferred to practice speaking over any other activity and rated their Spoken English class as having the greatest interest to them. So, the potential exists for students to be active in discussions and to benefit from this method, if it is clear that their teachers expect them to. Personally, I found that Chinese students were just as eager to discuss things as any other students I have taught, once they understood how a discussion works and what their role was.

One additional factor inhibits discussion in China—the political system. Every Chinese knows that there are certain issues one never discusses, in the true sense of the term, and that among them are Marxist-Leninist doctrine, modern Chinese history, and the Chinese political system. In these areas, politically-acceptable answers have been fashioned and promulgated by the government in such a way so as to preclude any real discussion. One memorizes these answers and believes them unflinchingly; one does not raise questions and discuss them. This process, powerful as it is in achieving political control, spills over into other facets of Chinese life, including education. In short, it is difficult to discuss anything if one does not have the freedom to formulate opinions and arrive at whatever conclusions the discussion may lead to.

A second reform commonly mentioned in the press was the need for more audiovisual aids. Though such aids would certainly appeal to students, who reported them among their favorite materials and activities, they would not ensure that teachers did anything significantly different in the way they taught. The English section used a surprising array of audiovisual aids already, including a fully equipped language laboratory, video recorders, films, etc. The way they were used, however, was quite old-fashioned: they became surrogate lecturers, presenting information to passive student listeners. Though the quality of the presentation was often better than that of live teachers, it was the same old teaching methods at work.

An Agenda for Reform

Though I wish the Chinese nothing but success in their efforts to improve curriculum and instruction, I cannot be overly optimistic, judging from the results of this study. Fundamental political and social barriers stand in the way of significant reforms, and these have apparently received little thoughtful attention. The reforms attempted so far have barely scratched the surface. Further, they have all come from the top with little regard for the opinions of teachers and students. Powerful as it has proved to be in China, the government will not likely succeed in simply dictating new methods of instruction. Teachers will only change when they are convinced that their traditional social role is no longer useful, and begin to think of their students in new roles. Students will support any efforts that involve them more actively in the learning process, and give them greater freedom. They are also the most likely source of agitation for reform, as their demonstrations for freedom attest. But the government's quick crackdown makes clear that students' ideas for reform are not welcome and will be fiercely opposed. University administrators are caught in the middle. They see the need for reform, but feel hamstrung, waiting for initiatives from above while also prodding reluctant teachers to accept them and trying to keep students in line.

So, what should be done? I asked students and teachers to state what they would change about the department, if they could change anything they wanted. Both provided me with a thoughtful list of suggestions for improvement. Among the suggestions that students made, the following were the most commonly cited:

(1). More audiovisual materials, especially from abroad
(2). More choice of course offerings, including more electives
(3). Give students more freedom and let them have more say in what and how they learn
(4). Eliminate some basic skills courses and replace them with more Advanced courses
(5). Provide opportunities for independent study
(6). Make class attendance optional
(7). Replace ineffective teachers and improve the training and skill of others
(8). Be sure teachers are available to talk to students out of class
(9). Require everyone in the department to use English only, both in and out of class

When teachers were asked what they would change, they came up with the following ten suggestions:

(1). Make better materials available in sufficient quantity, including more audiovisual and foreign materials

(2). Encourage students to be more independent and prepare them for life-long learning by providing basic learning skills

(3). Let students take courses in other departments at the university

(4). Put greater emphasis on learning to speak English

(5). Reduce the number of hours students spend in class (now 20 to 30 hours per week)

(6). Recruit teachers who can teach linguistics, literature, humanities and education, thus broadening the department's curricular focus

(7). Improve teacher training and encourage more active classroom methods of instruction

(8). Encourage teachers to conduct research, instead of just teaching, and provide them the time to do it

(9). Improve the physical plant by providing larger classrooms, a full-sized library, more language labs, office space, etc.

(10). Make the library available to all students

All of these suggestions are worth considering. In fact, they would form the basis for a very productive discussion in the English department. What is lacking from these lists, and the government's accounts of its reforms, is a clearly specified plan to bring about these changes.

Upon the completion of my research, the administration asked me to make some suggestions of my own. I recommended they do three things: conduct more research, implement changes in a planned and orderly way, and encourage student and teacher participation in the reform effort.

If schools in China encouraged more research, something that few currently do, this would not only help to build educational theory in China, but could serve as the basis for thoughtfully planned reforms aimed at clearly specified problems. Too often, education reformers plunge in without a clear grasp of the reality they wish to change or the consequences of their actions.

My suggestion that the university implement reforms in a planned way meant establishing goals that appeal to everyone, considering a variety of means to reach these goals and the possible effects of each, and making the long-term commitment necessary to allow for results that only emerge over time. All too often in the past the government has announced with loud fanfare some new reform movement, only to have it quietly fizzle out a few months later with few concrete results.

It is for this reason that I believe my final recommendation is the most important: involve students and teachers in reform, and more broadly, in the management of education. This would help to dispel their considerable apathy and even despair, and give them a greater stake in the educational process. Moreover, any meaningful reform of the curriculum and teacher education requires the cooperation of students and teachers to succeed. Without their support and involvement, reformers may end up spinning their wheels.

China is a nation of great potential which is faced with many challenges. Its youth are its most precious resource. They deserve the best education possible, and China needs to provide it if it hopes to succeed in regaining its preëminent role in the world.

References

1. Su Wen Ming, ed., *A Nation at School* (Beijing, 1983), p. 19.
2. "The English Language: Out to Conquer the World," *U.S. News and World Report* **98**:6 (1985), p. 50.
3. Zhong He, "U.S. Investment in China," *China's Foreign Trade* 11 (1985), p. 10.
4. "The Enlgish Language...," op. cit., p. 50.
5. "China Students March for U.S.-Style Democracy," *Los Angeles Times* (12/17/86), I, p. 5.
6. John Goodlad, *A Place Called School: Prospects for the Future* (New York, 1984), and John Goodlad and Assoc., *A Study of Schooling in the United States: Technical Reports, Numbers One to 29* (Los Angeles, 1979–1981).
7. Ralph Tyler, *Basic Principles of Curriculum and Instruction* (Chicago, 1950).
8. Dell Hymes, "Models of Interaction of Language and Social Setting," *Journal of Social Issues* **23**, (1967), pp. 8–28, and *Foundations in Sociolinguistics: An Ethnographic Approach* (Philadelphia, 1974), pp. 10–23.
9. Goodlad, *A Place Called School*, op. cit., p. 30.
10. For more on criterion-referenced measurement, see James Popham, *Criterion-Referenced Measurement* (Englewood Cliffs, N.J., 1978).
11. John Goodlad, ed., *Curriculum Inquiry: The Study of Curriculum Practice* (New York, 1979), p. 49.
12. Tyler, *Basic Principles*, op. cit., p. 84.
13. Ibid., p. 45.
14. Ibid., p. 105.
15. Ibid., p. 63.
16. J. Gumperz and Dell Hymes, eds., *Directions in Sociolinguistics* (New York, 1972), pp. 1–10.
17. See, for example, Chang Hsin Pao, *Commissioner Lin and the Opium War* (New York, 1964); John K. Fairbank, *The United States and China*, 1st ed. (Cambridge, Mass., 1958); John K. Fairbank and Teng Ssu Yu, *China's Response to the West*, 2 vols. (Cambridge, Mass., 1954); Mary Wright, *The Last Stand of Chinese Conservatism* (Stanford, Calif., 1957); and Immanuel C.Y. Hsu, *China's Entrance into the Family of Nations* (Cambridge, Mass., 1960).
18. Hosea Morse, *The International Relations of the Chinese Empire*, 3 vols. (London, 1910–1918).
19. Arthur Hummel, *Eminent Chinese of the Qing Period*, 2 vols. (Washington, D.C., 1943–44).
20. Poon Kan Mok. *The History and Development of Teaching English in China* (New York, 1951). A dissertation, originally written in 1935.
21. Ibid. p. 14.
22. Ibid., pp. 33–35.
23. Ibid., p. 40.
24. Ibid., pp. 66–69. Also see William Hung's translation, "Huang Tsun-Hsien's Poem 'The Closure of the Educational Mission in America'," *Harvard Journal of Asiatic Studies* 6 (1955), for an interesting view of the short-lived Yale-China educational exchange program.
25. Ibid., p. 71.
26. Knight Biggerstaff, *The Earliest Modern Government Schools in China* (Ithaca, N.Y., 1961), p. 12.
27. Mok, *History and Development*, op. cit., p. 78.
28. Biggerstaff, op. cit., pp. 32, 122.

29. Peter Duus, "Science and Salvation in China: The Life and Work of W.A.P. Martin 1827–1916," *Papers on China* **10,** p. 112.

30. Ibid.

31. Mok, op. cit., p. 97.

32. Duus, op. cit., p. 113.

33. Biggerstaff, op. cit., p. 127.

34. Ibid., p. 129.

35. Duus, op. cit., p. 114.

36. Biggerstaff, op. cit., p. 34.

37. Ibid., p. 134.

38. Ibid., p. 113.

39. Duus, op. cit., p. 115.

40. Biggerstaff, op. cit., p. 131.

41. Ibid., pp. 78–80.

42. Ibid., p. 81.

43. Mok, op. cit., p. 153.

44. Ibid., pp. 88–90.

45. Biggerstaff, op. cit., p. 136.

46. Ibid., p. 150.

47. See Hsiao En Cheng, *The History of Modern Education in China* (Beijing, 1932); Anthony C. Li, *The History of Privately Controlled Higher Education in the Republic of China* (Washington, D.C., 1954); Jessie Lutz, *The Role of Christian Colleges in Modern China Before 1928* (Ithaca, N.Y., 1955) and *China and the Christian Colleges, 1850–1950* (Ithaca, N.Y., 1959); W.A.P. Martin, *A Cycle of Cathay* (New York, 1900); Paul Monroe, *A Report of Education in China* (New York, 1922); W. Tchishin Tao and C.P. Chen, *Education in China* (Shanghai, 1925); William Fenn, *Christian Higher Education in Changing China* (Grand Rapids, Mich., 1976); Cyrus Peake, *Nationalism and Education in Modern China* (New York, 1932); and for those who read Chinese, Gu Chang Sheng, *Chuan Jiao Shi Yu Jin Dai Zhong Guo* (Shanghai, 1981).

48. Gu, cited immediately above, p. 333.

49. Jessie Lutz, *The Role of the Christian Colleges in China Before 1928* (Ithaca, N.Y., 1955).

50. Ibid., p. 20.

51. Ibid., p. 97.

52. Gu, op. cit., p. 239.

53. Mok, op. cit., p. 114.

54. Ibid., p. 116.

55. Ibid., p. 108.

56. Ibid., p. 117.

57. William P. Fenn, *Christian Higher Education in Changing China 1880–1950* (Grand Rapids, Mich., 1976), p. 123.

58. Ibid., p. 123.

59. Ibid.

60. Ibid.

61. Gu, op. cit., p. 333.

62. W. Tchishin Tao and C.P. Chen, *Education in China* (Shanghai, 1925), p. 38.

63. Anthony C. Li, *The History of Privately Controlled Higher Education in the Republic of China* (Washington, D.C., 1954), p. 13.

64. Gu, op. cit., p. 228.

65. Mok, op. cit., p. 177.

66. Cyrus H. Peake, *Nationalism and Education in Modern China* (New York, 1932), p. 67.

67. Ibid.

68. Ibid., p. 60.

69. Ibid., p. 61.

70. Ibid., pp. 85–86.

71. Tao and Chen, *Education in China*, op. cit., p. 38.

72. Peake, *Nationalism and Education*, op. cit., p. 147.

73. Fenn, op. cit., p. 115.

74. Ibid., p. 120.

75. Ibid., p. 85.

76. China Educational Commission of the Mission Boards and Societies in China, *Christian Education in China* (New York, 1922), p. 14.

77. Ibid., p. 15.

78. Fenn, *Christian Higher Education*, op. cit., p. 195.

79. Ibid., p. 225.

80. Li, op. cit., pp. 106–114.

81. Ibid., p. 117.

82. See Dale Bratton, *Politics of Educational Reform in the PRC* (Ann Arbor, Mich., 1979); Theodore Chen, *Chinese Education Since 1949* (New York, 1981); Ruth Gamberg, *Red and Expert* (New York, 1976); John Hawkins, *Mao Tse Tung and Education* (Hamden, Conn., 1974) and *Education and Social Change in the People's Republic of China* (New York, 1983); Hu Shi Ming, *Interrelationship Between Education and Political Ideology Exemplified in China* (Ann Arbor, Mich., 1970); Ronald Montaperto and Jay Henderson, *China's Schools in Flux* (New York, 1979); Suzanne Pepper, "Chinese Education After Mao," *China Quarterly* **81** (1980), pp. 1–65, and "China's Universities," *Modern China* **8**:2 (1982), pp. 21–35.

83. Janene Scovel, *Curriculum Stability and Change: English Foreign Language Programs in Modern China* (Ann Arbor, Mich., 1982), p. 47.

84. Pepper, "Chinese Education After Mao" (cited in note 82 above), and Donald Ford, "Foreign Language Instruction in China," *Pasaa* (Thailand) **9**:1 (1981).

85. R.F. Price, *Education in Modern China* (London, 1979).

86. Ibid., p. 172.

87. Ibid., p. 180.

88. Ibid., p. 179.

89. Ibid., p. 173.

90. Ibid., pp. 181–182.

91. Ibid., p. 184.

92. Ibid., p. 182.

93. See Charles Fergusen, "Applied Linguistics in China," *Linguistic Reporter* **17**:4 (1975), pp. 3–10; W.P. Lehman, *Language and Linguistics in the PRC* (Austin, Texas, 1975); Timothy Light, "U.S. Applied Linguistic Delegation to the PRC," *Linguistic Reporter* **20**:7 (1978); National Public Radio, "Education in China" (Washington, D.C., 1979); Lois Wein, "International Perspective: English Language Instruction in China Today," *English Journal* **69**:2 (1980), pp. 15–19.

94. See Wendy Allen and David Cooke, "Bridging the Gap," *TESL Talk* **13**:2 (1982), pp. 23–31; Ann Bishop, *English Language Teaching by Foreigners in Harbin* (Austin, Texas, 1981); Barbara De Mille, "Teaching in China," *ADE Bulletin* **73** (1982); Donald Ford, "Education in China: Lofty Ambitions, Grim Reality," *Monsoon* **3**:9 (1980) and "Foreign Language Instruction in China," *Pasaa* (Thailand) **9**:1 (1981); M. Grannis et al., " 'Shake a Leg' English in China," *English Around the World* **20** (1979); E.D. Kennedy, "Teaching English Language in China," *Linguistic Reporter* **21**:8 (1979); Donald Murray, "Culture Trading on the Old Silk Road," *Today's Education* **70**:4 (1981); Charles Scott, "Some First Impressions of EFL Teaching in China," *TESOL News* **14**:6 (1980).

95. In particular, see Robert Barendsen, "The 1978 College Entrance Examination in the PRC" (Washington, D.C., 1979); R.F. Price, "Some English Language Textbooks from China," *English Language Teaching Journal* **33**:4 (1979), pp. 15–23; Scovel, *Curriculum Stability and Change*, op. cit., p. 47.

96. Barendsen, op. cit., p. 56, pp. 108–110.

97. Price, "Some English Language Textbooks from China," op. cit., pp. 15–23.

98. Scovel, op. cit., p. 47.

99. Pepper, "Chinese Education After Mao," op.cit.

100. See Allen and Cooke, op. cit. (note 94), and Ford, "Foreign Language Instruction in China," op. cit.

101. This figure is based on the author's own estimate. There is no official figure available.

102. John Hawkins, "Educational Reform and Development in the People's Republic of China," in P. Altbach, R. Arnove and G. Kelly, eds., *Comparative Education* (New York, 1982), p. 428.

103. "Ti Chu Ji Chu Jie Duan Ying Yu Zhuan Ye Ke Cheng She Zhi Gai Jin Fang An," *Wai Yu Yu Yan Jiao Xue Ze Liao Bao Dao [Foreign Language Teaching Information Bulletin]* **1** (1984), pp. 5–9.

104. See "Colleges Outline Job Placement Reform," *China Daily* (3/13/85), p. 3, and "Leading University Announces Changes," *China Daily* (4/4/85), p. 3.

105. This is particularly true of the party and military press, but even the English language *China Daily* made its only mention of Christmas day in 1984 by running a large photo of homeless street people in New York City.

106. Dell Hymes, "Models of Interaction of Language and Social Setting," *Journal of Social Issues* **23** (1967), pp. 8–28, and Dell Hymes, C.B. Cazden, and V.P. Johns, eds., *Functions of Language in the Classroom* (New York, 1972).

107. D.H. Brown, *Principles of Language Learning and Teaching* (Englewood Cliffs, N.J., 1980), p. 204.

108. G.P. Moore, "Chinese Students' Protests Are Far from Academic," *Los Angeles Times* (5/3/81), II, p. 5.

109. Chen Guan Feng, "Success in Future Tied to Teachers' Vital Role," *China Daily* (2/25/85), p. 1.

110. Su Shaozhi, "Free Exchange of Thought Leads to Academic Progress," *China Daily* (2/12/85), p. 4.

111. "Hiring Away Teachers Endangers Education," *China Daily* (5/13/85), p. 4.

112. "Experts Worried Over Status of Education," *China Daily* (4/8/85), p. 4.

113. "Zhong Gong Zhong Yang Guan Yu Jiao Yu Ti Zhi Gai Ge de Jue Ding" [Decision of the Central Committee of the Chinese Communist Party Regarding Educational Reform], *Renmin Ribao* [*People's Daily*] (5/29/85), pp. 1–3.

114. Neither did Jaspar Utley; see his "The Performance Gap," *Wai Yu Jiao Xue Yu Yan Jiu* [Foreign Language Teaching and Research] **61:1** (1985), pp. 66–69.

115. "Teacher's Day," *China Daily* (1/29/85), p. 4, and "Colleges Introduce 'Contract Teaching'," *China Daily* (3/19/85), p. 4.

116. "Colleges Introduce 'Contract Teaching'," cited immediately above.

Bibliography

Allen, Wendy, and David Cooke. "Bridging the Gap: Materials Development in China," *TESL Talk* **13**:2, Spring 1982.

Anderson, E.J. *Factors Determining Success in Teaching English to Chinese*. Ph.D. Dissertation. University of Chicago, 1924.

Atkinson, Martin. "Language Learning and the Linguistic Environment," *Wai Yu Jiao Xue Yu Yan Jiu* **49**:1, 1982.

Barendsen, Robert. *Education in the PRC: A Selective Annotated Bibliography of Sources in English*. Washington, D.C.: Office of International Education, 1981.

_____. "The English Language Test Used by the PRC to Select Candidates for Study Abroad in 78–79." Washington, D.C.: U.S. Department of Education, 1980.

_____. "The 1978 National College Entrance Exam in the PRC," Washington, D.C.: U.S. Office of Education, 1979.

Beijing Jing Shan School. Dept. of Scientific Educational Research. "Tan Tan Women de Ban Xue Si Xiang" [Discussion of Our Guiding Thoughts in Running Schools], *Jiao Yu Yan Jiu* **1,** January 1981.

Biggerstaff, Knight. *The Earliest Modern Government Schools in China*. Ithaca, N.Y.: Cornell University Press, 1961.

Bing Wu. "Beijing Foreign Languages Institute and Its English Teaching." Beijing, China: ERIC ED205049, 1981.

Bishop, Ann. *English Language Teaching by Foreigners in Harbin*. M.A. Thesis. University of Texas, 1981.

Bratton, Dale. *Politics of Educational Reform in the PRC*. Ph.D. Dissertation. Ann Arbor, Mich.: University Microfilms International, 1979.

Brown, H. Douglas. *Principles of Language Learning and Teaching*. Englewood Cliffs, N.J.: Prentice-Hall, 1980.

Buck, Pearl. *Tell the People: Talks with James Yen About the Mass Education Movement*. New York: John Day Co., 1945.

Campbell, Russell. "Design, Development and Initial Evaluation of Three ESP Programs in the PRC." Paper delivered to TESOL Convention, 1981.

Chang Hsinpao. *Commissioner Lin and the Opium War*. New York: W.W. Norton, 1964.

Chang Pengchun. *Education for Modernization in China*. New York: Teachers College, Columbia University, 1923.

Chen Guanfeng. "Education Commission Gets Greater Power," *China Daily*, June 26, 1985.

_____. "Success in Future Tied to Teachers' Vital Role," *China Daily*, February 25, 1985.

Chen Hui. "Diao Dang Xue Sheng Xue Ying Yu de Xing Qu" [Raise Students' Interest in Learning English], *Beijing Wan Bao*, March 24, 1985.

Chen, Theodore H.E. *Teacher Training in Communist China.* Washington, D.C.: U.S. Office of Education, 1960.

Chen, Theodore. *Chinese Education Since 1949.* New York: Praeger, 1981.

Cheung Lokang. "Teaching English in China," *English Journal* **68**:3, March 1979.

China Educational Commission of the Mission Boards and Societies in China. *Christian Education in China.* New York: Committee of Reference and Counsel of the Foreign Missions Conference of North America, 1922.

"China Students March for U.S.–Style Democracy," *Los Angeles Times,* I, December 17, 1986.

Cicourel, A.V., S. Jennings, K. Leifer, R. MacKay, H. Mehan and D. Roth. *Language Use and School Performance.* New York: Academic Press, 1974.

"Colleges Introduce 'Contract Teaching'," *China Daily,* March 19, 1985.

"Colleges Outline Job Placement Reform," *China Daily,* March 13, 1985.

"Colleges Urged to Look After Students," *China Daily,* February 9, 1985.

Cowan, J.R., R. Light, B.E. Mathews, and G.R. Tucker. "English Language Teaching: A Recent Survey," *TESOL Quarterly* **13**:4, December 1979.

Delamont, S., and M. Stubbs, eds. *Explorations in Classroom Observation.* London: Wiley, 1976.

DeMille, Barbara. "Teaching in China," *ADE Bulletin* **73,** Winter 1982.

Dewey, John. *Experience and Education.* New York: Macmillan, 1939.

—————. *Impressions of Soviet Russia and the Revolutionary World, Mexico, China, Turkey.* New York: Teachers College, Columbia University, 1929.

Dow, Marguerite. "The Influence of the Cultural Revolution on the Teaching of English in the PRC," *English Language Teaching Journal* **29**:3, April 1975.

Dungworth, David. "The Future of English as a World Language," University of Manchester, England, 1978.

Duus, Peter. "Science and Salvation in China: The Life and Work of W.A.P. Martin 1827–1916," in *Papers on China,* Vol. 10. Cambridge, Mass.: Harvard University East Asia Program, October, 1956.

"Education Reform," *China Daily,* May 24, 1985.

"The English Language: Out to Conquer the World," *U.S. News and World Report* **98**:6, 1985.

"Experts Worried over Status of Education," *China Daily,* April 8, 1985.

Fairbank, John King. *The United States and China.* Cambridge, Mass.: Harvard University Press, 1958.

Fenn, William P. *Christian Higher Education in Changing China 1880–1950.* Grand Rapids, Mich.: William B. Eerdmans, 1976.

Ferguson, Charles. "Applied Linguistics in China," *Linguistic Reporter* **17**:4, April 1975.

Flower, Katherine. "Television in China," *Media in Education and Development* **16**:1, March 1983.

Ford, Donald. "Education in China: Lofty Ambitions, Grim Reality," *Monsoon* **3**:9, October 1980.

—————. "Foreign Language Instruction in China," *Pasaa* (Thailand) [Language] **9**:1, 1981.

Fox, Melvin. *Language and Development: A Retrospective Survey of Ford Foundation Language Projects, 1952–1974.* New York: Ford Foundation, 1975.

Fraser, Stewart. *China: A Select Bibliography.* New York: Wiley, 1972.

Fu, Gail. *A Hong Kong Perspective: English Language Learning and the Chinese Student.* Ann Arbor: Univ. of Michigan Comparative Education Dissertation Series, 1975.

Gamberg, Ruth. *Red and Expert: Education in Revolutionary China.* New York: Schocken Books, 1976.

Giglioli, Pier P. *Language and Social Context*. London: Penguin, 1972.

Goodlad, John (ed.). *Curriculum Inquiry: The Study of Curriculum Practice*. New York: McGraw-Hill, 1979.

_____. *A Place Called School: Prospects for the Future*. N.Y.: McGraw-Hill, 1984.

_____, and Assoc. *A Study of Schooling in the United States: Technical Reports*. Los Angeles: IDEA, 1979–1981.

Grannis, M., et al. " 'Shake a Leg' English in China," *English Around the World* 20, May 1979.

Gregory, Peter, et al. *China: Education Since the Cultural Revolution: A Selected Annotated Bibliography*. San Francisco: Eric ED064463, 1981.

Gu Chang-Sheng. *Chuan Jiao Shi Yu Jin Dai Zhong Guo* [Missionaries and Recent China]. Shanghai: People's Publishing House, 1981.

Gumperz, J., and Dell Hymes, eds. *Directions in Sociolinguistics: The Ethnography of Communication*. New York: Holt Rinehart Winston, 1972.

Hamilton, D., and R. McAleese, eds. *Understanding Classroom Life*. Windsor, England: NFER Publishing, 1978.

Hawkins, John. *Education and Social Change in the People's Republic of China*. New York: Praeger, 1983.

_____. *Mao Tse-tung and Education: His Thoughts and Teachings*. Hamden, Conn.: Shoestring Press, 1974.

Hsiao Encheng. *The History of Modern Education in China*. Beijing: Beijing University Press, 1932.

Hsu, Immanuel C.Y. *China's Entrance into the Family of Nations: The Diplomatic Phase, 1858–1880*. Cambridge, Mass.: Harvard University Press, 1960.

Hu Chang Tu, ed. *Chinese Education Under Communism*. New York: Teachers College Press, Columbia University, 1974.

Hu Menghao. "College Moves with the Times," *China Daily*, January 24, 1985.

Hu Shi Ming. *Interrelationship Between Education and Political Ideology Exemplified in China: A Critical Analysis of Educational Policy and Curriculum Trends*. Ph.D. Dissertation. Ann Arbor, Mich.: University Microfilms, 1970.

Hu Wen Jing. "Tan Tan Liu Nian Zhi Zhong Dian Zhong Xue Ying Yu Jiao Xue de Mu Di" [Discussion of the Purpose and Demand for Keypoint Middle Schools English Study], *Ren Min Jiao Yu*, June 1982.

Hu Wen Zhong and David Crook. "University Studies Move with Times," *China Daily*, March 14, 1985.

Hummel, Arthur, ed. *Eminent Chinese of the Ching Period (1644–1912)*. (2 vols.) Washington, D.C.: U.S. Government Printing Office, 1943–44.

Hung, William. "Huang Tsun-Hsien's Poem 'The Closure of the Educational Mission in America'," *Harvard Journal of Asiatic Studies* 18:1, June 1955.

Hymes, Dell. *Foundations in Sociolinguistics: An Ethnographic Approach*. Philadelphia: University of Pennsylvania Press, 1974.

_____. "Models of Interaction of Language and Social Setting," *Journal of Social Issues* 23, 1967.

_____, C.B. Cazden, and V.P. John, eds. *Functions of Language in the Classroom*. New York: Teachers College Press, 1972.

Jia Qiang. "Pioneering Professor Promotes 'Open' Education," *China Daily*, March 1, 1985.

Kennedy, G.D. "Teaching English Language in China," *Linguistic Reporter* 21:8, May 1979.

Klein, M. Frances. *A Study of Curriculum Decision Making in Eighteen Selected Countries*. Los Angeles: IDEA, 1978.

Kwong, Julia. *Chinese Education in Transition: Prelude to the Cultural Revolution.* Montreal: McGill–Queens University Press, 1976.

Lambert, Wallace. *Language, Psychology and Culture: Selected Writings of Wallace E. Lambert.* (A. Dil, ed.) Stanford: Stanford University Press, 1972.

_____, and J. Gardner. *Attitudes and Motivation in Second Language Learning.* Rowley, Mass.: Newbury House, 1972.

Lehmann, W.P. *Language and Linguistics in the PRC.* Austin: University of Texas Press, 1975.

Li, Anthony. *The History of Privately Controlled Higher Education in the Republic of China.* Washington, D.C.: Catholic University of America Press, 1954.

Li Xiao Zhu. "Shi Yi Suo Yuan Xiao Ying Yu Zhuan Ye 1984 Nian Bi Ye Ban Ying Yu Neng Li Ce Shi Jie Guo Gen Xi" [Analysis of English Ability Test Results of the 1984 Graduating Class from English Departments of 11 Institutes and Colleges], *Wai Yu Jiao Xue Yu Yan Jiu* **61:**1, 1985.

Liu Xiao Chuan. *Introducing English Poetry to Chinese College Students.* Ph.D. Dissertation. Ann Arbor, Mich.: University Microfilms, 1954.

Liang Bai Ping. "Exam System 'Merely Tests Memory'," *China Daily,* April 18, 1985.

Light, Richard. "Training Teachers Across Cultures: Report on the Fulbright Program in China," ERIC ED202212, 1980.

Light, Timothy. "U.S. Applied Linguistic Delegation to the PRC: A Report," *Linguistic Reporter* **20:**7, April 1978.

Lutz, Jessie G. *China and the Christian Colleges, 1850–1950.* Ithaca, N.Y.: Cornell University Press, 1959.

_____. *The Role of Christian Colleges in Modern China Before 1928.* Ph.D. Dissertation. Ithaca, N.Y.: Cornell University, 1955.

Magner, Thomas. "The Study of Foreign Languages in China," *Modern Language Journal* **58:**8, December 1974.

Martin, W.A.P. *A Cycle of Cathay; or China, South and North.* New York: Revell, 1900.

Mehan, H. "Structuring School Structure," *Harvard Educational Review,* **48:**1, February 1978.

_____, C.B. Cazden, et al. "The Social Organization of Classroom Lessons," *CHIP Report 67.* University of California–San Diego: Center for Information Processing, 1976.

Ministry of Education, Beijing. "Guan Yu Ying Yu Ming Ti," [Concerning Questions on the English (Entrance) Exam], *Ren Min Jiao Yu,* **8,** August 1982.

Mishler, Elliot. "Meaning in Context: Is There Any Other Kind?" *Harvard Educational Review* **49:**1, February 1979.

Mok, Poon Kan. *The History and Development of the Teaching of English in China.* Ph.D. Dissertation. Columbia University, 1951.

Monroe, Paul. *A Report of Education in China.* New York: Institute of International Education, 1922.

Montaperto, Ronald, and Jay Henderson, eds., with Ralph Tyler et al. *China's Schools in Flux: Report by the State Education Leaders Delegation.* White Plains, N.Y.: M.E. Sharpe, 1979.

Moore, G.P. "Chinese Students' Protests Are Far from Academic," *Los Angeles Times,* I, January 5, 1987.

Morse, Hosea Ballou. *The International Relations of the Chinese Empire.* London: Longman, Green, 1910–1918. (3 vols.)

Murray, Donald. "Culture Trading on the Old Silk Road," *Today's Education* **70:**4, November-December 1981.

National Public Radio. "Education in China: Parts 1–6," ERIC ED174554, 1979.

"New System Proposed for Colleges," *China Daily*, April 23, 1985.

Oller, John, and T. Chihara. "Attitudes and Attained Proficiency in EFL: Adult Japanese Speakers," *Language Learning* **28**:1, 1978.

_____, J. Hudson, and P. Liu. "Attitudes and Attained Proficiency in ESL: A Sociolinguistic Study of Native Speakers of Chinese in the U.S.," *Language Learning* **27**:1, 1977.

Parker, Franklin. *What Can We Learn from the Schools of China?* Bloomington, Ind.: Phi Delta Kappa Educational Foundation, 1977.

Peake, Cyrus H. *Nationalism and Education in Modern China.* New York: Columbia University Press, 1932.

Pepper, Suzanne. "China's Universities," *Modern China* **82,** April 1982.

_____. "Chinese Education After Mao," *China Quarterly* **81**:1, March 1980.

Popham, W. James. *Criterion-Referenced Measurement.* Englewood Cliffs, N.J.: Prentice-Hall, 1978.

Price, R.F. *Education in Modern China.* (2nd edition) London: Routledge and Kegan Paul, 1979.

_____. "English Teaching in China: Changes in Teaching Methods 1960–66," *English Language Teaching,* **26**:1, October, 1971.

_____. "Some English Language Textbooks From China," *English Language Teaching Journal,* **33**:4, July 1979.

"Reforms Aim to Reinforce Weak Links in Education," *China Daily*, May 29, 1985.

Sampson, Gloria P. "Exporting Language Teaching Methods from Canada to China," *Wai Yu Jiao Xue Yu Yan Jiu* **61**:1, 1985.

Scott, Charles. "Some First Impressions of EFL Teaching in China," *TESOL News* **14**:6, December 1980.

Scovel, Janene. *Curriculum Stability and Change: English Foreign Language Programs in Modern China.* Ph.D. Dissertation. University of Pittsburgh, 1982.

Seybolt, Peter, comp. *Revolutionary Education in China: Documents and Commentary.* White Plains, N.Y.: International Arts and Sciences Press, 1973.

Sinclair, Coulthand. *Toward Analysis of Discourse: the English Used by Teachers and Pupils.* Oxford: Oxford University Press, 1975.

Song, Pulin. "Jiao Cai, Jiao Fa, Xue Fa" [Teaching Materials, Teaching Methods, and Learning Methods], *Jiao Yu Yan Jiu* **10,** October 1981.

Spindler, G.D. *Education and Culture: Anthropological Approaches.* New York: Holt Rinehart Winston, 1963.

Spolsky, Bernard. *Educational Linguistics: An Introduction.* Rowley, Mass.: Newbury House, 1978.

Strong, K.A.B. "Language Teaching in China," *Babel* **9**:2, July 1973.

"Students Show New Values," *China Daily*, June 24, 1985.

Su Shaozhi. "Free Exchange of Thought Leads to Academic Progress," *China Daily*, February 12, 1985.

Su Wenming, ed. *A Nation at School: China Today, Number Five.* Beijing: Beijing Review Publications, 1983.

Tan Li. "Leading University Announces Changes," *China Daily*, April 4, 1985.

Tao, W. Tchishin, and C.P. Chen. *Education in China.* Shanghai: Commerical Press Limited, 1925.

Teng Ssuyu, and John K. Fairbank. *China's Response to the West.* Cambridge, Mass.: Harvard University Press, 1954. (2 vols.)

Thelen, Herbert. *The Classroom Experience.* New York: Wiley, 1981.

"Ti Chu Ji Chu Jie Duan Ying Yu Zhuan Ye Ke Cheng She Zhi Gai Jin Fang An,"

[Formulation of a Plan to Reform Course Offerings in Elementary English], *Wai Guo Yu Yan Jiao Xue Ze Liao Bao Dao* 1, 1984.

Trudgill, Peter. *Sociolinguistics: An Introduction to Language and Society.* London: Penguin, 1983.

Trueba, H.T., G.P. Guthrie, and K.H. Au (eds.). *Culture and the Bilingual Classroom: Studies in Classroom Ethnography.* Rowley, Mass.: Newbury, House, 1981.

Tyler, Ralph W. *Basic Principles of Curriculum and Instruction.* Chicago: University of Chicago Press, 1950.

United States Information Agency. "The Study of English in the PRC," ERIC ED136609, 1975.

Urhegyi, Jaspar. "The Performance Gap," *Wai Yu Jiao Xue Yu Wan Jiu* 61:1, 1985.

Wang Dongtai. "Universities to End Free Tuition System," *China Daily*, May 31, 1985.

Wang Kun. "English and Other Foreign Language Teaching in the PRC," *College English* 43:7, November 1981.

Wang Tingfang. "Tan Tan Wai Yu Jiao Xue de Xin Li Xue Ji Chu [Discussion of the Psychological Foundation of Foreign Language Teaching], *Jiao Yu Yan Jiu* 11, November 1982.

Wein, Lois. "International Perspective: English Language Instruction in China Today," *English Journal* 69:2, February 1980.

Wright, Mary. *The Last Stand of Chinese Conservatism: The T'ung-Chih Restoration, 1862–1874.* Stanford, Calif: Stanford University Press, 1957.

Wu Fusheng. "Three Lessons in Education," *China Daily*, February 22, 1985.

Xu Jinhai. "Yu Wen Jiao Xue Yao Jiang Bian Zheng Fa" [Chinese Language Teaching Must Stress Dialectics], *Shanghai Jiao Yu*, December 1982.

Xu Yongnian. "Xiao Xue Yu Wen Jiao Cai Zhong de Wei Wu Bian Zheng Fa Wen Ti" [The Question of Dialectical Materialism in Primary School Chinese Language Curriculum], *Shanghai Jiao Yu*, December 1982.

Yen, Maria. *The Umbrella Garden; A Picture of Student Life in Red China.* New York: Macmillan, 1954.

Zais, Robert S. *Curriculum Principles and Foundations.* New York: Harper & Row, 1976.

Zhang Jianzhang. "Educational Reform in China's Middle School English." Paper delivered to Conference on Foreign Language Teaching, Japan, ERIC ED205026, 1980.

Zhang Mei Jin. "Dui Bian Xie Jiao Yu Xue Jiao Cai de Ji Dian Kan Fa" [Some Views on the Compilation of Teaching Materials in Pedagogics], *Jiao Yu Yan Jiu* 5, May 1982.

"Zhong Gong Zhong Yang Guan Yu Jiao Yu Ti Zhi Gai Ge de Jue Ding" [Decision of the Central Committee of the Chinese Communist Party Regarding the Reform of the Educational System], *Renmin Ribao*, May 29, 1985.

Zhong He. "U.S. Investment in China," *China's Foreign Trade* 11, 1985.

Zhou Yougao. "Textbooks to Fit New Needs," *China Daily*, February 11, 1985.

Zhu Ciliu. "On the Precis Approach, *Wai Yu Jiao Xue Yu Yan Jiu* 54:2, 1983.

Index

Administration's decision making role 103
Administrator interview results 43
Administrator survey results 41
Administrators: decision making power
    42; views of 41
Advanced English courses 122, 143
Allocation of time 159
Americans 2, 46; American Accents 5;
    American ESL textbooks 107;
    American influence in China 23;
    American teachers 5, 27, 46
Attendance 129, 150
Audiolingual approach to language learn-
    ing 27, 34, 36, 40, 79, 93, 95, 191
Audio taping 105
Audio-visual aids 202

Basic skills 32, 45
Beginning English courses 63, 64
Bilingual education 21
Boredom, students and 88, 116
Boxer Rebellion 18
Britain 93
British Broadcasting Corporation 5
British English 5
British instructors 5

Catholic missionaries 22
Chapter outlines 10
China: official policy toward English 15;
    response to English 12
Chinese 73, 100, 115
Chinese Central Television Network 5
Chinese Christians 24
Chinese communists 25, 29
Chinese government's attitude toward
    foreign schools 23
Chinese materials translated into English
    26
Chinese motives for learning English 16

Chinese nationalism 24
Chinese teachers of English 122, 143
"Chinglish" 5, 55
Christian colleges, origins of 19
Christian education, objectives of 20
Christianity 16
Civil Service Examination 22
Civil War 23, 25
Class climate 50, 69, 116, 118, 128, 129,
    140, 149, 150, 161, 193
Class monitor 64, 117
Classrooms 71; breaktime 128, 149; behav-
    ioral regularities 8; heat and light 82
College entrance examinations 5, 27
College major of teachers 45
Communicative activities 39
Communicative approaches to language
    learning 40, 191
Communicative competence 10, 41
Communist Party organizations' influence
    43
Confucian ethic 193
Confucian scholars 17
Confucius 1, 193
Contemporary English Curriculum: 1976–
    1986 27
Contract system in the universities 195
Course load 31; offerings 55
Courses: usefulness of 60
Courses chosen for observation 64
Criterion-referenced testing 8, 9
Criterion-referenced reading test 103, 120
Cross-cultural experiences 54
Cultural exchanges 3
Cultural Revolution 25, 27, 29
Curricular decision making 7, 47
Curricular decisions 8
Curricular organization 9
Curricular problems 188
Curriculum: components of 63; continu-
    ity 70, 110; curriculum development 7;

curriculum planning 26; curriculum reform 27; definitions of terms 9; domains of curriculum inquiry 7, 8; effectiveness 74; future prospects 201; integration 70, 82, 110, 137, 158; reform of 50; sequence 70, 110; space, use of 71; theory of 8

Department goals 45
Decision making 43, 44; decision making process 193
Deng Xiaoping 3, 27, 187
Department administrators 41, 194, 196
Department goals 42
Dewey, J. 23
Dickens, C. 5
Dictation 80, 105
Differences between teachers and students 60
Direct method of instruction 47, 136, 157, 190
Discourse analysis 63, 71, 83, 86, 98, 100, 130, 139, 151, 160; results of 73, 114; statistics generated by 99
Discussion 68, 102, 106, 135, 156, 202; example of 125, 146
Dissatisfaction 198
Drawing inferences 75
Drill and practice 68, 99, 109, 124, 145; example of 95

Educational objective 9
Educational reform movement 11
Educational system 1
Electives 56
Elite universities 6
English series 40, 102; objectives of volumes 3 and 4 37; organization of volumes 3 and 4 40; textbook, second year 37; texts in volumes 1 and 2 36; texts in volume 3 78; texts in volume 4 38
English: Pidgin 14; spoken 90
English as medium of instruction 20
English curriculum 26
English department specific curriculum 32
English instructors, views of 44
English language 34, 37, 41
English language curriculum in China 28
English language textbooks used in China 28
English literature 10
English literature courses 122, 143

English syntax 35, 38
English teachers 58, 201
Evaluation 10, 40, 96, 99; of students 37, 126, 147; weaknesses in 81, 111
Explication of text 67
Extensive Reading, first year 64; class climate of 73; decisions about materials 74; difficulty level of materials 74; materials 66; objectives in observed lesson 72; organization of course 69; reading materials 66; spatial conditions 71; student talk 73; videotape 71; vocabulary activity 69
Extra-curricular activities 43

Facilities 48
First modern school system 22
Foreign domination 13
Foreign ideas 26
Foreign investment 4
Foreign language courses 16
Foreign languages 4
Foreign schools 22
Foreign teachers 6, 52, 122, 143
Foreign trade 3
Foreigners 4
Formal classroom style 100

Goals of the curriculum 56
Goodlad, J. 7, 63
Goodlad-Tyler conceptual framework 7
Government's view of curriculum 31
Grammar 40, 77
Grammar-translation approach 34, 40, 79, 190; example of 79
Grouping patterns 69, 81, 110, 127, 148
Growth of English: 1842–1900 14

Hidden curriculum 8, 71, 87
History of English 10
History of English language learning 6, 12
Homework 80, 111
Humor 140
Hymes D. 8, 71

Implicit curriculum 100, 113, 114, 139, 160
Importance of course offerings 56
Ineffective teachers 203
Inefficiency 192
Instructional decision making 46
Instructor Interviews 47

Integration as an organizational element 85

Intensive Reading I 33, 37; audio taping 98; class climate 87, 88, 101; content 78; curricular decision making 89; first year 76; learning opportunities 84; materials for the course 93; problems with 104; second year 91; spatial setting 97; statistics compiled from the discourse analysis 86; teaching group 89; textbook 33; tone of the discourse 100; tone of the lesson 87; use of classroom space 82; use of time 83; videotaped lesson 89; written evaluation 96

Interest in subject 51

Interviews 10, 43; with administrators, teachers and students 30

Japanese language 2
Junior-level faculty 197

Knowledge of results 52
Kuomintang 24, 25; and Communist parties 24

Language laboratory 104, 105, 112
Learning activities 54, 67, 78, 94, 99, 109, 113, 125, 134; inappropriateness 75
Learning experiences 34, 35, 37
Learning styles 55, 116
Lecture as a teaching strategy 107, 109
Lectures 136, 157
Liang Chichao 18
Libraries 20
Listening comprehension 104; content of the lessons 108; cultural context 120; discourse, channel of 115; formal style 115; objectives of the course 106; student decision making 117; use of time 112

Management of university education 43
Mao Tse-tung 1, 3, 27
Martin, W.A.P. 16, 17, 21
Marxism 3
Materials 53
May 4th (1919) Movement 24
Memorization 5
Ministry of Education 23, 24, 25, 30
Missionaries 12; conflict over schools 23;

in China 10, 19; missionary education 24; missionary schools 14, 19
Modern education 19
Modernization 6, 19, 200
Motives for learning English 57

Naturalistic observations 63
Notional-functional approach to language learning 93, 107

Objectives 31, 34, 37, 65, 77, 99, 113
Observation 8
Open door policy 3, 27, 57
Oral evaluation 68, 81, 85, 111
Oral translation 85
Organization of Curriculum 81, 110, 137, 158
Outdated textbooks 188
Overall assessment of the department 60

Pedagogical practices 29
Physical resources 198
Poetry 123, 144
Poor behavior of students 101
Precis writing 39
Preferences of teachers and students 58

Question-answer 135, 156
Questionnaires 10, 30, 31
Questions asked by students 84

Radical politics 4
Reading comprehension skills 36, 37, 38 90
Reading skills 36, 38, 75
Reading test, results of 75
Reforming Chinese education 9, 195; resistance of Chinese teachers toward 27
Relations between China and English-speaking countries 12
Research methodology 7, 9
Research purposes 6
Research significance 9
Retelling 68
Role-playing 39
Russia 2, 25

Satisfaction 8, 9, 42, 43; with the cur-
    riculum 43
Science and technology 4
Senior-level faculty 197
Selected Readings of American and
    British Literature 132; allocation of
    time 138; content 134; objectives of the
    course 133; spatial elements of this
    course 138; written evaluations 137
Self-strengthening theory 16, 17
Sentence combining 39
Short stories 134, 155
Sociolinguistics 10
Special economic zones 3
St. John's University 20, 21, 24
State Education Commission 2, 30, 31,
    34, 46, 195, 196, 201
Structural linguistics 123, 144
Student achievement 8
Student decision making 48, 50, 89, 102,
    197; example of 102
Student demonstrations 186, 198
Student dissatisfaction 57, 102, 199; with
    the English curriculum 58
Student participation 43, 47
Student preferences 49
Student protests 199
Student questions 80
Student survey 10; results of 48
Student talk 73, 83, 86, 99, 113, 128, 138,
    139, 149, 159, 160
Stylistics 122; content of the class 124;
    course materials 124; difficulty level 141;
    objectives of the course 124; purposes
    of the course 123; student participation
    128; topic sequence 126
Sun Yatsen 24

Teacher concern 52; education 187, 190;
    satisfaction 48; talk 83, 128, 138, 149, 159

Teacher Survey Results 45
Teacher-student relationship 193
Teachers, social status of 193
Teachers University 30, 43
Teaching methodology 143; content of
    the class 145; content 155; course
    materials 145; critical comments by
    teacher 115; difficulty level 162; learning
    activities 146, 155; objectives of the
    course 145, 154; purposes of the course
    144; spatial elements of the course 159;
    student participation 149; topic se-
    quence 147; written evaluations 158
Teaching methods 26, 33
Teaching strategies 54, 59, 67, 79, 95,
    102, 109, 135, 156
Technical Institutes 6
Tengzhou College 22
Textbooks 5
Time use: in class 70, 97
Tong Wen Guan (Government
    Translators School) 15, 18, 19
Tourist industry 3
Trade schools 6
Trade with China 3, 13
Translation 5, 40, 47, 68, 76, 96, 109; as
    a teaching strategy 34, 35, 68; of
    Western books 20; translation clause 15
Tyler, R. 7, 33, 63, 70, 93, 110

Unequal treaties 14

Videotaping 83, 139, 160
Vocabulary 36

Wartime colleges 24
Writing skills 39; lack of 90